Lucy Waverman's
COOKING SCHOOL
COOKBOOK

Lucy Waverman's
COOKING SCHOOL COOKBOOK

HARPER & COLLINS

Toronto

First published 1988
by Collins Publishers
100 Lesmill Road, Don Mills, Ontario

Canadian Cataloguing in Publication Data

Waverman, Lucy.
    The cooking school cookbook

ISBN 0-00-215429-3

1. Cookery.   I. Title.

TX715.W38 1988   641.4   C88-093998-2

Editor: Shelley Tanaka
Design: Catherine Chafe
Illustrations: Sally J.K. Davies and Catherine Chafe

Printed and bound in Canada

Second Printing

Some of the recipes in this book originally appeared in the Toronto *Sun*,
Canadian Living Magazine, *Toronto Life* and *City and Country Home*.

Acknowledgments

I owe a debt of gratitude to many people for their help in writing this book, but especially to my husband, Bruce MacDougall, for his unwavering support; Emma, Katie and Alex, who were my best critics; Florence Minz Geneen, who helped create some order in the original manuscript; my father, Ben Geneen, and my brother, David Geneen, for being there; Kate Stein, who learned to cook by testing the recipes in this book; Zoe Cormack Jones, who encouraged me to get started; Simmie Clarke and Shirley Hawkins, for their comments and advice; Shelley Tanaka, my editor, for her limitless patience and excellent counsel—without her there would be no book; and, finally, to all my cooking school students for their enthusiasm and loyalty.

To Sophie and Pearl

Contents

Foreword

I come from a line of women who believed that cooking good food was the best way to show love. In addition, the preparation and presentation of food became our careers.

My grandmother Sophie Geneen, widowed at a young age with eight children to support, turned her hand to what she knew best—the kitchen—and opened a hotel and restaurant in Glasgow, Scotland. Her superb cooking built her a fine reputation throughout Britain, and Geneen's Hotel quickly became the place to eat in Glasgow. It also became the center of Jewish activity within the community—the place where everyone celebrated their weddings and bar mitzvahs. During World War Two, it was a haven for Jewish servicemen from all over the world seeking home-cooked food and comfort.

Sophie was an imposing figure. Tall, austere, her arms folded across her chest, she ruled everything, including her kitchen, with a firm hand. Her underlying gentleness was apparent in her caring for others less fortunate, and her reputation for generosity surpassed even her food and hospitality. When she died, the media called her the Mother of Glasgow.

My mother, Pearl, is Sophie's daughter-in-law. Marrying my father, who was brought up in the hotel, created grave problems for her. He was used to a full menu at dinner and expected excellent food, three courses and good service. My mother quickly decided that the way to a peaceful marriage was to learn to cook as well as her mother-in-law. She started with the basics and rapidly moved on to experimenting and innovating. Eventually she became a cook with a style all her own. Never any good at chicken soup or brisket, she became a superb French chef with a creative touch that emerged long before the trend to California chic.

When we emigrated to Canada in the fifties, my mother started one of Toronto's first cooking schools. Eventually she turned her talents to retailing, with a highly successful kitchen shop on Toronto's Yorkville Avenue.

Mother's impact on the cooking community has been both colorful and extensive. Even today, her former students tell me that her recipes have stood the test of time. Some of them are in this book.

Cooking is a necessity, a joy and a source of comfort. I have inherited many good feelings, excellent teaching and a passion for good food from my family. I am privileged to have had this heritage passed on to me as a career, and I hope through using this book, others will enjoy it as much as I do.

Lucy Waverman
The Cooking School
Toronto, 1988

Introduction

Many of my cooking school students have admitted that they felt like strangers in their own kitchens when they started to cook. First, they were confused by cooking jargon. "Fold in egg whites," "roast until done" and "deglaze the pan" are common enough expressions, but they can be baffling for beginners. Instructions such as "stock lasts for five days" were also confusing. What happened to it after that, students wanted to know. Would it explode in the refrigerator?

Second, beginning cooks were terrified at the thought of doing something wrong, and turning all that effort into disaster. What could they do if they added too much salt, or didn't have the right number of onions that a recipe called for? What could they do when the mayonnaise curdled or the roast was raw? Could they fix cream that had been beaten to butter? Could a recipe be frozen or made ahead? And why couldn't they manage to make a decent pastry?

The Cooking School Cookbook deals not only with the methods of good cooking, but also the art of correcting mistakes. It features spendidly simple recipes suitable for both everyday cooking and entertaining. Helpful tips, step-by-step technique descriptions and troubleshooting sections play a prominent role. The book is intended to be both a practical primer for the beginner and a concise refresher for the more expert.

During my seventeen years of teaching at The Cooking School in Toronto, I always stressed basic cooking techniques. When I started giving cooking classes, some students who had cooked previously enrolled in the Intermediate or Advanced classes. Ninety percent returned to do the Preliminary course, because they learned that real cooking involved more than the ability to read a recipe!

This book is organized like my cooking courses. The first section deals with the kitchen—how to equip it with pots and pans and how to stock the shelves of a store cupboard and the herb cupboard. This section will put your mind at ease over cooking instructions. You'll learn how to chop an onion, how to hold a knife, how to substitute different ingredients when you don't have the ones called for, and the art of seasoning. You'll learn not to be afraid of the salt and pepper shaker and always to taste, taste, taste.

The second part of the book focuses on the techniques of cooking, with basic recipes to illustrate these techniques. The third section contains more than 100 tasty, easy recipes that have been the mainstay of my cooking career, and which I still use today in cooking for family and friends.

Finally, there is glossary, which will explain all the terms used. By working your way through the book, you will gradually feel comfortable and in control in the kitchen.

Cooking has been the focus of my work life since 1972, although I fell into it by accident. I was looking for a part-time career while I raised my children, so during my husband's sabbatical year in England, I took the opportunity of attending the Cordon Bleu Cookery School in London.

It was quite an experience. I was registered in the Advanced Certificate course, which required chef's papers or previous experience in restaurants or catering. The school was looking for professionals whose skills they could hone. I was certainly less professional than most, having had experience in my mother's cooking school but not much else!

The Cordon Bleu training was rigid, classical and structured. There were no electrical kitchen tools, electric mixers or, heaven forbid, food processors. Imagine making breadcrumbs by rubbing stale bread through a fine sieve! However, tedious as it was at times, I learned that once you know the basic cooking techniques, you can then go on to explore and invent. Without the basics, experimentation and creativity are out of reach.

The training, my own research and lots of eating over the years have given me definite opinions about food, cooking techniques and tastes. I love strong flavors and spicy tastes. Gray food, with little color or texture, leaves me cold. I like clear tastes and I like to know what I am eating. "Wet" food, with interesting sauces, appeals to me the most. I usually stress that fresh is best; however, out-of-season food coming from other countries may look good but fall short in flavor. Tomatoes in December are cardboard; I would substitute good-quality canned ones.

During my travels to Hong Kong and India, I became fascinated by oriental cuisines, which combine fresh, high-quality ingredients with the ingenious use of spices. I have incorporated some of these techniques into my own cooking. From my Scottish heritage comes my love of baking. But love alone doesn't produce a flaky pie crust. I've included some time-honored baking recipes that promise one hundred percent success.

Finally, as a mother and generally busy person, I've kept preparation time to a minimum.

So whether you are a student fending off life in the fast-food lane, getting started and looking for new and exciting recipes that work, or a serious cook who likes to understand the whys of a recipe, I feel this book has a lot to offer. *The Cooking School Cookbook* will help you accomplish almost anything you want in your kitchen.

Part 1

The Kitchen

·1·
Kitchen Equipment

chef's knife   sharpening steel

serrated edge knife

Good kitchen equipment makes a big difference to food preparation and cooking. Sharp knives and heavy pots help the work go faster and more efficiently. You are less likely to cut yourself with a sharp knife because it slices neatly and quickly. Heavy pots mean that sauces or custards don't burn and make double boilers obsolete.

The following equipment list is designed as a guide for anyone who is starting out, as well as filling in a few gaps for those whose kitchens are already equipped. Buying good-quality equipment is a life-long investment and can only improve your cooking performance.

KNIVES

• **Chef's knife:** Buy either an 8-inch (20 cm) or a 10-inch (25 cm) chef's knife. This knife will do all the chopping, dicing and mincing of vegetables and meat.

Buy high-carbon stainless steel, if available, because it keeps a sharper edge than ordinary stainless steel. If the knife is not kept sharp, it will bruise or mash the food. The larger the knife you can handle, the more efficient you will find it. Good knives are properly balanced (try holding several to discover which one has the best feel) and are shafted, meaning the metal runs through the entire handle.

• **Serrated edge knife:** This knife, with its tiny serrations, is used for cutting fruits. The serrated edge grips the skin, making it more effective than a straight-edged knife.

• **Carving and slicing knife:** This knife is used for carving meat. The stainless-steel blade should be long—11 inches (27 cm)—and flexible for the best control.

• **Paring knife:** Use this small knife for

12

paring fruits and vegetables. It should feel comfortable in your hand.

• Do buy a sharpening steel to restore the edge to your knives and keep them sharp. Use it each time you use your knife. To sharpen your knives, hold the steel horizontally. With the knife at a 45 degree angle to the steel, run the knife along the steel from handle to point in one stroke. Repeat about six times on each side.

• When the knife edge eventually becomes dull, have it professionally sharpened. Check the Yellow Pages for a professional knife sharpener. Do not use the man with the bell who pushes a knife-sharpening unit through the streets. Because of the coarseness of these units, they give an edge to the knife that is temporary, and will quickly wear down your knife.

• Do store knives in a knife rack or hang them on a magnetic board. Don't keep knives in drawers where they bang against each other and are a safety hazard.

POTS AND PANS

• Pots and pans are produced in different materials and at varying prices. My preference is to have several kinds of pots in various materials for more flexibility. Most pots come with lids, but if they don't, buy the covers separately.

• **Copper lined with tin or nickel** is the finest material to use in the kitchen because of its heat retention properties, but it is not always practical in terms of price or the time needed to clean and polish it.

• **Stainless steel** is excellent for stockpots or roasting pans but, because it is not a porous material, it can develop "hot spots"—areas where food will keep sticking. Copper-bottomed stainless steel is a good heat conductor, but it does not completely eliminate the hot-spot problem.

• **Anodized aluminum**, an aluminum material that has a protective Teflon-like coating electroplated or bonded into it, is non-stick and scratch resistant. It is excellent for sauce and milk-cooking pots. Although uncoated aluminum is good for certain kitchen processes, it is not versatile because the acids in some foods react with the aluminum and sully the taste of the dish. There is also speculation that using aluminum pots could affect your health over a long period of time.

• **Enamel** is good for stockpots because it is reasonably inexpensive. Unfortunately, it is not quite heavy enough for sauce pots.

• **Teflon-coated** pots and pans have an advantage because of their non-stick properties, but they are generally made of thin material and are therefore poor conductors of heat. They also become scratched, and the coating can peel off and get into the food. And you have to use special non-scratch utensils to go with them.

You'll need the following pots and pans:

• **One 12- to 14-quart (12 to 14 L) stockpot:** This pot is used for making stock and large quantities of soup, or boiling pasta. A steamer insert is used to steam vegetables or fish. Buy enamel or stainless steel.

• **One 4 1/2-quart (4 L) pot:** This pot is used for cooking vegetables or large amounts of sauce. Buy stainless steel or anodized aluminum.

• **Two or more 1 1/2- or 2 1/2-quart (1 or 2 L) pots:** These pots are used for sauces, melting chocolate, custards and other small-quantity cooking. I would highly recommend anodized aluminum, because it eliminates the need for a double boiler.

A 9-inch (23 cm) serrated knife doubles as a bread knife, as well as being excellent for slicing cold meats.

Do not put good knives in the dishwasher, as it will blunt them.

Using a Sharpening Steel
Hold the steel horizontally. With the knife at a 45 degree angle to the steel, run the knife along the steel from the heel to the point of the knife, in one stroke. Turn the knife over and do the other side.

Heavy pots conduct heat evenly. They heat up quickly, maintain the heat and cool down fast when removed from the stove, which is essential for good cooking.

• One 4- to 6-quart (4 to 6 L) Dutch oven: This is useful for stove-to-oven cooking, for stews and other slow-cooking recipes. You should buy heavy, cast-iron enamel for best results. They are attractive enough to use as serving dishes as well.

• One rectangular roasting pan with a rack: You should buy stainless-steel or cast-iron enamel roasting pans, because they can also be used on top of the stove to make gravy. The rack is necessary to elevate the food while it is being roasted.

• One 10- or 12-inch (25 or 30 cm) shallow frying pan: If you are planning to cook for more than two, buy the larger size. It is used for frying, deep-frying and sautéing. If a lid is available, it is a good investment. Buy cast iron, copper or anodized aluminum for the best results. Metal handles allow the skillet to go in the oven, although if the handles get too hot you may have to use a pot holder.

• One small 6- or 7-inch (15 or 18 cm) frying pan: This is used for eggs, omelets, crêpes and small-scale cooking. Cast iron or steel are the best materials. Since these are porous materials, they become non-stick with use, but they must be seasoned before using.

TOOLS OF THE TRADE

• One wooden cutting board: Buy as large a board as your space permits. It is needed to protect your knives and counters. Use for all chopping and slicing needs. If you cut meat or poultry, you should clean the board with a little liquid bleach after using to prevent bacteria from breeding. White plastic boards can be washed with soap and water.

• One stainless-steel whisk: Buy a 10-inch (25 cm) stainless-steel whisk, because it will not rust in the dishwasher. A whisk is used for whisking sauces or egg whites.

• One multipurpose stainless-steel grater: A grater is used for cheese, chocolate or citrus rind.

• Stainless-steel mixing bowls: These bowls come in several sizes, including a large one for beating egg whites. Because stainless steel conducts heat, in an emergency you can stick the bowl on top of the stove. Plastic is my least favorite kitchen material. Although it looks wonderful, because it absorbs odors it seems to impart a subtle taste to the food. (If you drink coffee out of a plastic mug rather than a china one, you can tell the difference.)

• One 10-inch (25 cm) stainless-steel colander: This can also double as a steamer insert.

• Wooden spoons: Wooden spoons are necessary for mixing, tasting and stirring. They don't conduct heat like metal spoons, avoiding the problem of seared fingers. Buy at least two.

• Food mill: The predecessor of the blender and food processor is useful for mashing or pureeing. It purees soups and sauces, too, making it an obvious choice if your budget doesn't run to a food processor or blender.

• Basic kitchen utensils: A slotted spoon for removing food from liquids; a ladle for soups and serving; a metal spatula for smoothing the tops of gratins and cakes; a swivel vegetable peeler for peeling apples, potatoes and carrots; metal tongs for turning meats; kitchen scissors for a multitude of kitchen tasks.

BAKING EQUIPMENT

• Measuring spoons: These spoons are used for measuring small amounts of liquids and solids.

• Dry measuring cups: These cups are used for measuring flour and sugar. They are designed to be filled to the top, then leveled off for accurate measuring. They come in both imperial and metric meas-

Seasoning Pans

Cast iron and steel are good heat conductors and are slightly porous, but they rust easily. To avoid this, season them with oil right after you buy them. Pour ½ inch (1.25 cm) oil into the pan and bake in a 200 F (90 C) oven for 2 hours. Cool and discard the oil.

After each use, sprinkle the pan with salt and wipe clean with a paper towel, but don't wash. Then wipe the pan with oil before storing. If you need to wash the pan, re-season it before storing and using.

ures. When following a recipe, make sure that you use either metric or imperial measures; don't switch from one to the other.

• **Liquid measuring cups:** These cups are used for measuring all liquids. Do not use them for dry measures.

• **One 9-inch (23 cm) false-bottom tart pan:** Buy heavy tin, which has a porous finish and, through use, will become non-stick. Use it for quiches, tarts and pies. The base can double as a lid on pots.

• **Two heavy cookie sheets:** Heavy-bottomed dark steel cookie sheets stop the base of cookies from burning. Heavy tin is also satisfactory. Make sure that the sheets will fit your oven. Cookie sheets have a lip at one end; jelly roll pans have a lip all the way around. They can double as cookie sheets.

• **One 9- or 10-inch (23 or 25 cm) springform pan:** This is used for cheesecakes, cakes and frozen desserts.

• **One standard muffin tin, 2½ × 1-inch (7 × 2.5 cm):** This muffin tin is used for muffins, Yorkshire puddings or large tarts.

• **One small muffin tin, 1 × 1-inch (2.5 × 2.5 cm):** Use these for mini muffins and tartlets. The best material is heavy tin or aluminum.

• **One 9 × 5-inch (2 L) loaf pan:** These are used for breads, quickbreads and cakes. Buy tin pans; they are better conductors of heat than glass.

• **Two 9-inch (23 cm) round cake pans:** These pans are used for double or single layer cakes.

• **One 8-inch (20 cm) square cake pan.**

• **One 13 × 9-inch (3.5 L) baking dish.**

• **One 16-inch (40 cm) rolling pin:** Preferably made of one piece of wood.

• **Pastry brush:** This is used to brush on glazes and syrups.

• **Two large wire cooling racks:** Coolings racks are needed for cooling cookies and cakes.

• **Fine mesh strainer:** This can double as a flour and sugar sifter.

• **Rubber spatula:** Necessary for scraping bowls and spreading icings.

OVEN TO TABLE DISHES

• **Three oval or square ovenproof gratin dishes** in small, medium and large sizes for baking, reheating and serving foods.

• **One 6-inch (15 cm) round soufflé dish** for puddings, crème caramel and soufflés.

ELECTRICAL EQUIPMENT

Food processors are excellent for large family needs or people who cook a lot; otherwise a blender or food mill is sufficient. Unless baking is your passion, a small handheld mixer is adequate. Otherwise a large table model with several different beater attachments is desirable, but not necessary.

THE STORE CUPBOARD

What you have on your cupboard shelves can make or break you when preparing a meal. It provides the luxury of being able to cook without having to run out to the store.

The store cupboard should stock basic ingredients and seasonings for everyday cooking.

The following list includes ingredients that you will use both in the recipes in this book and for your own cooking needs. You can vary the list according to your own style.

Choosing Bakeware
Heavy aluminum bakeware is excellent if it is coated with a dark wash or non-stick material that has been bonded into the aluminum. Stainless-steel baking equipment warps easily and is expensive.

Rectangular baking pans can double as lasagna pans or gratin dishes.

Cooking Ingredients

Good-quality chicken and beef bouillon cubes (read the ingredients and make sure there are chicken and beef in them), ketchup, Tabasco, Worcestershire sauce, oriental soy sauce, salt and peppercorns for the peppermill, tomato paste, dry mustard, vegetable oil, olive oil, red and white wine vinegar, white vinegar.

Optional Extras

Balsamic vinegar, fruit-flavored vinegar, sesame oil, nut oils, Chinese chili paste.

Baking Ingredients

Baking powder, baking soda, all-purpose flour, whole wheat flour, raw bran, rolled oats, cornstarch, arrowroot, dried fruits, vanilla extract, almond extract, icing sugar, brown sugar, granulated sugar, cocoa, molasses, gelatin, unsweetened chocolate, bittersweet or semisweet chocolate.

Cupboard Staples

Long-grain rice, short-grain rice, dried pasta in various shapes, lentils, barley, dried beans, Salmon, tuna, jams, honey, peanut butter, anchovies, canned chicken and beef broth, canned tomatoes, tomato paste, pimientos, olives, capers.

Refrigerator Staples

Mayonnaise, shortening, horseradish, Dijon mustard, butter, margarine.

THE HERB AND SPICE CUPBOARD

Herbs and spices change the flavor of foods, giving the distinctive finishing touches to a sauce or dish. Using them is an art, but certain basic rules apply.

Herbs are the leaves and stems of certain plants. They are always better fresh, but unfortunately most are not always available fresh unless you live in a major city. In trying to suggest a basic store cupboard of herbs, I have included the most popular herbs, both fresh and dried.

Herbs are affected by sunlight. It drains the flavor from them. Do not store them in glass jars on the counter. They may look attractive, but the herbs will taste like dust in no time. Store herbs in dark jars or in a cupboard. Dried herbs last for about six to nine months. Always buy the leaf variety, not the ground herb, which has little flavor and loses what it does have quickly. It is better to buy from herb and spice shops that have a high turnover, because you have a greater chance of the herbs being fresh. You cannot tell how long some of the supermarket supplies have been on the shelves.

Spices are the seeds, roots or bark of plants. For the freshest flavor, all whole spices can be ground in a spice mill or coffee grinder, although fresh ground spices are acceptable.

Basil: The Italian herb with a sharp, licorice-like taste and a sweet, minty smell. It spices up tomato sauces, tomato salads, Italian dishes, chicken and veal. Fresh basil is readily available in the summer and fall, as well as being easy to grow in the garden.

Bay leaf: This dried leaf of the bay tree flavors soups and stews. Remove it from the dish before serving.

Cayenne: The ground seeds and pods of fiery red peppers give a zing to food. Cayenne is hot but does not have much depth of flavor. Use it sparingly unless you love hot food.

To substitute dried herbs for fresh, use one-third the amount. For example, 1 tbsp (15 mL) fresh herbs = 1 tsp (5 mL) dried.

Both dried herbs and spices should be rubbed through your fingers before being added to a recipe. This releases the oils and flavor.

Chives: Chives are often available fresh, and can be grown in pots. Their mild onion flavor and pretty appearance make them ideal for garnishes.

Cinnamon: Cinnamon gives that familiar fragrant flavor to apple pies, rice, mulled wine, cookies and sweet breads. It comes ground or in sticks. Use the sticks to flavor rice and curry dishes; remove them before serving.

Cloves: This pungent spice flavors apples, oranges, sweet breads, Christmas cakes and curries. It comes as whole cloves and ground.

Dill: Its slightly licorice flavor is good with dips, salmon and scones, while its feathery leaves make a lovely garnish. Buy fresh, if available; dried dill tends to have little taste.

Coriander: The seed is round and has a strong, nutty smell and a sweet but tongue-tingling taste. It is used in pickles and Indian food. Fresh coriander, also known as Chinese parsley or cilantro, is a herb with a fragrant, flowery taste. It is never dried.

Cumin seeds: They have a nutty aroma and fragrant taste and are essential in East Indian food.

Garlic: Always buy fresh. To use, peel it and chop. The longer garlic is cooked, the milder the flavor. For a strong garlic flavor, add it to a dish just before serving. Garlic crushed through a garlic press is stronger in taste than chopped garlic. Look for fat, firm cloves with no green sprouts. Store it in dish on the counter. It will not last as long when refrigerated.

Curry powder: Curry powder is a mixture of spices used for making curries or flavoring other dishes. Although it is available commercially, making your own is easy. Combine 1 tbsp (15 mL) ground coriander, 1 tbsp (15 mL) ground cumin, 1 tsp (5 mL) ground cloves, 1 tsp (5 mL) ground cinnamon, 1 tsp (5 mL) ground cardamom and ¼ tsp (1 mL) cayenne pepper.

Ginger: The gnarled ginger root is peeled and chopped before using. Look for smooth-skinned, firm roots. Its hot taste flavors Chinese and Indian dishes, cakes and puddings. Ground or powdered ginger is not a substitute for fresh ginger. Use only if it is specifically called for in a recipe.

Marjoram: Its pungent flavor is similar to a mild sage, although it comes from the oregano family. Use it in poultry stuffings, sausages, veal dishes and pizza.

Mint: There are many varieties of mint, which is usually available fresh. Taste before you buy to decide what you like. It is exceptional with lamb, sauces and as a garnish for fruit. Freeze mint in the fall to use during the winter.

Nutmeg: Nutmeg is the dark-brown fruit encased by an outer shell called mace. Mace is milder than nutmeg, but they can be used interchangeably. Freshly grated nutmeg has lots more flavor than the ground variety. It perks up white sauce, cauliflower, apple dishes and rice.

Oregano: Also known as wild marjoram, oregano has a sharp taste. Greek oregano has the most mellow flavor. It flavors Italian food, tomato sauces, chicken, stews and chilis.

Paprika: Paprika comes from a mild variety of chili pepper. Some of it is sweet, some slightly bitter. Hungarian paprika is the best; the others have little flavor. Use with chicken, goulash and veal.

Parsley: Always buy fresh. Use it chopped up as a garnish for almost any savory dish. It is an essential ingredient in a bouquet garni. To keep parsley fresh, wash it, shake dry and place in a jar with a tight-fitting lid. It will keep for two weeks. Italian parsley has a flat broad leaf and more flavor than the curly variety.

Rosemary: The spiky rosemary leaf is used to flavor lamb, chicken and potatoes.

Sage: One of the strongest-flavored herbs, its pungent taste is used in stuffings or with potatoes.

Tarragon: Make sure you buy French tarragon, with its lemony, anise flavor—not the Russian variety, which has no taste at all. Tarragon dries well. It enhances poultry, fish, eggs, sauces and salad dressings.

Thyme: Thyme has a strong, spicy flavor and is used to flavor stews, stuffings, beef dishes and anything made with red wine. Thyme dries well.

·2·
How to Read a Recipe

Cooking is gratifying. Preparing a meal that everyone enjoys makes you feel good. But if you lack basic knowledge and confidence, your masterpiece can turn into a mess. Unfortunately, reading the recipe can be the first problem. Cooking terms such as julienne, large dice, mince or fold can confuse and intimidate new cooks. So understanding basic kitchen processes and knowing the meaning of cooking terms is essential for success.

Before you begin, get organized. Read through the whole recipe and get out everything you will need. Measure out the ingredients and have your pots and pans ready. Now you are ready for the recipe. Read it again.

MEASURING

People often get nervous about cooking because they worry about measuring properly. Meticulous measuring is a must in baking, but creative measuring in cooking will usually not harm the recipe. If two onions are needed and you only have one, don't let it stop you; the final dish will have less onion flavor, but will still work. Similarly, ½ cup (125 mL) more or less stock in soup or a sauce will not make an enormous difference to the dish.

If you feel imaginative and confident, use the recipes as a guide to create your own dish. If you want to add something or try something different—do it.

However, there are some ingredients that depend on scientific reactions with the food to work properly. Baking powder, yeast or baking soda must always be measured accurately.

When measuring flour, sugar or other dry ingredients for baking, use metal measuring spoons or cups. (Plastic retains odors.) Fill them to heaping, then level off with a knife.

Butter and other fats can be measured by the leveling-off method, by cut-

As a rule of thumb, add ½ tsp (2 mL) salt and ¼ tsp (1 mL) pepper per pound (500 g) of meat or per 2 cups (500 mL) liquid. Pepper in this book refers to freshly ground black pepper.

How to Chop an Onion

1 Cut the onion in half. Slice horizontally to—but not through—the root, three or four times.

2 Make vertical slices down through the onion.

3 Use the heel of the knife to slice down through the previously made cuts.

How to Chop Parsley

Holding the tip of the knife down on the board with your fingers, chop through the parsley heads with the heel of the knife until finely chopped.

ting butter while it is still in the brick, or by water displacement. To measure by displacement, place 1½ cups (375 mL) water in a measuring cup; then add butter or fat until the water reaches 2 cups (500 mL). When you drain off the water, you will be left with ½ cup (125 mL) butter. My preference is to weigh solid fats, but you need a kitchen scale and must know, for example, that ½ cup (125 mL) fat weighs 4 oz (125 g).

SEASONING

I cannot stress enough how important it is for all cooks to *taste*. It makes the difference between a good dish and an outstanding one. By tasting you will understand what is lacking and how to fix it. Most people have good palates but lack confidence. If you think something tastes good, trust your palate rather than relying completely on the recipe.

In this book, the terms salt and pepper to taste are often used. As it is difficult to assess another person's tolerance for seasonings, I have left it up to your own judgment. As well, if your pot is bigger or smaller than mine, it will affect the amount of reduction in the recipe, making it impossible for me to know the amount of seasoning you will need. Remember, if it tastes bland, first try more salt, then more herbs. Pepper in this book refers to freshly ground black pepper.

CHOPPING AND CUTTING

Recipes often instruct you to chop the onion or dice the carrot, and if you don't know what these terms mean, you'll feel defeated before your start.

Dice = to cut into ¼ inch (5 mm) cubes

Chop = to cut into small even-sized pieces

Finely chop = to chop into tiny pieces

Grate = to shred food very finely by scraping on a rough- or sharp-edged grater

Julienne = to cut food into thin, matchstick-sized pieces

Mince = to chop so finely that the ingredients look like dust

Shred = to cut food into long thin slivers

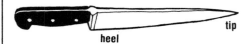

heel   tip

How to Use a Chef's Knife

The correct hand position for using a chef's knife is to shake hands with the knife handle. Your fingers will curl around the handle. Use the heel of the knife (the part nearest the handle) for the chopping and cutting. Although the tendency is to pull the knife toward you, always slice away from you for better balance and efficiency.

How to Chop an Onion

This is a basic cooking technique feared by many because of the effect the onion fumes have on your eyes. The best way to aviod crying, other than wearing a gas mask, is to use a sharp knife that slices cleanly through the onion, preventing the juices from running out.

• Peel the onion. Then cut the onion in half through the root. Lay the flat surface of the onion on a cutting board.

• With a sharp chef's knife, slice the onion horizontally to, but not through, the root, three or four times. By not cutting through the root, the onion will hold together.

• With the tip of the chef's knife, slice down through the onion several times.

• Holding the onion firmly, use the heel of the knife to slice down through the previously made cuts. The onion is now chopped. The finer you want it, the closer together the cuts.

EQUIVALENTS

If you cook from lots of cookbooks, you'll find that ingredients are often listed in different ways. Some are listed by weight, as in pounds or kilograms of carrots; some in volume, as in cups or liters of carrots. Even more confusing are butter and cheese measurements, which can be given in cups, pounds, tablespoons or milliliters.

Here is an easy guide to help you sort out whether the three apples in the drawer will be enough to make the recipe that calls for one pound.

Butter, shortening, cream cheese, cottage cheese
1 lb (500 g) = 2 cups (500 mL)
8 oz (250 g) = 1 cup or 16 tbsp (250 mL)
4 oz (125 g) = ½ cup or 8 tbsp (125 mL)

Flour
1 lb (500 g) = 3½ cups (875 mL)

Eggs
12 to 14 egg yolks = 1 cup (250 mL)
8 to 10 egg whites = 1 cup (250 mL)

Nuts
4 oz (125 g) chopped nuts = ¾ cup (175 mL)
4 oz (125 g) ground nuts = 1 cup (250 mL)

Raisins and dried fruits
1 lb (500 g) = 3 cups (750 mL)

Sugar
1 lb (500 g) granulated sugar = 2½ cups (625 mL)
1 lb (500 g) packed brown sugar = 3 cups (750 mL)
1 lb (500 g) icing sugar = 4 cups (1 L)

Fruit
1 lb (500 g) apples = 4 cups (1 L) sliced = 3 medium
1 lb (500 g) bananas = 1½ cups (375 mL) mashed = 3 medium
1 lb (500 g) peaches = 3 cups (750 mL) sliced = 4 medium

Meat
1 lb (500 g) cooked meat = 3 cups (750 mL) chopped

Rice
1 lb (500 g) rice = 2½ cups (625 mL)

Vegetables
1 lb (500 g) cabbage = 4 cups (1 L) shredded
1 lb (500 g) carrots = 3 cups (750 mL) sliced = 1⅓ cups (325 mL) pureed = 5 medium
1 lb (500 g) cauliflower florets = 4 cups (1 L)
1 lb (500 g) mushrooms = 6 cups (1.5 L) sliced
1 lb (500 g) onions = 3 cups (750 mL) sliced or chopped = 3 medium
1 lb (500 g) potatoes = 6 cups (1.5 L) sliced or chopped = 6 medium
1 large rutabaga = 4 cups (1 L) chopped
1 lb (500 g) raw spinach = 1½ cups (375 mL) cooked
1 lb (500 g) tomatoes = 2 cups (500 mL) chopped = 3 medium

SUBSTITUTIONS

Suppose you want to make a chocolate cake that calls for chocolate, cake and pastry flour, sugar, baking powder and eggs. You look in your cupboards and your refrigerator and you only find eggs. But you are craving a chocolate cake and nothing else will satisfy. Look again. Do you have cocoa, all-purpose flour, honey, baking soda and cream of tartar?

When you find you don't have the necessary ingredients for a recipe, look for substitutions. Some substitutes are common, such as butter or margarine for shortening; others are less so. Using substitutions won't give exactly the same results, but you will get a reasonable facsimile.

1 tbsp (15 mL) flour for thickening = 1½ tsp (7 mL) cornstarch, arrowroot or rice flour

1 cup (250 mL) cake and pastry flour = ⅞ cup (220 mL) all-purpose flour

How to Chop Carrots, Zucchini, Parsnips, etc.

1 Cut a small sliver off one side of the carrot. Lay the flat side of the carrot on the cutting board. Slice the carrot thinly.

2 Pile the slices on top of each other and cut into matchstick-sized pieces.

3 Gather the pieces together and slice through into small bits.

Metric is becoming more and more common in Canada. Here is a brief table of equivalents to help you translate imperial to metric and vice versa. When following a recipe, make sure that you use only one set of measurements—either imperial or metric.

1 tsp = 5 mL
1 tbsp = 15 mL
2 tbsp = 25 mL
¼ cup = 50 mL
½ cup = 125 mL
¾ cup = 175 mL
1 cup = 250 mL
4 cups = 1 L
4 oz = 125 g

Oven Temperatures

Fahrenheit	Celsius
300	150
325	160
350	180
375	190
400	200
425	220
450	230

1 cup (250 mL) self-rising flour (flour that already contains baking powder) = 1 cup (250 mL) all-purpose flour plus 1 tsp (5 mL) baking powder and ¼ tsp (1 mL) salt

1 cup (250 mL) all-purpose flour = ¾ cup (175 mL) rye or whole wheat flour

1-oz (30 g) square of unsweetened chocolate = 3 tbsp (45 mL) cocoa plus 2½ tsp (12 mL) butter

1 cup (250 mL) brown sugar = 1 cup (250 mL) granulated sugar plus ¼ cup (50 mL) light molasses

1 cup (250 mL) granulated sugar = 1 cup (250 mL) brown sugar, packed = 2 cups (500 mL) icing sugar = 1 cup (250 mL) honey or corn syrup (reduce the remaining liquid in recipe by ¼ cup/ 50 mL)

1 cup (250 mL) sour milk or buttermilk = 1 cup (250 mL) milk mixed with 1 tbsp (15 mL) vinegar or lemon juice

1 cup (250 mL) milk = ½ cup (125 mL) evaporated milk plus ½ cup (125 mL) water = 1 cup (250 mL) fruit juice, in baking

1 egg in batter = ½ tsp (2 mL) baking powder

1 tsp (5 mL) baking powder = ¼ tsp (1 mL) baking soda plus ½ tsp (2 mL) cream of tartar

1 cup (250 mL) buttermilk = 1 cup (250 mL) plain yogurt

1 cup (250 mL) sour cream = 3 tbsp (45 mL) butter plus ⅞ cup (220 mL) sour milk

1 cup (250 mL) cream cheese = 1 cup (250 mL) cottage cheese plus ¼ cup (50 mL) margarine or butter

4 cups (1 L) homogenized milk = 4 cups (1 L) skim milk plus 3 tbsp (45 mL) cream

2 cups (500 mL) tomato sauce = ¾ cup (175 mL) tomato paste plus 1 cup (250 mL) water

1 cup (250 mL) tomato juice = ½ cup (125 mL) tomato sauce plus ½ cup (125 mL) water

1 tsp (5 mL) lemon juice = ½ tsp (2 mL) vinegar

1 lb (500 g) apples = 1 lb (500 g) any hard fruit such as pears

1 lb (500 g) strawberries = 1 lb (500 g) any other berries

1 tbsp (15 mL) fresh herbs = 1 tsp (5 mL) dried herbs

1 tsp (5 mL) dry mustard powder = 2½ tsp (12 mL) prepared mustard

1 tbsp (15 mL) shortening = 2 tsp (10 mL) vegetable oil

1 tbsp (15 mL) liquor = 1 tbsp (15 mL) fruit juice

Part 2

Techniques of Cooking

·3·
Cooking with Water

Water is the most common cooking medium in the kitchen—it is used for boiling pasta or rice, steaming vegetables, or poaching eggs.

For the novice cook, understanding the techniques of cooking with water will help to accomplish the most basic kitchen processes.

Boiling

Boiling is one of the easiest and most basic of kitchen techniques. In boiling, the liquid maintains a steady roll with large popping bubbles and lots of steam. Technically water boils at 212 F (100 C). This temperature is substantially lower than broiling or frying temperatures, which is why meats cannot be browned by boiling. Turning up the heat will not raise the temperature of the liquid. A boil is a boil, whether it is full, rapid or rolling. The term a "gentle boil" usually means a simmer—the temperature is reduced to about 190 F (90 C), and the bubbles come up more slowly. A wisp of steam comes off the surface, and the liquid is undulating rather than turbulent. At a simmer, the food is cooked more slowly, which is a great advantage when you are cooking tough meats, which need a long, slow cooking time to tenderize the tough fibers.

Boiling is probably the oldest cooking technique after roasting. Roasting came first because few utensils were needed—meat was simply skewered on a stick. Boiling required a receptacle, so it wasn't until pottery was invented that boiling became widely used.

Boiling is a moist method of cooking suitable for eggs, vegetables, pasta, rice and grains. Boiling is also used to seal in juices in some meat and poultry dishes.

Boiling is sometimes used to seal in juices of meat and poultry—the meat is immersed in boiling water before being simmered. French *pot au feu* or *poule au pot*, English boiled beef, American New England boiled dinner and Jewish corned beef are all examples of boiled meat dishes.

Equipment
• A large heavy pot for boiling spaghetti; a smaller pot for other boiling needs; for cooking rice you will need a heavy pot with a tight-fitting lid.

• A colander for draining.

BASIC BOILING TIPS

• Always use lots of water. On high heat, bring the water to a full boil. (To bring the water to a boil more quickly, leave the lid on the pot until the liquid boils.) Add 1 tsp (5 mL) salt per 8 cups (2 L) water.

• Immerse the vegetables, pasta or eggs in the boiling water, but do not cover. Boiling is always done uncovered to allow the steam to escape.

• When the food is cooked, drain through a colander.

EGGS

People who love boiled eggs are usually particular as to how long they are boiled. A three-minute large egg is runny, a four-minute egg is starting to set around the edges of the yolk, and a five-minute egg has a creamy center. Hard-boiled eggs are cooked through in the middle.

Egg-Boiling Tips
• Eggs can be white, brown or freckled. The color depends on the breed of chicken. Certain breeds lay brown eggs; others white. Brown eggs have slightly harder shells, making them better for boiling.

• Refrigerate the eggs until the day before they are needed. They will cook more evenly at room temperature, and there is less chance of the shell cracking. If you forget to remove the eggs from the refrigerator, place them in a bowl of warm water for 15 minutes before boiling.

• Use enough water to cover the eggs. Bring the water to a boil on high heat.

• If the egg cracks in the water, pour about 1 tsp (5 mL) salt directly into the water on the crack. The salt will help to seal the crack.

• Time the eggs from the moment the water returns to a full boil. The cooking times given are for large eggs.

• To center the yolk for deviled eggs, rotate the eggs with a spoon for the first minute of cooking time.

• Hard-boiled eggs with greenish-black rings around the yolk are overcooked, dry and less flavorful. When the eggs are cooked, a harmless gas is formed that eventually turns the yolk green. To avoid this, cook the egg for the specified amount of time, then plunge it into cold water to stop the cooking process.

• Hard-boiled eggs can be difficult to peel; sometimes part of the white comes away with the shell. To avoid this, peel the egg from the fat end. Breaking into the air space dislodges the membrane attached to the white, and the shell should slip off more easily.

If an egg floats and will not stay immersed in water, it is bad. Remove it and discard.

Soft-Boiled Eggs

For breakfast, serve these eggs with "soldiers"—buttered toast cut into strips. They are perfect for dipping into the runny yolk. Eat the eggs immediately or they will continue to cook in their shells.

| 2 | large eggs, at room temperature | 2 |

1. Bring a small pot of water to a boil on high heat. Add the eggs, turn the heat down to medium-high and boil for 3 to 4 minutes.

Serves 1

Hard-Boiled Eggs

Hard-boiled eggs can be tossed into salads, chopped for a sandwich, used as a garnish or stuffed for an hors d'œuvre. Leave the cooled cooked eggs in their shells until needed. They will keep for about three days in the refrigerator.

6   large eggs   6

1. On high heat, bring a medium pot of water to a boil. One by one, place each egg on a large spoon and slip it gently into the water. Allow the water to come back to a boil, then turn the heat down to medium-high. Boil the eggs for 12 minutes from the time the water comes back to a boil.

2. Plunge the eggs into cold water to stop the cooking. Leave them in cold water until the eggs are cool to the touch. If using immediately, peel the eggs. If you peel the eggs but don't use them until later, place them in a bowl of cold water so they don't dry out.

VEGETABLES

Although boiling is an easy technique, many cooks are afraid to boil vegetables. We've all had vegetable disasters—limp, brown-tinged beans, soggy cabbage or mushy cauliflower. Overcooked vegetables have no texture, little taste and are of scant nutritional value, since most of the nutrients have been cooked out into the water. However, boiling vegetables is easy if you follow a basic rule of thumb. Root vegetables that grow under the ground (carrots, potatoes, turnips, parsnips, sweet potatoes) should go into cold salted water and be brought to the boil. This will cook the firm flesh through evenly.

Vegetables that grow above the ground (broccoli, green beans, cauliflower, snow peas, corn, asparagus) should go into a large amount of salted water that has already been brought to the boil. The vegetables need enough room to move around in the boiling water so they will cook evenly and quickly. They should be boiled until they are crisp-tender—slightly soft but with some bite remaining. Drain them and pour about 2 cups (500 mL) cold water over to stop the cooking so that they maintain their color and texture. Drain again, then serve.

Vegetable-Boiling Tips

• Because vegetables are all different sizes and textures, the cooking times vary. Bite into one to try. Usually green vegetables take about 4 to 8 minutes; root vegetables take 15 to 20 minutes. When ready, drain and refresh by pouring cold water over them to stop the cooking.

• Boil vegetables in salted water. Add 1 tsp (5 mL) salt per 8 cups (2 L) water.

• Don't store "wet" vegetables such as mushrooms, zucchini, beansprouts or cucumbers in plastic bags. These vegetables exude water which cannot evaporate in plastic, and the vegetables become mushy. Store in paper bags or leave loose.

• When boiling squash, treat it as a root vegetable if you are cooking it with the skin on; if you are peeling it first, treat it as a green vegetable.

• Vegetables such as zucchini, spinach, mushrooms, eggplant, celery and cucumber are too watery to be boiled. Steam or sauté them instead (see Chapter 5).

Deviled Eggs

Cut hard-boiled eggs in half lengthwise and scrape out the yolks. Grate the yolks and combine with mayonnaise, a pinch of cayenne and mustard. With a teaspoon, stuff the yolks back into the egg whites.

Marinated Eggs

Toss warm hard-boiled eggs with enough olive oil to moisten. Season with a pinch of thyme or tarragon. Leave refrigerated for a few hours or up to two days. Slice and serve in salads.

Egg Salad

Chop hard-boiled eggs finely; mix with mayonnaise, salt and pepper. Use as egg salad in sandwiches.

Mimosa Garnish

This garnish looks like the yellow mimosa flowers. Grate the yolks over cauliflower, broccoli or asparagus as a garnish.

Marmalade Glazed Carrots

Serve these carrots with roast or fried chicken or pork. Make them ahead and reheat, covered, on medium heat for about 5 minutes, or until hot.

1 lb	carrots, thinly sliced	500 g
2 tbsp	butter	25 mL
2 tbsp	orange marmalade	25 mL
	Salt and freshly ground pepper to taste	

1. Place the carrots in a pot with cold salted water to cover. On high heat, bring the water to a boil. Turn the heat down to medium-high and boil until the carrots are crisp-tender, about 5 minutes. Drain in a colander, reserving ¼ cup (50 mL) cooking liquid.

2. Heat the butter in the pot on medium heat. Stir in marmalade, reserved cooking liquid and carrots. Simmer together until the liquid forms a glaze, about 3 minutes. Season well with salt and pepper.

Serves 4

New Potatoes with Lemon and Garlic

These potatoes are wonderful with any lamb dish. New potatoes have not had time to form the starches and sugar of older potatoes, so they are fresh-flavored and creamy.

2 lb	new potatoes	1 kg
2 tbsp	butter	25 mL
2	cloves garlic, finely chopped	2
	Grated rind of 1 lemon	

1. Scrub the potatoes. Place in a pot of cold salted water to cover and bring to boil on high heat. Turn the heat down to medium-high. Boil until tender, about 10 to 15 minutes. Drain.

2. In a frying pan, melt the butter on high heat. Add the garlic and lemon rind and cook, stirring, for 30 seconds, or until the garlic softens.

3. Add the potatoes and toss with the lemon-garlic mixture.

Serves 6

Vegetables that have hard, woody stalks, such as broccoli and asparagus, should be peeled with a knife or vegetable peeler before cooking. Removing the peel ensures that the vegetables cook evenly and quickly.

GRAINS

Cooks are often afraid to buy grains because they don't know what they are or how to cook them. It's a shame, because grains can be tasty, inexpensive and nutritious.

The grains we eat most—wheat, rice, barley, oats, rye and corn—are all members of the grass family. Buckwheat, which is actually a plant related to rhubarb and sorrel, is also usually included in this category.

Barley

Most people know little about the advantages of barley, except for the fact that it is used as a base for beer and whiskey. Barley is easy to cook, can be used in a number of different dishes, and has an interesting nutty taste. Most of the barley found in supermarkets is pearl barley—the polished grain of whole barley with the bran removed. Pearl barley comes in coarse, medium and fine grinds. Pot barley has not had the outer bran layer removed. It is full of fiber but harder to find. Look for it in health food stores.

Bran

Bran is the coarse outer covering of wheat. This outer husk is added to recipes to increase the fiber content. On its own, bran tastes terrible. It has a shorter shelf life than other grains.

Buckwheat

Buckwheat is not a true grain because it does not come from grass. It is found in two forms—groats and flour. Roasted buckwheat groats are a staple in Eastern European countries, where it is called kasha, and is popular in pilafs or salads. Buckwheat flour, which may be light or dark in color, is often mixed with all-purpose flour because it has a strong, nutty taste, giving a distinctive buckwheat flavor even when the buckwheat flour comprises only 10 percent of the total flour content in a recipe.

Bulgur

Bulgur is the Turkish word for cracked wheat berries. It is made by cracking kernels of partially cooked or roasted wholewheat berries. Bulgur is known as the rice of the Middle East. It usually comes in three grinds: coarse, medium and fine. Medium and fine grinds are used in salads; the coarse grain is used in pilafs. Bulgur's fine nutty flavor complements meat, poultry and fish.

Couscous

A North African specialty, this is finely cracked wheat that is cooked, then dried. The taste of couscous is similar to ground pasta. Couscous is best served with spicy meat and vegetables.

Oats

Oats are rich in B vitamins, and are higher in protein and fats than most grains. Grains of oats are surrounded by a husk that has to be removed. The resulting kernels are called groats.

Rolled oats are made from steaming and flattening whole oat groats.

Quick-cooking rolled oats are the product of steaming and flattening pre-cut oat groats. They are rolled thinner than regular rolled oats. The nutritional loss means they are not worth buying for the 5 minutes saved in cooking time. If a recipe calls for quick-cooking rolled oats and you only have regular rolled oats, just cook them about 10 minutes longer.

Instant oatmeal is quick-cooking rolled oats pulverised into tiny pieces.

Storing Grains

Store grains in airtight containers in a cupboard. Although they do not spoil, they will dry out over time. Therefore, the longer they have been stored, the longer they will take to cook.

Unusual Grains

Triticale is a cross between wheat and rye. It was developed by scientists to help supplement the world's food supply. Triticale is high in protein and lysine, an essential amino acid. Amaranth is another unusual grain that is high in protein and amino acids but has little gluten content. It is usually eaten as a breakfast cereal.

Cooking Grains

Grains should be added to water that has already been brought to the boil, because the intensity of the heat causes the grains to swell quickly. With this method you will end up with separate grains, not a sticky mass.

For fluffy grains, start with twice the amount of boiling water as grains (except in the case of barley which needs three times the amount), and avoid stirring, which loosens the starch and produces a gummy mess. The grains should absorb all the water and not need draining.

Before cooking grains, rinse them under cold running water and remove any remaining hulls. Each type of grain takes a different amount of time to cook. Test by tasting one after 20 minutes (40 minutes for barley); if it is still too hard, replace the lid and continue to cook until tender. Add ¼ cup (50 mL) hot water if the grain is drying out to prevent scorching. If the grains are tender but some water still remains, uncover and continue to cook until the water has evaporated.

You can change flavors in cooking grains by adding spices. Try 1 tsp (5 mL) ground cumin, ground coriander, paprika, chopped fresh ginger or garlic per cup (250 mL) of grain. Add these to the water when the grain is sprinkled in.

Basic Boiled Grain

4 cups	water	1 L
½ tsp	salt	2 mL
2 cups	grain	500 mL

1. Put the water and salt in large pot and bring to a boil on high heat.

2. Add the grain, stir once and cover. Turn the heat to low. Do not lift the cover.

3. Check the grain after 20 minutes. When water has been absorbed, turn off the heat and let rest for 5 minutes. Fluff with a fork before serving.

Serves 6

_____

Grain Cooking Timetable

Barley	40 minutes
Buckwheat groats	25 minutes
Bulgur (cracked wheat)	20 minutes
Couscous	20 minutes
Oats	15 minutes

RICE

Cooking rice leaves many people frustrated, especially when the rice turns out sticky, gummy or undercooked. I once did a phone-in food show that turned into a two-hour free-for-all, with dozens of callers defending their method of cooking rice, and an equal number calling to tell me why that method had failed.

There are different forms of rice, depending on how much the grain has been processed, and the size and shape of the grain.

When the inedible husk is removed from the rice kernel, you are left with brown rice. It is more nutritious than white rice because the outer layer of fibrous bran remains. Brown rice takes twice as long to cook as white rice and has a nuttier flavor and chewier texture.

Parboiled (converted) rice has been through the process of cooking the brown rice to seal in the nutrients before removing the bran. Parboiled rice is a slightly darker color than ordinary white rice. After cooking, each grain remains separate.

Rice can be long grain, medium grain or short grain.

Long-Grain Rice

Long-grain rice has a slender grain. The longer the grain, the more expensive the rice. This type of rice is excellent for Middle Eastern pilafs. Once cooked, the grains should be slightly firm and separate. Basmati, a nutty, delicate Indian rice, is the finest example of long-grain rice, as well as the most expensive.

Medium-Grain Rice

Medium-grain rice is used for Chinese and Japanese dishes, because when cooked it is slightly sticky—perfect for handling with chopsticks.

Short-Grain Rice

Short-grain rice has a round grain, which swells considerably on cooking. It has a creamy texture and is the basis of the best rice puddings. It will absorb considerably more liquid than medium- or long-grain rice. Arborio is a super-absorbent, pearl-like Italian short-grain rice used for risottos (see page 152).

Rice-Cooking Tips

• Wash long- or medium-grain rice before cooking to remove the surface starch. Short-grain rice doesn't need washing. To wash the rice, put it in a colander and rinse under cold running water. The water will appear murky. When the water runs clear, the rice is ready.

• Use a heavy pot with a tight-fitting lid that will not allow steam to escape. If the pot is made of a light material, the rice will scorch; if the lid is not tight enough, too much steam will escape, and the rice will be undercooked.

• One cup (250 mL) uncooked rice will make approximately 3 cups (750 mL) cooked rice.

Plain Boiled Rice

When cooking long-grain rice, use twice as much water as rice. When cooking medium-grain rice, use equal amounts of water and washed rice. And when cooking short-grain rice, use three times as much liquid as rice. (With short-grain rice, the creamier you want it, the more liquid used—for rice pudding, for example, up to five times as much milk could be used for a really creamy pudding.)

Add ½ tsp (2 mL) salt for every cup (250 mL) rice.

Put the water, rice and salt in a heavy pot and bring to a boil on high heat. Cover, turn the heat to low and cook until tender, about 20 to 25 minutes.

Always Right Rice

I learned this method of rice cooking at the Cordon Bleu; it always works beautifully. You can cook any amount of rice this way, as long as you have a big enough pot.

This rice also reheats well. To reheat, spread the cooked rice on a cookie sheet, dot with butter, cover with foil and reheat in 350 F (180 C) oven for 15 minutes.

2 tsp	salt	10 mL
1 cup	long-grain rice	250 mL
2 tbsp	butter	25 mL

1. Bring a large pot of water to a boil on high heat. Add the salt and sprinkle in the rice. Return to a boil, then reduce the heat to medium-high and boil steadily, uncovered, for 12 minutes. Drain.

2. Turn the heat down to low. Rinse the rice with warm water and shake dry. Return the rice to the pot, cover and steam for 5 minutes.

3. Stir in the butter and add salt and pepper to taste.

Serves 3

Steamed Rice

It is important to wash the surface starch off rice before cooking. Equal amounts of rice and water plus a heavy pot with a tight-fitting lid result in perfect oriental steamed rice. After removing the rice from the heat, it can remain covered in the pot for up to 30 minutes before serving.

2 cups	medium-grain rice	500 mL
2 cups	water	500 mL

1. In a colander, wash the rice until the water runs clear. Put the rice and water in a pot. Cover.

2. Bring to a boil on high heat, then turn the heat down to low.

3. Steam for 20 minutes without removing the cover. Taste the rice and steam for another 5 minutes if needed.

Serves 4

One cup (250 mL) uncooked rice equals approximately 3 cups (750 mL) cooked rice.

PASTA

Pasta is the name for an assortment of different-shaped noodles made with flour, water and sometimes eggs that are becoming an integral part of our national diet. *New York Times* food writer Craig Claiborne called it the "pastarization" of America.

The Chinese lay claim to being the original pasta-makers; the story is told of Marco Polo traveling back from his adventures in China with Chinese noodles in his luggage. The Italian court became addicted to them, and Italian chefs themselves soon perfected the art of noodle-making!

Pasta can be fresh or dried. Dried pasta is made with semolina, which is a flour ground from durum wheat, the hardest wheat grown. Fresh pasta is usually made with all-purpose flour, eggs and a little olive oil.

There is a widespread belief that fresh pasta is better than dried. However, unless fresh pasta is made by the old-fashioned method of rolling the dough six times through smaller and smaller openings of a pasta machine so that the dough is worked and the texture becomes ethereal, then it's a myth, in my opinion. Good-quality dried Italian pasta made with semolina is infinitely preferable to lesser-quality fresh pasta made by the extrusion method. The extrusion method uses a machine that works the dough together but does not roll it. The pasta is then extruded in various shapes out of the machine (this is acceptable for short pastas, but not for long noodles).

The finest dried pasta comes from Italy. It seems to have better elasticity and more bite than North American varieties. Dried Italian pasta also does not become as soft and gooey when cooked too long.

I never use frozen pasta, because the texture changes during the freezing process. I prefer to use dried.

In general, strongly flavored tomato and meat sauces, spicy sauces and seafood need the body of dried pasta, since dried pasta does not absorb the sauce the way fresh pasta does. The rich sauce sits on the pasta and complements it. Fresh pasta usually goes best with cream sauces, light vegetable mixtures and cheese and cream combinations, because the pasta absorbs the flavor.

The little pasta shops springing up everywhere make pasta in many flavors and colors, from beet-red and spinach-green to squid-ink black. Because of the small amount of ingredients used to create these colored pastas, they don't taste much different, but they do look appealing.

Pasta comes in many different shapes, lengths, colors and thicknesses. There are over five hundred different varieties. Thick ribbon pastas like linguine or fettuccine are best for cream sauces, which cling to them. Tubular pastas such as penne are for thin but spicy sauces that will seep through the holes. Spiral pastas like fusilli or pasta shells are used for salads or for sauces with small pieces of vegetable or meat that get captured in them. Very light sauces go on fine pastas like vermicelli. Flat sheets of pasta are used for lasagna or cannelloni.

Pasta-Boiling Tips

• Bring a stockpot of salted water to boil. The pot must be large enough for the pasta to move around freely, so that the surface starch is removed. Add 1 tsp (5 mL) salt to each 4 cups (1 L) water.

• If you are cooking dried pasta, add 1 tsp (5 mL) salt and 1 tsp (5 mL) olive oil to each 4 cups (1 L) water. The oil will prevent the water from boiling over and stop the pasta from sticking together.

• When the water has come to a full boil, add the pasta slowly to keep the water temperature steady (the water shouldn't stop boiling).

• Fresh pasta will take about 2 minutes to cook; dried from 8 to 10 minutes.

Al dente refers to pasta that is tender but with a little bite left.

• Test the pasta by tasting it—there should be a little bite still left.

• When cooked, drain the pasta in a colander. It is not necessary to rinse with water. Toss the pasta with butter or olive oil, if desired, then stir together with the sauce. Serve immediately.

• One pound (500 g) of dried pasta feeds 4 to 6 people.

Spaghetti with Meat Sauce

The classic spaghetti. Spoonfuls of dark-red meaty sauce poured over twisted strands of noodles is a winner in every household. My spaghetti sauce is essentially just meat and tomato sauce, but it does have a splendid flavor.

2 tbsp	olive oil	25 mL
1 lb	lean ground beef	500 g
1	onion, finely chopped	250 mL
1	clove garlic, finely chopped	1
1 tsp	salt	5 mL
½ tsp	freshly ground pepper	2 mL
1 tsp	dried basil	5 mL
¼ cup	red wine	50 mL
1	5½-oz (156 mL) can tomato paste	1
2	28-oz (796 mL) cans plum tomatoes, undrained	2
pinch	hot pepper flakes	pinch
1 lb	dried spaghetti	500 g

1. In a large pot, heat the oil on high heat. Add the ground beef, onions and garlic and cook, stirring, until the meat loses its pinkness and the onions are soft, about 10 minutes. Add the salt, pepper and basil.

2. Stir in the red wine and tomato paste.

3. In a food processor or blender, puree the tomatoes with their juice. Pour into the meat and stir together. Bring to a boil.

4. Reduce the heat to medium-low. Add the pepper flakes. Simmer, uncovered, for 1 hour, or until the sauce thickens.

5. Bring a stockpot of salted water to a boil. Add the spaghetti and boil until *al dente*, about 8 to 10 minutes. Drain well. Pour the sauce over the pasta and serve with grated Parmesan cheese.

Serves 6

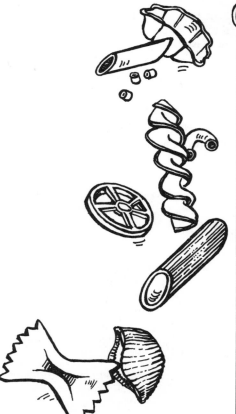
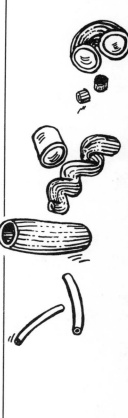

Poaching

With the new tendency toward lighter eating, poaching is a technique that is right back in style, because it uses no fat. Poaching is a delicate cooking method that's easy to perfect with practice and by following a few basic guidelines.

Technically, poaching means cooking in a liquid at 170 to 180 F (75 to 80 C) —a temperature at which liquid "shivers" but does not bubble. The liquid is usually water, but can also be tomato juice, stock, wine, beer or milk.

Poaching is used to cook fragile foods like eggs, fish and fruit. Higher temperatures would cause the foods to break down, change texture or overcook. It's a healthy, low-calorie way to cook and allows delicate foods to retain their subtle flavor.

Equipment
• A deep frying pan or wide pot for poaching eggs.

• A slotted spoon or potato masher to lift the poached ingredients out of the water.

• A metal fish poacher is a lovely treat, but they are expensive; I use a roasting pan set over two burners with a rack placed inside.

EGGS
What better brunch dish is there than a perfectly poached egg sitting on a bed of steamed spinach and covered with a lemony Hollandaise (see page 51)? Poached eggs are a brunch-time boon, since they can be made ahead and reheated when needed.

• Use fresh eggs, otherwise the white will tend to separate from the yolk, giving a tentacle-like appearance to the egg.

• Fill a large pot with 6 inches (15 cm) water and bring to a boil on high heat. Once the water is boiling, turn the heat to low and add 1 tbsp (15 mL) vinegar. This will help to keep the white attached to the yolk.

• Break the egg into a saucer. With a large spoon, make a whirlpool in the center of the pot. Remove the spoon and slip the egg from the saucer into the whirlpool. The white will slowly encase the yolk. Leave for 3 minutes, making sure the water stays below a simmer with only a few bubbles breaking.

• Slip a potato masher or slotted spoon under the egg and lift it out of the water. If you want to eat the egg immediately, place it in dish of warm water until all the eggs are poached.

• If the poached eggs are to be eaten later, slide them gently into a dish of cold water once they are cooked. Repeat with the remaining eggs and allow the eggs to cool. Refrigerate the poached eggs in the water, covered, for up to three days. To reheat, bring a frying pan filled with 1 inch (2.5 cm) water to a simmer. Slide the eggs into the water and simmer for 3 minutes.

• If you have lots of eggs to poach, try poaching them in a frying pan. Bring 2 inches (5 cm) water to a boil on high heat and add 1 tbsp (15 mL) vinegar. Turn the heat to low. Break four eggs into separate saucers. Slide each one into the frying pan. Poach for 3 minutes.

• Avoid metal egg poachers. Because the egg is placed inside these metal egg cups, the water does not touch the egg. This means the eggs steam, and they will have a slightly tougher texture.

FRUIT

The basis of poaching fruit is a sugar syrup which gives extra flavor and sweetness. Sugar syrups can be light or heavy, depending on the amount of sugar used (heavier syrups contain more sugar). Fruits that have lots of juice, such as plums, cherries and peaches, need a slightly heavier sugar syrup to compensate for the added juice that seeps out of the fruit. Fruits with less juice, such as pears and apples, need a lighter syrup.

Poached Peaches

This poaching method can also be used for other fruits, such as plums, apples and pears.

4 cups	sugar syrup	1 L
1 tbsp	grated lemon rind	15 mL
6	peaches, peeled and halved	6

1. In a heavy pot, combine the sugar syrup and lemon rind. Bring to a boil on high heat.

2. Add the peaches and turn the heat down to low. Cover and poach for 5 to 10 minutes, or until a knife slips easily into a peach.

3. Remove from the heat and let cool. Store in the sugar syrup until needed.

Serves 6

FISH

• Fillets, steaks or whole fish poach equally well. Poaching is best for non-oily fish such as sole, halibut, cod, salmon and snapper. Coarse-grained fish such as mackerel or grouper will fall apart when cooked this way. These fish are better grilled or barbecued.

• To oven-poach fish, preheat the oven to 450 F (230 C). Place the fish on a large sheet of foil. Season with a sprinkling of lemon juice, pinch of dried herbs (such as thyme, tarragon or dill) and dot with butter. Fold the foil loosely but securely around the fish, making sure there are no air holes. Bake for 5 minutes per ½ inch (1.25 cm) of thickness.

• To poach fish on the stove, fill a frying pan or wide pot with 2 inches (5 cm) of fish stock, water or a combination of water and white wine. Season the liquid with salt, pepper and a pinch of dried tarragon, dill or thyme. Bring the liquid to a boil and turn the heat to low. Immerse the fish in the poaching liquid and poach until white juices rise to the top and the fish becomes opaque—about 5 minutes per ½ inch (1.25 cm) of thickness. Do not cook until the fish flakes easily with a fork, or it will be overcooked.

Sugar Syrup
Combine 4 cups (1 L) water and 3 cups (750 mL) granulated sugar in a heavy pot and bring to a boil on high heat. Lower the heat to medium-high and boil for 2 minutes for a light syrup, or 5 minutes for a heavy syrup. Cool and refrigerate until needed. Makes 6 cups (1.5 L).

To calculate the poaching time for fish, measure the fish vertically at its thickest point. Poach for about 5 minutes per ½ inch (1.25 cm) of thickness.

Poached Sole

2 tbsp	finely chopped onion	25 mL
¼ cup	dry white wine	50 mL
½ cup	fish stock or chicken stock	125 mL
4	sole fillets	4
1 tbsp	butter	15 mL
	Salt and freshly ground pepper to taste	

1. Put the onion, wine and stock in a large frying pan. Bring to a boil on high heat. Reduce the heat to low.

2. Add the fish to the liquid. Cover and cook for 10 to 12 minutes, or until the fish has lost its transparent look and the juices that rise to the top are opaque. With a slotted spoon, gently lift the fish out of the liquid and place on a platter.

3. Turn the heat under the frying pan up to high and boil the liquid until it is reduced and slightly thickened, about 3 minutes. Remove from the heat. Swirl in the butter and season with salt and pepper. Serve the sauce over the fish.

Serves 4

Steaming

Steaming is a fat-free, slow method of cooking in which food is directly exposed to concentrated steam. The food cooks more slowly than the boiling or poaching methods because steam is less dense than water. Steaming is a healthy method of cooking, because the nutrients are retained instead of being boiled out into the cooking water.

Foods most often steamed are vegetables, fish, Christmas puddings and some grains.

Equipment
• Although you can use a colander set in a pot, steaming is more efficient if you use the special stainless-steel steamers that expand to fit inside different-sized pots.

• A large pot with a tight-fitting lid to keep the steam from escaping.

• A wok with a cover and Chinese steaming baskets are great if you want to steam several dishes at once; these inexpensive baskets stack on top of one another—buy only one cover because only the top basket needs it.

Basic Steaming Tips
• If you are steaming vegetables, place them directly in the steamer or colander.

• Place delicate food like fish directly on its serving platter and then steam. This helps to keep the food from falling apart and preserves the juices that are served with the dish. Use a wide wok or pot and elevate the dish on a ring or trivet (an empty tuna can with the base and top removed works well).

• To steam, fill the wok or pot with about 1 inch (2.5 cm) water. Bring the water to a boil on medium heat. Use only enough water to produce steam.

• Insert the steamer or colander. Make sure the water does not touch the bottom of the steamer or dish, or the food will not cook evenly (the food on the bottom will cook more quickly than the food on top). Cover and steam.

• While steaming, occasionally check the water level. Add more water if needed. If the water evaporates completely, the cooking stops, and the pot will burn.

Steamed Vegetables with Lemon Sauce

Remember to peel the rough outer skin of broccoli stalks so that the vegetable cooks evenly.

1	small head broccoli, cut into florets	1
1	small head cauliflower, cut into florets	1
	Juice of 1 lemon	
3 tbsp	butter	45 mL
1 tbsp	finely chopped fresh dill	15 mL

1. Fill a large pot with 1 inch (2.5 cm) water. Bring the water to a boil on medium heat.

2. Peel the broccoli stalks. Place the broccoli and cauliflower in a steamer basket and place the basket in the pot. Cover and steam until the vegetables are crisp-tender, about 5 to 8 minutes.

3. Meanwhile, heat the lemon juice in a frying pan over high heat. Boil until it is reduced to 1 tbsp (15 mL). Reduce the heat to low and whisk in the butter and dill. Pour the sauce over the vegetables.

Serves 6

Steamed plum pudding is a traditional part of the Christmas dinner. These puddings are made with a high quantity of dried fruit combined with nuts, suet (the firm fat surrounding beef kidneys), flour and liquid. They are steamed for several hours, soaked with brandy, stored for a month to mature, then resteamed on Christmas day, producing a sticky, dark, boozy, filling finale to a great feast.

Steamed Fish

Steaming is a low-calorie, flavorful way to cook fish. Both the French and Chinese are masters at steaming.

French Style:

1 lb	sole fillets	500 g
½ tsp	salt	2 mL
2 tbsp	butter	25 mL
2 tbsp	lemon juice	25 mL
1 tbsp	finely chopped parsley	15 mL

1. Sprinkle the fish with salt. Place in a shallow heatproof dish.

2. Pour about 1 inch (2.5 cm) water into a frying pan larger than the dish and bring to a boil on high heat. Place the dish on top of a trivet in the frying pan. Turn the heat down to medium.

3. Dot the fish with the butter and sprinkle on the lemon juice and parsley. Cover and steam for 15 minutes, or until white juices rise to the top.

Serves 3 to 4

Chinese Style:

1 lb	sole fillets	500 g
2 tbsp	vegetable oil	25 mL
2	green onions, finely chopped	2
1 tbsp	finely chopped fresh ginger	15 mL
2 tsp	soy sauce	10 mL

1. Place the fish in a shallow heatproof dish.

2. Pour about 1 inch (2.5 cm) water in a frying pan slightly larger than the dish and bring to a boil on high heat. Place the dish on top of a trivet in the frying pan. Turn the heat down to medium.

3. Pour the oil on the fish and sprinkle with the remaining ingredients. Cover and steam for 15 minutes, or until white juices rise to the top.

Serves 3 to 4

·4·
Cooking with Stock

My mother always made stock. When I was growing up, the stockpot bubbled away daily as Mother fed it roast bones, ends of onions, bits of tomatoes and other leftovers. For me there has never been a mystique to stock-making, because I'm used to it.

Unfortunately, not many people grow up with a stockpot today; bouillon cubes are much more likely to occupy a place on the shelf in most modern kitchens. However, stocks are basic to good cooking. Essentially they are flavored liquids that add body and soul to other dishes. They are simple to prepare and are the basis of the best sauces, soups and stews.

Beef stocks are used in beef-based soups, such as beef and barley, beef and lamb stews, gravies for roasted red meat, and reduced sauces. Chicken stock is used in vegetable soups, sauces for light meats such as chicken or veal, and in fish dishes, if fish stock is unavailable. Fish stock is used in fish soups and chowders, sauces

for fish recipes, fish stews, or for poaching fish or seafood.

You can, of course, use canned beef or chicken broth, or even bouillon cubes. But homemade stocks cost less, taste better and have no additives or preservatives. (Read the ingredient list on a bouillon cube box, and see if you still want to use it.)

There are three basic stocks: beef stock, chicken stock and fish stock. The methods for making them are almost identical. Only the ingredients change.

Equipment

• A large enamel or stainless-steel stockpot; the pot should hold at least 12 quarts (12 L).

• A slotted spoon or wire mesh strainer to skim the fat from the stock. A colander to strain the stock when it is cooked.

Instant Stock
You can improve stock substitutes by combining 2 bouillon cubes with 5 cups (1.25 L) cold water in a large pot. Add a sliced onion, sliced carrot, and a chopped celery stalk. Bring the stock to a boil on high heat, then reduce the heat to low and simmer for 30 minutes. Makes 4 cups (1 L).

STOCK-MAKING TIPS

• Try to buy soup bones with a small amount of meat on them — 5 lb (2.5 kg) bones will make about 6 to 8 cups (1.5 to 2 L) stock.

• The best vegetables to include in stock are onions, carrots and celery. If you don't have the amount called for in the recipe, don't worry; more or less will not drastically affect the final flavor. You can also add parsnips for a sweeter flavor. Instead of discarding leek tops and green onion tops, save them for stock.

• Herbs and spices included are whole peppercorns, thyme and a bay leaf. Use peppercorns, not ground pepper, because ground pepper clouds the liquid.

• All stock should be started in cold water, otherwise the albumin in the bones is less likely to harden and rise to the top as a gray scum.

• The amount of cold water varies with the amount of bones you start with. A good rule of thumb is to make sure the bones are covered by 1 inch (2.5 cm) of water before bringing it to boil.

• When the water comes to a boil, skim off the gray scum that rises to top. You will have a clearer stock.

• Simmer stock at a low heat with a few bubbles coming up to the surface. Cooking stock at a boil produces a cloudy liquid and leaves a fatty taste.

• Don't salt stock during cooking. When the liquid is reduced, it may be too salty. Add salt after the stock has been added to a recipe.

• Stock will not have an intense flavor unless it has been reduced. Unreduced stock can be used for making soup and most sauces, but if you want a more concentrated flavor, as in reduced sauces, simmer the stock down. For example, 6 cups (1.5 L) stock reduced to 3 cups

As you use vegetables in other recipes, keep the ends and roots. Freeze them and add to stocks.

(750 mL) will give a rich, strong-tasting stock.

• Cool stock after cooking; strain, then refrigerate.

• Refrigerate strained stock for up to five days. Let the fat congeal on top to help preserve it. If you bring stock back to the boil every other day, it should keep indefinitely.

• If you notice your stock bubbling in the refrigerator, or if it has a lemony taste, it has gone sour and should be discarded.

• To keep stock for a longer time, remove the congealed fat and freeze 1-cup (250 mL) or 2-cup (500 mL) amounts in plastic bags or containers. The stock will keep for six months frozen, but after this it will lose flavor. If you need smaller amounts, freeze it in ice cube trays in 2 tbsp (25 mL) portions, and then bag.

Beef Stock

The key to good beef stock is a friendly butcher who will supply you with bones. They may be given away free if you are a repeat customer. Supermarkets sell soup bones at the meat counter. If you feel flush, buy a piece of cheap meat such as shortribs for a meatier flavor. Try to include a veal knuckle in beef stock because this will make the stock gelatinous and more flavorful.

Roasting bones until they are deep brown gives a rich, appealing color to the stock. Onion skins contain a natural dye which also helps to improve the color—don't peel the onions.

Beef stock is used in beef-based soups, such as beef and barley, as gravy for roasts and reduced sauces. It is the basis for beef and lamb stews. Stock can also be made with cooked bones from a roast.

5 lb	beef bones	2.5 kg
1	veal knuckle	1
4	carrots, cut in chunks	4
2	onions, unpeeled, quartered	2
2	celery stalks, without leaves, cut in thirds	2
12 cups	cold water	3 L
1	tomato, quartered	1
1	bay leaf	1
1	sprig fresh thyme, or ½ tsp (2 mL) dried	1
2	stalks parsley	2
6	peppercorns	6

1. Preheat the oven to 450 F (230 C).

2. In a large roasting pan, roast the beef bones and veal knuckle for 30 minutes. Add the carrots, onions and celery and roast for another 30 minutes. Place the bones and vegetables in a large stockpot.

3. Skim any fat from the roasting pan and add 1 cup (250 mL) water. On high heat on the stove, deglaze the pan by scraping up any brown bits. Add to the stockpot. Pour in the remaining water, adding more cold water if necessary to cover the bones by 1 inch (2.5 cm).

4. Bring the stock to a boil on high heat. With a slotted spoon, skim the gray scum off the top and discard.

5. Add the tomato, bay leaf, thyme, parsley and peppercorns. Turn the heat to low and simmer, uncovered, for about 5 hours, or until the stock is reduced by half.

6. Cool the stock. Strain into a large bowl, cover and refrigerate.

Makes about 6 cups (1.5 L)

Chicken Stock

For chicken stock use chicken backs, necks, and add a few wings for extra flavor. Any uncooked leftover chicken necks or bones can be frozen for up to six months and tossed into your stock. Because chicken stock is a light color, don't brown the bones. The light color in a sauce complements light meats.

When the stock is made with a whole chicken or is reduced down even more, it becomes chicken soup. The cooked chicken can be used in chicken pies, salads or other dishes calling for cooked chicken.

Chicken stock is used in vegetable soups, sauces for light meats such as chicken or veal and in fish dishes if fish stock is unavailable.

4 lb	chicken backs and necks	2 kg
	Cold water	
1	onion, peeled and quartered	2
2	carrots, cut in chunks	2
2	stalks celery, cut in thirds	2
1	parsnip, cut in chunks, optional	1
1	clove garlic, unpeeled, optional	1

1. Place the chicken bones in a large stockpot. Add enough cold water to cover the bones by 1 inch (2.5 cm). Bring to a boil on high heat. With a slotted spoon, skim the foam from the top.

2. Reduce the heat to low and add the remaining ingredients. Simmer, uncovered, for 4 hours, or until the stock is reduced by one-third.

3. Cool the stock and strain into a large bowl. Cover and refrigerate.

Makes about 6 cups (1.5 L)

Chicken stock can be made with a cooked chicken carcass. It will be a darker color because the bones are cooked, but it will be full of flavor.

Fish Stock

A good homemade fish chowder is a heartwarming dish, but it needs a base of fish stock—the least familiar stock because it is not made or needed as often as the others. Buy fish bones from the fishmonger; they always have them. A fish head will give the stock added body, if looking at it doesn't bother you.

2 lb	fish bones and heads	1 kg
12	peppercorns	12
1	onion, peeled and sliced	1
1	carrot, cut in chunks	1
3	stalks parsley	3
1 tsp	dried thyme	5 mL
1	bay leaf	1
8 cups	cold water	2 L
1 cup	dry white wine	250 mL

1. Place all the ingredients in a large stockpot. Bring to a boil on high heat and skim the scum off the top. Reduce the heat to low and simmer, uncovered, for 45 minutes.

2. Strain the stock and return to the pot. Boil down to 4 cups (1 L) for further strength.

Makes 4 cups (1 L)

Stock Substitutes

Stock substitutes in the form of bouillon cubes or canned broths cannot be boiled down because they contain too much salt and monosodium glutamate (MSG). In a pinch, use good-quality bouillon cubes, which are usually more expensive than the poorer-quality ones. Look for chicken or beef listed as a main ingredient; not chicken or beef flavor.

Canned beef or chicken broth work fine. They have a little better flavor than bouillon cubes. Bottled clam juice will work for fish stock, but I find it salty.

Most of the recipes in this book, with the exception of the reduced sauces, will work with stock substitutes.

From Stocks to Soups

From an elegant cream soup to start off a formal dinner party to a thick, meaty meal-in-one-pot, soup is a soul-satisfying, nourishing food.

Anything edible can be turned into soup. Simmer in some chicken stock a handful of carrots spiced with some curry powder; or add a few elderly zucchini perked up with apples and watercress; combine leftover salad with a tin of kidney beans and some pasta—the combinations are endless and exciting.

Every couple of weeks, I make refrigerator soup using leftover vegetables, both cooked and uncooked, adding in leftover rice or pasta and finishing with the tomato paste that invariably remains from another recipe. I add a few favorite herbs and create my own soup of the day.

There are many different kinds of soups—thick creamy soups, vegetable soups, hearty soups made with grains, tomato soups. Soups are so varied that many cookbooks have been written just on that subject! Different kinds of soups, however, involve different methods of preparation.

CREAM SOUPS

Cream soups taste rich and elegant, and they are easy to make. Any vegetable makes a good cream soup. Combinations of vegetables, such as turnip and squash, are appetizing, too. Often onions, leeks or green onions are added to intensify the flavor.

• Cook the vegetables in some oil or butter before adding the stock, for better flavor.

• Cook the vegetables and stock together until the vegetables are softened but not overcooked. Overcooking tends to weaken the flavor of the vegetables. Blend or puree in a food processor, blender or food mill. Add cream and simmer together for a few minutes.

• Use any cream from half-and-half (10 percent butterfat) to whipping (35 percent). However, remember that because of its high butterfat content, only whipping cream can be brought to the boil; other creams will curdle and separate. This does not change the flavor, but it looks unappetizing to see little flecks of white in the soup.

• If the soup is too thick, thin it with a little extra stock or cream.

• If you are adding spices (curry powder, cumin, nutmeg, etc.), they should be cooked with the butter; herbs (thyme, tarragon, basil) should be added with the stock. Add salt and pepper to taste at the end.

• Cut all the vegetables the same size to make sure they cook evenly. Whether they are large or small is unimportant, as long as they are uniform.

• Green vegetables are lacking in starch, so a thickener can be added. I like to thicken cream soups with a root vegetable, like potatoes, rather than flour or cornstarch. Potatoes give smoothness without detracting from the flavor or texture. Flour and cornstarch can detract from the natural flavors and produce a texture like canned soup.

• Another thickening technique is to increase the amount of the vegetables used in the soup so it thickens itself. The flavor is more intense and the texture is lighter than if potatoes are used.

Cream of Vegetable Soup

The basic recipe for all cream soups.

2 tbsp	vegetable oil or butter	25 mL
1	onion, peeled and chopped	1
1	potato, peeled and chopped	1
1 lb	vegetables, coarsely chopped	500 g
3 cups	chicken stock	750 mL
¼ cup	whipping cream	50 mL
	Salt and freshly ground pepper to taste	

1. In large heavy pot, heat the oil or butter on medium heat.

2. Add the onion and potato. Cook, stirring, until the onion is slightly softened, about 2 minutes. Add the vegetables, stir together and cook slowly for a further 5 minutes.

3. Pour in the stock and bring to a boil on high heat. Reduce the heat to low and simmer, uncovered, for 20 minutes, or until the vegetables soften.

4. Puree the soup in a blender or food processor. Return to the pot. Add the cream. Bring to a boil on high heat. Reduce the heat to low and simmer for 5 minutes. Season with salt and pepper to taste.

Serves 6

Cream of Vegetable Soup Variations

Carrot and Curry Soup

Add 1 lb (500 g) chopped carrots to pot with onion and potato. Season with 1 tsp (5 mL) curry powder.

Apple, Zucchini and Watercress Soup

Combine 2 peeled and chopped apples, 1 lb (500 g) unpeeled and chopped zucchini and 1 bunch watercress leaves. Add to the pot with the onion and potato.

Cucumber Soup

Add 1 chopped English cucumber to the pot with the onion and potato. Season with 1 tsp (5 mL) ground cumin.

Asparagus Soup

Add 1 lb (500 g) peeled and chopped asparagus and 3 chopped leeks to the pot with the onion and potato. Season with 1 tbsp (15 mL) lemon juice.

Cream Soup Garnishes

• Chop up some of the blanched vegetable used to make the soup and sprinkle on top. (This is always a good psychological move so people will recognize what kind of soup it is before they start eating!)

• Sprinkle with chopped green onion or chives, or use a dollop of sour cream. Or sprinkle with crumbled bacon.

• Homemade (see page 56) or store-bought croutons can be sprinkled on top at the last minute.

• Streak whipped cream on top of each serving. Swirl in a pattern for an interesting effect.

• Grate cheese on hot soup, so it begins to melt.

TOMATO-BASED SOUPS

Tinned cream of tomato soup was a staple in my family. It tasted fine to me, and for years I never realized that it came out of a can. However, once I started to make the real thing, I couldn't go back to the canned soup. The same thing will probably happen to you.

Making tomato soup with canned tomatoes is a compromise we have to make during most of the year because of the poor quality of imported fresh tomatoes.

Tomato Orange Soup

Add the grated rind and juice of half an orange plus 1 tsp (5 mL) granulated sugar to the basic tomato soup recipe after the cream has been added. Bring to a boil and simmer for 5 minutes to blend the flavors. Float a thin slice of orange on top for an attractive garnish.

Tomato Basil Soup

For an intense basil flavor, add 1 tbsp (15 mL) tomato paste and 2 tbsp (25 mL) chopped fresh basil to the basic soup recipe after the cream has been added. Bring to a boil and simmer for 5 minutes. Serve hot or cold.

Basic Tomato Soup

A basic tomato soup can be dressed up to suit any occasion by changing the herbs and flavorings. It freezes well, so I keep it on hand in the freezer for a quick first course. If the soup has a slightly acidic taste, mellow it with a pinch of sugar.

2 tbsp	butter	25 mL
1	onion, chopped	1
1	carrot, peeled and chopped	1
1	1-inch (2.5 cm) strip lemon rind	1
2 lb	tomatoes, cut in quarters, or 1 28-oz (796 mL) can tomatoes, undrained	1 kg
3 cups	chicken stock	750 mL
1	bay leaf	1
6	peppercorns	6
1 tsp	granulated sugar	5 mL
½ tsp	salt	2 mL
¼ cup	whipping cream, optional	50 mL

1. In large heavy pot, heat the butter on medium-high heat. Add the onion, carrot and lemon rind. Cook, stirring until the vegetables are slightly softened, about 2 minutes.

2. Add the tomatoes, stock, bay leaf, peppercorns, sugar and salt. Bring to a boil, reduce the heat to low and simmer gently for 30 minutes. Remove the bay leaf and lemon rind.

3. Puree in a food processor or blender. Return to the pot, add the cream and simmer for 5 minutes. Serve hot or cold.

Serves 8

COLD SOUPS

Cold soups are refreshing before a barbecue or simple summer meal. They are often made in the same manner as cream soups and then chilled. Serve cold soups in chilled glass mugs or pottery bowls and use contrasting garnishes. Garnish with refreshing tidbits such as chopped ginger, slices of lime, or leaves of fresh herbs.

Curried Apple and Avocado Soup

Test the avocado for ripeness. If it has a slight give when pressed, buy it. Unripe avocados have a bitter flavor. To ripen, place them in a paper bag in a dark place for two to three days.

This soup is a lovely pale-green color and has a spicy flavor that complements the richness of the avocado. Stem ginger in syrup can be bought in bottles at the supermarket.

¼ cup	butter	50 mL
1	onion, chopped	1
1	¼-inch (5 mm) slice ginger, peeled and chopped	1
2 tsp	curry powder	10 mL
1	tart green apple, peeled and chopped	1
1 tsp	orange marmalade	5 mL
4 cups	chicken stock	1 L
1	avocado, peeled and chopped	1
½ cup	whipping cream	125 mL
½ tsp	nutmeg	2 mL
	Salt and freshly ground pepper to taste	
2	pieces stem ginger in syrup, slivered, optional	

1. In a medium pot, heat the butter on medium heat until sizzling. Add the onion and cook, stirring, until soft but not brown, about 3 minutes. Add the ginger, curry powder and apple. Cook for 1 minute, stirring.

2. Add the marmalade and chicken stock. Simmer for 10 minutes. Puree the soup in a food processor or blender. Add the avocado and puree again.

3. Pour the mixture into a bowl and stir in the cream, nutmeg, and salt and pepper to taste. Chill well. Garnish with ginger slivers.

Serves 6

Trouble-shooting

If your soup tastes uninteresting or underseasoned, here are some soup-savers to perk it up:

- **Salt:** A dash or two improves a lackluster flavor in all soups.

- **Pepper:** Freshly ground black pepper adds spice. If you have white pepper, use it for white soups, but don't worry if you don't; black is fine.

- **Garlic:** One clove, finely chopped and added 10 minutes before the end of the cooking time, stops any soup from being flat.

- **Tomato paste:** A tablespoon adds body and flavor to any soup.

- **Cayenne:** Adds heat and is especially effective in thick soups made with dried beans.

- **Curry powder:** A few pinches will add a background flavor to cream soups and dried bean soups.

- **Lemon or lime juice:** A few drops will liven up all soups.

- **Herbs:** A teaspoon of tarragon, basil, chives or thyme will perk up a monotonous flavor in cream or tomato soups.

FROM STOCKS TO SAUCES

Sauces define and highlight a dish. In earlier times, sauces were used to mask the taste of inferior food. Today, they serve to enhance rather than over-shadow.

Sauces are often intimidating to the novice, but there is nothing mysterious about them if some simple techniques are followed. Basically, sauces are pre-pared by using ordinary ingredients such as stock, milk or wine. The thickness is determined by the ingredient used to bind them together—flour, egg yolks, butter, cream, arrowroot or cornstarch. Herbs, spices, onions, garlic, flavored vinegars and fruit juices season them. Using these elements, you can create limitless possibilities for flavor, texture and taste.

Because lighter food is currently fash-ionable, heavier flour-thickened sauces are considered out of style. But don't discard these classics; they are the basis of many fine dishes.

The current approach to sauces is based on reducing ingredients to pro-duce a lighter, more intensely flavored sauce. However, these reduced sauces require homemade stock for the best results; flour-thickened sauces don't need the same quality of stock.

Equipment
• A small or medium heavy pot.

• A wire whisk to beat in the liquid.

• A wooden spoon to stir everything to the boil.

FLOUR-BASED SAUCES
• The base for flour-thickened sauces is called a roux. A roux is a mixture of equal parts butter and flour, whisked together on medium heat until com-bined, then cooked for a minute or two. This paste-like mixture should have the consistency of pancake batter. The longer the roux is cooked, the darker it becomes. Use a creamy-colored roux for white sauces, golden-colored for chicken stock sauces and dark-brown for brown sauces. Margarine or oil can be substituted for butter.

• A roux made with 2 tbsp (25 mL) butter and 2 tbsp (25 mL) flour will make a medium-thick sauce when 1 cup (250 mL) liquid is added.

• Use a whisk to stir the roux together to prevent lumps. If the roux is too thick and dry-looking, add a little extra fat.

• Gradually whisk the liquid into the roux until it is well combined and there are no lumps. Bring to a boil, continuing to stir with a wooden spoon. If you don't stir, the sauce will be lumpy and stick to the bottom of the pan. Turn the heat down to low and simmer for 2 minutes to combine the flavors.

• If the sauce is too thick and gluey for your purposes, add more milk or stock to thin it down; if it is too thin, simmer down to the required thickness.

• If the roux has not been cooked long enough, the sauce will taste floury.

• A lightly cooked roux with milk added is called a white or béchamel sauce; with chicken stock added, it is a velouté sauce.

• A rich, nutty, dark-brown roux with beef stock added is called a brown sauce or sauce espagnole.

• Flour-based sauces all reheat well. They will keep in the refrigerator for five days. They can also be frozen. To keep a skin from forming, place plastic wrap on the surface of the sauce while it is still hot. Let the sauce cool at room tem-perature, then refrigerate. Remove the wrap when the sauce is needed.

To keep a skin from forming on sauces, place plastic wrap on the sur-face of the sauce while it is still hot. Let the sauce cool at room tempera-ture, then refrigerate. Remove the wrap when the sauce is needed.

White Sauce

This elegant sauce is the most useful of the classic French sauces because it can be adapted to so many dishes. It is the basis of cheese sauce, cream sauce and onion sauce.

2 tbsp	butter	25 mL
2 tbsp	all-purpose flour	25 mL
1 cup	milk	250 mL
pinch	nutmeg	pinch
	Salt and freshly ground pepper to taste	

1. In a heavy pot on medium heat, melt the butter.

2. Remove the pot from the heat and whisk in the flour, making sure there are no lumps. Return to the heat and cook, stirring, for 1 minute. Whisk in the milk; bring the sauce to a boil, whisking to prevent lumping.

3. Turn the heat to low and simmer slowly for 2 minutes. Season with nutmeg, salt and pepper.

Makes 1 cup (250 mL)

Velouté Sauce

This sauce enhances the flavor of poultry, fish or veal. It is made in the same way as the white sauce, but using stock instead of milk. Cook the roux until it is straw-colored, about 3 minutes. The sauce should be a toffee color when finished and have a slightly nutty smell and flavor.

2 tbsp	butter	25 mL
2 tbsp	all-purpose flour	25 mL
1 ¼ cups	chicken stock	300 mL
	Salt and freshly ground pepper to taste	

1. Melt the butter in a heavy pot on medium heat.

2. Whisk in the flour. Cook, stirring occasionally, until the flour turns a toffee color, about 2 minutes.

3. Whisk in the stock. Bring to a boil, stirring. Reduce the heat to low and simmer for 5 minutes. Season well with salt and pepper.

Makes 1 ¼ cups (300 mL)

Cheese Sauce

Add 1 tsp (5 mL) Dijon mustard and ½ cup (125 mL) grated Cheddar or Swiss cheese to the basic white sauce recipe. Stir until the cheese melts. This is a great sauce for vegetables, macaroni and cheese, or eggs.

Cream Sauce

Add ¼ cup (50 mL) whipping cream and 1 tbsp (15 mL) finely chopped parsley to the basic white sauce recipe after it comes to a boil. Simmer together for 2 minutes. Try this richer version over chicken, fish or vegetables.

Onion Sauce

Chop 1 onion and cook gently in 1 tbsp (15 mL) butter for about 10 minutes, or until very soft. Add to the basic white sauce after the milk has been added, then bring to a boil. Use over veal, lamb or with fried eggs.

Mushroom Sauce

In small frying pan, heat 1 tbsp (15 mL) butter on high heat. Add 4 oz (125 g) sliced mushrooms and cook, stirring, until slightly softened. Stir in 1 tbsp (15 mL) lemon juice. Add to the cooked velouté sauce.

Rich Cream Sauce

Whisk ¼ cup (50 mL) whipping cream into the basic cooked velouté sauce. Simmer together for 3 minutes. Serve with veal or chicken.

Red Wine Sauce

Combine ¼ cup (50 mL) dry red wine, 2 chopped shallots or green onions and 1 cup (250 mL) rich brown sauce. Simmer together for 5 minutes. Serve with filet, roast lamb or duck.

Devil Sauce

Combine 2 tbsp (25 mL) brandy, 1 tbsp (15 mL) tomato paste, pinch cayenne and 1 tsp (5 mL) Worcestershire sauce to 1 cup (250 mL) rich brown sauce. Simmer for 5 minutes. Serve with grilled steak or hamburgers.

Rich Brown Sauce

The most strongly flavored of the basic sauces, this brown sauce is great to have on hand in the freezer to liven up ordinary meats or to add to the gravy for a roast. The secrets are to chop the vegetables all the same size so they cook evenly, and to cook the oil and flour to a rich brown color that smells nutty. The first time I made this sauce, I cooked the roux until it was black, believing that darker is better. Needless to say, the whole sauce tasted burnt.

3 tbsp	vegetable oil	45 mL
1	small onion, chopped	1
1	carrot, chopped	1
1	stalk celery, chopped	1
2 tbsp	all-purpose flour	25 mL
3 cups	beef stock	750 mL
1 tsp	tomato paste	5 mL
3	mushroom stalks	3
1	bay leaf	1
2	sprigs parsley	2
pinch	dried thyme	pinch

1. Heat the oil in a pot over medium heat. Add the onion, carrot and celery. Cook, stirring, until the vegetables are brown around the edges, about 6 minutes. Remove from the heat.

2. Stir in the flour, return to the heat and continue to cook, stirring occasionally, until the flour is dark brown and smells nutty, about 3 minutes.

3. Add the stock and the remaining ingredients. Bring to a boil, reduce the heat to low and simmer for 45 minutes. Strain and cool. Remove the fat before using.

Makes about 3 cups (750 mL)

REDUCED SAUCES

These flavorful light sauces go hand in hand with today's emphasis on light eating. They enrich the fine tastes of good-quality meats, poultry and fresh fish but, unless the cream and butter are omitted, they are not lower in calories or cholesterol than flour-based sauces.

• Use homemade stock as a base— chicken, fish or beef. The gelatinous consistency of homemade stock helps to thicken the sauce.

• An acid such as wine, vinegar or lemon juice is needed to bind the sauce. Fruit-flavored vinegars can be used, too.

• Reduced sauces are made by boiling down their ingredients—an acid, stock, and cream or butter—one at a time for maximum flavor and a smooth consistency.

• Reduced sauces are often finished with whipping cream, which will thicken but not curdle when boiled.

• Only unsalted butter can be whisked in on low heat after the sauce is made. The butter binds the sauce and thickens it. Do not let the butter boil, or it will separate.

• Bouillon cubes and canned stocks are too salty when reduced.

• Reduced sauces can be made ahead of time and reheated when needed.

• When meat, chicken or fish have been cooked in the frying pan, make sure you deglaze the pan with the acid. Deglaze means to scrape up all the little concentrated brown bits (coagulated juices) that are stuck to the bottom of the pan. They will improve the flavor of the sauce.

Light Cream Sauce

You can change the flavor of this sauce by adding herbs such as thyme or tarragon, or several chopped shallots along with the wine. This sauce is terrific with chicken, veal or fish because it enhances their light flavors. Often these sauces don't need salt and pepper because of the natural salt in the stock. Taste after it's made and then decide.

¼ cup	dry white wine	50 mL
2 cups	chicken stock	500 mL
½ cup	whipping cream	125 mL

1. In a pot, boil the white wine over medium heat and reduce to 1 tbsp (15 mL).

2. Add the chicken stock and reduce the wine and stock to ½ cup (125 mL).

3. Add the cream and reduce until sauce thickens and coats the back of a spoon.

Makes ¾ cup (175 mL)

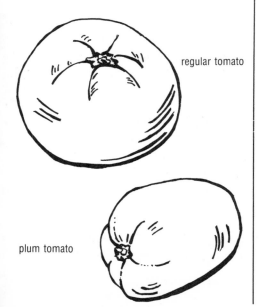

regular tomato

plum tomato

Basic Tomato Sauce

This is another basic sauce to serve with sausages or chicken. It is also the basis for tomato soup and many Italian dishes. Add a couple of spoonfuls to hamburgers or other sauces to add flavor.

⅓ cup	olive oil	75 mL
1 cup	finely chopped onion	250 mL
1	clove garlic, finely chopped	1
1	5½-oz (156 mL) can tomato paste	1
2	28-oz (796 mL) cans plum tomatoes	2
	Salt and freshly ground pepper to taste	

1. In a large pot, heat the oil on high heat. Add the onions and cook, stirring, until softened but not browned, about 2 minutes. Add the garlic and cook, stirring, for about 1 minute.

2. Stir in the tomato paste.

3. In a food processor or blender, puree the tomatoes and their juice. Pour into the pot. Stir together and bring to a boil.

4. Turn the heat to medium-low. Add the salt and pepper. Simmer for 45 minutes, or until the sauce thickens.

Makes 5 cups (1.25 L)

Fresh Tomato Sauce

Often called a concasse of tomatoes or tomato coulis, this uncooked sauce is superb over fresh pasta.

6	tomatoes	6
1 tbsp	olive oil	15 mL

1. Bring a pot of water to boil. Cut slits in the stem ends of the tomatoes, then plunge them into the boiling water. Boil for 30 seconds.

2. Remove the tomatoes and pour cold water over them until they are cool enough to handle. Peel off the skins. Cut in half crosswise and squeeze out the seeds.

3. Coarsely chop and mix with the olive oil.

Makes about 1½ cups (375 mL)

BUTTER-BASED SAUCES

Hollandaise Sauce

Hollandaise, the most delightful sauce to savor with poached eggs, fish and chicken, instills fear in cooks—fear of curdling, fear of not thickening. But don't give it a second thought; Hollandaise is one of the easiest sauces to make and to fix if something goes wrong.

• Start with room temperature egg yolks and unsalted butter.

• Cook the sauce in a heavy pot or a double boiler on low heat to prevent the egg yolks from curdling.

• If, after cooking, the sauce is not thick enough, continue to beat over low heat until thickened.

• If the sauce curdles (separates into a scrambled egg mixture) beat in an ice cube. Because of the sudden lowering of the temperature, the sauce will uncurdle and come together again.

• You can make the sauce ahead of time and refrigerate it for up to 3 days; just be sure to reheat it, whisking constantly, in the top of a double boiler over simmering water.

Beurre Blanc

Like a Hollandaise without the egg yolks, this tangy sauce thickens on the emulsion principle. Reduce the wine and then slowly whisk in the butter. Don't overheat, otherwise the butter will separate.

If you wish, season a beurre blanc with 1 tsp (5 mL) dried herbs or 1 tbsp (15 mL) chopped fresh herbs, depending on what the sauce will be used with. Beurre blanc goes well with fish, shellfish and vegetables, but serve only a small amount, as it is quite rich. If red wine is used instead of white, the sauce is called a beurre rose.

3	shallots, chopped	3
1 cup	dry white wine	250 mL
1 tbsp	lemon juice	15 mL
1 tbsp	whipping cream	15 mL
⅔ cup	butter, at room temperature	150 mL

1. In a frying pan over high heat, reduce the shallots, wine and lemon juice until 2 tbsp (25 mL) remain.

2. Reduce the heat to low. Whisk in the cream. Then whisk in the butter, one-third at a time, until the butter is incorporated and the sauce thickens.

Makes 1 cup (250 mL)

Hollandaise Sauce

Serve this sauce with eggs, salmon, fish and vegetables for a rich and satisfying dish.

3	egg yolks, at room temperature	3
2 to 3 tbsp	lemon juice	25 to 45 mL
¾ cup	butter	175 mL
pinch	salt	pinch
pinch	cayenne pepper	pinch

1. In a small heavy pot over low heat, whisk together the egg yolks, 1 tbsp (15 mL) lemon juice and 1 tbsp (15 mL) butter. Continue to whisk until the butter melts.

2. Whisk in the remaining butter, 2 tbsp (25 mL) at a time, waiting until the butter is incorporated before adding the next addition.

3. Season with the remaining lemon juice, salt and cayenne.

Makes 1¼ cups (300 mL)

Food Processor Hollandaise

A fast and easy method for making foolproof Hollandaise in the food processor or blender. The key to the technique is to make sure the butter and lemon juice are bubbling before pouring into the processor. The heat is necessary to thicken the egg yolks. (Less butter is used in food processor Hollandaise than in Hollandaise prepared conventionally.)

If the Hollandaise fails to thicken, pour it into a heavy pot and whisk over low heat until thickened.

3	egg yolks, at room temperature	3
pinch	salt	pinch
pinch	cayenne pepper	pinch
½ cup	butter	125 mL
2 to 3 tbsp	lemon juice	25 to 45 mL

1. In a blender or food processor, combine the egg yolks, salt and cayenne; process until blended.

2. In a small pot, melt the butter with the lemon juice until bubbly but not browned. Remove from the heat.

3. With the machine running, slowly add the hot bubbling butter through the feed tube and process for 30 seconds, or until smooth and thickened.

Makes about ⅔ cup (150 mL)

Hollandaise should be served lukewarm. If you make it a little ahead of time, keep it warm in a Thermos for an hour.

Béarnaise Sauce

The base of a Béarnaise sauce is a reduction of wine, shallots or green onions, and peppercorns. This cuts the richness of the Hollandaise and gives it a piquant flavor. Serve this full-bodied sauce with any cut of roast or barbecued beef. (You can substitute the white parts of two green onions for the shallots.) Crush the peppercorns by placing between two sheets of waxed paper and bashing them with a pot.

¼ cup	white wine vinegar	50 mL
1 tbsp	water	15 mL
2	shallots, finely chopped	2
2 tsp	dried tarragon	10 mL
3	peppercorns, crushed	3
3	egg yolks, at room temperature	3
¾ cup	butter	175 mL
pinch	salt	pinch
pinch	cayenne pepper	pepper

If your salad dressing is too oily, add a pinch of salt. It will help to eliminate the oily taste.

1. In a heavy pot, combine the vinegar, water, shallots, tarragon and peppercorns. Bring to boil and cook over medium-high heat until reduced to 1 tbsp (15 mL).

2. Whisk the egg yolks into the reduction.

3. Whisk in the butter 2 tbsp (25 mL) at a time, waiting until the butter is incorporated before adding the next addition. Whisk until thickened. Season with the salt and cayenne.

Makes 1¼ cups (300 mL)

SALAD DRESSINGS

Salad dressings and mayonnaise are really cold sauces. They can glamorize an assortment of vegetables and meats with their piquant taste and smooth texture.

Salad dressings are also known as vinaigrettes. A vinaigrette is a combination of oil, vinegar, herbs and spices which, when combined together, form a tangy, thickened sauce to coat salad vegetables. The piquant flavor of the vinaigrette comes from the vinegar used. Remember that although salads are low calorie, salad dressings are not.

Equipment
• Use a medium bowl and wire whisk for whisking the dressing ingredients together; a blender or food processor for making large quantities of dressing.

Vinaigrette Tips
• **Oils:** An oil with flavor is essential for a good salad dressing. Use a good-quality olive oil or vegetable oil such as corn or safflower. Extra-virgin olive oil, although expensive, is a pure, green, delicately flavored and perfumed oil. It is made from the first pressing of the olives and has a low acidity. Use it on delicate salads to complement their flavor.

For a flavor change, try different oils. Oils such as hazelnut and walnut give a nutty taste. They combine well with fruit vinegars and are at their best on plain green salads that do not fight with their flavor.

• **Vinegars:** Different vinegars can open up a whole new panorama of tastes. Their sharp taste cuts through the oil. All vinegars can be used in salad dressings, but some are better than others. I find ordinary white vinegar too tart; it gives an acidic taste to the dressing. In my opinion, red and white wine vinegars, because they are less acidic, are the mainstay of salad dressings. White wine vinegar creates a pale, creamy vinaigrette; the red a more rosy-hued one. Herb-flavored vinegars such as tarragon or basil give a whole different variety of tastes. Fruit vinegars are light and fresh-tasting. Raspberry and blueberry vinegars work well with salads containing fruit. Balsamic vinegar, the least acidic vinegar, can be used on its own because of its rich, mellow taste, or combined with only a little olive oil. Try it on salads containing seafood or poultry.

Other acids such as lemon or lime juice can be used instead of vinegar.

• Use three parts oil to one part vinegar for best results.

• Use fresh herbs if you can; if using dried herbs, use one-third of the quantity, i.e., 1 tbsp (15 mL) fresh herbs = 1 tsp (5 mL) dried.

• Dijon mustard helps to emulsify the dressing as well as adding spiciness. An emulsion is the amalgamation of oil and vinegar to form a creamy dressing. Oil and vinegar, on their own, do not have the properties to emulsify; mustard or egg yolks act as the emulsifier.

• Always beat together seasonings and vinegar before slowly whisking in the oil. This will produce a thickened dressing.

• Make the dressing in quantity and store in the refrigerator for up to one month. It's much better, healthier and cheaper than store-bought dressing. Vinaigrette can be stored in a screw-top jar. Shake to re-emulsify it just before using.

• Don't use too much salad dressing on salads. They will lose their freshness and become wilted. Use about ⅓ cup (75 mL) dressing for 6 cups (1.5 L) lettuce.

• Use leftover salad, including the dressing, to make a refrigerator soup. Toss everything into a soup pot with some water, a bouillon cube and any other leftovers. Bring to boil. Simmer for about 15 minutes; puree in food processor. Serve topped with cheese or croutons.

Classic Vinaigrette

This is the basic salad dressing that can dress all salads. Make a large quantity by doubling or tripling the recipe, then add the herbs and spices when you use it for different salads.

2 tbsp	wine vinegar	25 mL
1 tsp	Dijon mustard	5 mL
⅓ cup	olive oil	75 mL
	Salt and freshly ground pepper to taste	

1. In a medium bowl, whisk together the wine vinegar and Dijon mustard. Slowly whisk in the olive oil until the dressing emulsifies. Season with salt and pepper.

Makes about ½ cup (125 mL)

Garlic Vinaigrette

Before beating in the oil, add 1 finely chopped clove garlic to the classic vinaigrette.

Creamy Garlic Vinaigrette

Before beating in the oil, add 1 finely chopped clove garlic and 1 tbsp (15 mL) whipping cream to the classic vinaigrette.

Tarragon Vinaigrette

Before beating in the oil, add 1 tsp (5 mL) dried tarragon to the classic vinaigrette.

Roquefort Vinaigrette

Before beating in the oil, whisk 1 tbsp (15 mL) Roquefort and 1 tbsp (15 mL) cream into the classic vinaigrette.

Herb Vinaigrette

Before beating in the oil, add 1 tbsp (15 mL) finely chopped fresh herbs (a mixture of chives, parsley, tarragon and basil) to the classic vinaigrette.

Spicy Lime Vinaigrette

In the classic vinaigrette, use 2 tbsp (25 mL) lime juice instead of the vinegar, and add three drops of Tabasco.

Low-Calorie Dressing

I developed this dressing when I was going on my regular diets to shed the excesses of enjoying food. It combines all the flavors of a good dressing without the calories or the heavy texture. This recipe makes a lot of dressing, but it keeps for two weeks in the refrigerator.

pinch	salt	pinch
¼ cup	white wine vinegar	50 mL
1 tsp	granulated sugar	5 mL
½ tsp	freshly ground pepper	2 mL
1	clove garlic, finely chopped	1
2 tsp	dried oregano	10 mL
½ tsp	dried basil	2 mL
½ tsp	dried tarragon	2 mL
1 tsp	lemon juice	5 mL
2 tsp	Worcestershire sauce	10 mL
½ tsp	Dijon mustard	2 mL
½ cup	water	125 mL
2 tbsp	corn oil	25 mL
1 cup	plain yogurt	250 mL

1. In a medium bowl, combine the salt, vinegar, sugar, pepper, garlic, oregano, basil, tarragon, lemon juice, Worcestershire sauce, mustard and water.

2. Slowly stir in the oil and the yogurt, then whisk vigorously until well blended.

Makes about 2 cups (500 mL)

Making Mayonnaise
In a bowl, whisk together 3 egg yolks, 1 tbsp (15 mL) lemon juice, 1 tsp (5 mL) dry mustard, ½ tsp (2 mL) salt and ¼ tsp (1 mL) freshly ground pepper. Drop by drop, pour in 1½ cups (375 mL) oil, whisking constantly, until the mixture thickens. Taste and add more lemon juice if desired. Makes about 1¾ cups (425 mL).

MAYONNAISE

In a mayonnaise, egg yolks are combined with a large quantity of oil to produce a thick dressing. The egg yolks help the sauce to emulsify. Mayonnaise is used as a sauce for cold foods and as a dressing for salads like tuna or salmon. I don't think there is anything to beat good homemade mayonnaise on poached salmon, or as the basis of a spicy, garlicky aioli dip. Flavored mayonnaises are especially good with cold foods, but they also adapt easily to hot ones. Serve mayonnaise beside hot foods instead of on top.

Equipment
• A bowl and whisk, or a food processor or blender.

Mayonnaise Tips
• Use fresh eggs. The fresher the eggs, the more quickly the mayonnaise will thicken. Try to buy newly laid eggs at markets. Their flavor is incomparable. Each egg yolk absorbs about ½ cup (125 mL) oil.

• If you don't like olive oil, use a good-quality vegetable oil such as corn oil or safflower oil.

• Use room temperature eggs and oil to prevent the mixture from curdling or separating.

• If you are whisking by hand, place a tea towel on the table and stand the bowl on it. This will prevent the bowl from sliding around.

• Whisk the oil into the egg yolks very slowly, drop by drop, until the mixture begins to thicken. Oil can then be added more quickly.

• If the mayonnaise curdles or doesn't thicken, beat another egg yolk in a separate bowl and slowly whisk the curdled mixture into it.

• Always taste for seasoning in case more salt, pepper or lemon juice is needed.

• Homemade mayonnaise will keep in the refrigerator for up to three days.

Food Processor Mayonnaise

If the mayonnaise separates or doesn't thicken, remove it from the blender or food processor. Place another egg yolk in the blender or food processor and, with the machine running, gradually pour in the separated mayonnaise. Using a whole egg instead of an egg yolk will result in a lighter mayonnaise.

2	eggs, at room temperature	2
2 tbsp	lemon juice or vinegar	25 mL
1 tsp	dry mustard	5 mL
½ tsp	salt	2 mL
¼ tsp	freshly ground pepper	1 mL
pinch	cayenne pepper	pinch
1½ cups	olive or vegetable oil	375 mL

1. In a blender or food processor, combine the eggs, lemon juice, mustard, salt, pepper, cayenne and ¼ cup (50 mL) oil.

2. With the machine running, slowly pour the remaining oil in a thin steady stream through the hole or feed tube. Taste and adjust the seasoning with more lemon juice if desired.

3. When finished, the thickened mayonnaise should be smooth and thick.

Makes about 1¾ cups (425 mL)

SALADS

To show off your salad dressings, here are some tips on the art of salad-making.

Salads should not be limp, tasteless, dull or insipid; they should be lively, palate-pleasing, nippy and beautiful to look at. Salads can be served as an appetizer, main course, or used as a palate cleanser between courses at an elegant dinner. They can be full of many different ingredients or made with one special component. Use your imagination in creating your house salads, or follow the suggestions below.

Salad Greens

• **Arugula** or rocket lettuce has a pronounced, slightly bitter flavor. It's one of today's trendy lettuces.

• **Belgian endive** has an elongated white stalk and pale-green buds. Look for closed heads without any discoloration. It has a slightly bitter taste with lots of crunch.

• **Boston** or butter lettuce, with its deep-green, soft leaves and buttery flavor, remains one of the most popular lettuces.

• **Chinese cabbage** has a mild cabbage flavor with pale-green, fringed leaves. Its crisp texture is attractive in salads.

• **Curly endive** tastes slightly bitter. Its curly leaves add some texture to a salad.

• **Escarole** is a variety of endive with broad, curly leaves. It has a faintly tart flavor and is good when lightly stir-fried and used in warm salads.

• **Hydroponic** lettuce is grown in water with no pesticides, fungicides, sulphites or preservatives. It is long-lasting, does not need washing and is great in sandwiches.

Cucumber and Dill Mayonnaise

This light, fresh-tasting mayonnaise is a must with broiled salmon. Or combine it with diced cooked chicken for an outstanding chicken salad.

Grate ½ English cucumber and add to 1 cup (250 mL) mayonnaise along with 3 finely chopped green onions and 2 tbsp (25 mL) finely chopped fresh dill. Season to taste with salt and pepper. Makes about 2 cups (500 mL).

Mayonnaise Verte

Try this colorful mayonnaise with broiled fish. Or thin it with a little cream and use as a dressing for potato salad.

In a food processor, combine 1 cup (250 mL) fresh spinach, ¼ cup (50 mL) parsley, ¼ cup (50 mL) watercress and 2 green onions. Process until finely chopped and combine with 1 cup (250 mL) mayonnaise, 1 tbsp (15 mL) white wine vinegar and salt and pepper to taste. Makes about 1½ cups (375 mL).

Aioli

For an unusual hors d'oeuvre tray, offer crudités on a large platter with aioli in the center served as a dip.

In a small bowl, beat together 1 cup (250 mL) mayonnaise with 3 finely chopped large cloves garlic, 1 tbsp (15 mL) lemon juice and salt and pepper to taste. Makes about 1 cup (250 mL).

• **Iceberg** lettuce has a firm head and crunchy texture, but not as much taste as other lettuces.

• **Red oak leaf** lettuce has red-tinged, mild-tasting leaves that add color to a mixed green salad.

• **Radicchio** is a bitter, red Italian lettuce that is very fashionable. It looks like a little red cabbage. Use it sparingly in salads for color and bite.

• **Romaine** is the traditional ingredient in a classic Caesar salad. Its leaves are dark and elongated, with a strong flavor.

• **Spinach** adds a pungent taste and dark-green color. It provides a good base for a salad that includes other strong ingredients such as bacon and onions.

• **Watercress** is a refreshing green used alone or mixed with other vegetables. It is also good in sandwiches. Use the leaves, not the stalks.

Salad Tips

• Make sure all the raw ingredients have been thoroughly washed—nothing is worse than a gritty salad.

• Using a salad spinner is the most efficient way to dry greens. Otherwise, wrap the greens in tea towels and refrigerate.

• Don't put washed greens in plastic bags; the moisture cannot escape and the greens will turn brown.

• Whenever possible, toss a salad with the dressing; this coats the salad more evenly than simply spooning the dressing over it.

• All salads spoil more quickly after they have been mixed with a dressing. Prepare the ingredients and the dressing separately and mix just before serving. Robust salads, with cold meat or strong vegetables, can be dressed with vinaigrette and kept in the refrigerator for 12 hours or so. However, the more delicate the ingredients, the less time they can be left to marinate.

• Sprinkle on all types of nuts—walnuts, pine nuts, almonds, pistachios.

• Green, red and Spanish onions, chopped or thinly sliced, add bite to a salad. Salt the red or Spanish onions first for 30 minutes, or marinate in wine vinegar to remove the strong taste.

• Grated or sliced hard-boiled eggs add protein to a salad.

• Add chopped black and green olives for color and flavor.

• Crumbled bacon or chopped ham provide crunch, taste and protein.

• Hard and soft cheeses such as Parmesan, chèvre, Cheddar or Swiss can be grated onto the salad to make it more filling.

• Sprinkle croutons over a salad just before serving.

Our House Salad

This is my favorite everyday salad. I use whatever greens are on hand. (As we are onion eaters, onions always sneak their way into our house salads!)

6 cups	mixed salad greens	1.5 L
1	red onion, thinly sliced	1
1/3 cup	Classic Vinaigrette (see page 53)	75 mL
1/4 cup	grated Parmesan cheese	50 mL

1. Combine the salad greens and onion.

2. Just before serving, toss with the vinaigrette. Sprinkle with the Parmesan and toss again.

Serves 4

Croutons

Remove the crusts from day-old bread. Cut the bread into ½-inch (1.25 cm) cubes. Lightly coat the bottom of a frying pan with oil and heat on high heat. Add the bread and toss in the oil until golden-brown on all sides. Drain on paper towels and sprinkle with salt and the herbs of your choice. Cool and store in plastic bags in the refrigerator; they should keep for three months.

Braising and Stewing

Braising and stewing are techniques that use a flavored liquid to cook less tender ingredients. A hearty beef stew brim full of vegetables is the most comforting of foods. Stews form an integral part of the cooking of every culture. The cheapest, toughest cuts of meat can be used to produce a robust, nutritious, flavorful dish demanding bread or other starches to sop up the gravy.

Before homes had electric or gas stoves, cooking was done over an open fire or wood stove. More sophisticated techniques such as roasting were reserved for the rich, who could not only afford finer cuts of meat, but also servants who could monitor the process over the open fire. The poor, on the other hand, tossed sinewy, fibrous leftovers into a covered pot and left them to cook while they worked. The dishes of the people, or peasant food—whether a curry from India, beef braised in red wine from France, soy sauce-bathed chicken from China or osso bucco from Italy—are all stews.

Braising and stewing are now interchangeable terms; both mean long, slow cooking in liquid, although traditionally braising was done on a bed of finely chopped vegetables while stewing was not. Today, braising usually refers to a single intact piece of meat, poultry, fish or vegetable, while stewing refers to the same process with the ingredient cubed. Both braising and stewing are usually done in the oven, because the heat is more even. Pot roasting is another term associated with long, slow cooking and usually refers to a single piece of meat or poultry that is browned, then baked, covered, without any added liquid. This method is good for slightly more tender cuts such as a sirloin tip or rump. Because the meat is more tender to begin with, it can be served medium-rare. Use the resulting liquid as a gravy.

Equipment

• The best equipment is a heavy pot, preferably cast-iron enamel, or a Dutch oven with a tight-fitting lid that can be used on top of the stove and in the oven. A tight-fitting lid is essential to prevent the liquid from evaporating and the stew from drying out. Failing this, use a frying pan to brown the meat and vegetables, then transfer to an ovenproof casserole.

STEWING TIPS

• The best cuts for stewing are the tougher ones, which have more flavor and texture than tender cuts. Muscles have to work hard to build up flavor, but become tougher as a result. Long, slow cooking in liquid makes tougher cuts tender and tasty. Tender cuts will dry out more easily. Don't be misled; more expensive meat does not mean better stews. The best cuts for stewing are beef chuck, shoulder, shanks and shortribs; veal shoulder and breast; pork butt, shoulder and leg; lamb shoulder, shank and breast; older poultry, preferably hens; thicker fish such as monkfish, grouper, halibut or squid.

• Trim off most of the fat, then either leave the meat whole or cut it into uniform pieces for even cooking. Meat is usually cut in 1- or 2-inch (2.5 or 5 cm) cubes. If you are stewing vegetables, make sure they are the same size.

• Brown the meat on all sides to seal in the juices, then season. Salting before browning causes the juices to leak out during the browning process. Remove the meat with a slotted spoon and reserve. If all the oil has been soaked up, add more and reheat before continuing to brown.

• It is not necessary to dust the meat with flour, but make sure it is dry so the oil does not splatter. To do this, pat the meat dry with paper towels.

• Heat a film of vegetable or olive oil on high heat until it is smoking, then add the meat a few pieces at a time. Butter cannot be heated hot enough for browning meat—it will burn. Don't crowd the pot while browning, or the heat will be lowered, causing the meat to release its juices and produce steam. This will result in a grayish, flat stew.

• After the meat is browned, lower the heat to medium and add the onions, if using. Cook, stirring, until transparent. Return the meat to the pot and add the liquid, making sure there is enough liquid to come halfway up the meat. Do *not* immerse the meat totally in liquid, or the gravy will be weak and thin.

• For the most successful stews with the strongest taste, use a pot that fits the amount of meat. Cubed stewing meat should sit in two layers, while one piece of meat should fit snugly inside the pot. Too large a pot causes the gravy to evaporate too quickly; too small means the meat cooks unevenly.

• Cooking can be done on top of the stove or in the oven, although I find that an oven provides a more even heat.

• After browning, use gentle heat to cook the meat slowly—325 F (160 C) is perfect for stews. Turning the heat up will not make the stew cook more quickly, and it will toughen the fibers of the meat. The meat is cooked when it can be pierced with a fork—usually about 2 hours for beef, 1½ hours for lamb and pork. Chicken takes 1 hour, depending on its age. Fish stews are cooked the same way as meat and poultry stews, but the fish cooks only for about 20 minutes.

• Liquid can vary from beef stock to tomato juice or wine. Different liquids give different-flavored gravies. Don't use water—it will make a weak gravy.

• Vegetables such as potatoes, carrots and whole onions can be added about 45 minutes before the meat is cooked. More tender vegetables such as zucchini, cabbage, mushrooms or peas are added about 15 minutes before the end of cooking time.

• Thicken the stew with flour, cornstarch or arrowroot. If you use flour, add it to the oil after the meat is browned and cook for 1 minute. Cornstarch and arrowroot are mixed with water, then stirred into the stew when it has finished cooking. I usually don't thicken my stews because of the extra calories, but if I am making one for a buffet, I will thicken it to make the gravy cling better to the meat.

• Alternative methods of thickening include boiling down the stewing liquid. This should only be done if you use homemade stock. Or you can thicken the stew by pureeing the stewing liquid with the vegetables that have been cooked in it. The latter method is currently popular because it is nutritious and lower in calories than using a starch.

• Stews reheat beautifully and taste even better the next day. They also freeze well.

Tam O'Shanter Beef Stew

This thick, hearty beef stew is an original recipe from my mother's cooking school. It's a filling one-dish meal. Substitute other vegetables, if you wish.

¼ cup	vegetable oil	50 mL
½ tsp	salt	2 mL
¼ tsp	freshly ground pepper	1 mL
¼ cup	all-purpose flour	50 mL
2 lb	beef chuck, cut into 2-inch (5 cm) cubes	1 kg
1	large onion, diced	1
1	clove garlic, finely chopped	1
1 cup	beef stock	250 mL
1	28-oz (796 mL) can tomatoes, with juice, chopped	1
2 tbsp	Worcestershire sauce	25 mL
3 tbsp	tarragon vinegar	45 mL
¼ tsp	Tabasco	1 mL
1	bay leaf	1
3	carrots, cut into ½-inch (1.25 cm) dice	3
3	potatoes, cut into ½-inch (1.25 cm) dice	3
¼	head cabbage, coarsely chopped	¼
½ cup	corn niblets, optional	125 mL

1. Preheat the oven to 325 F (160 C).

2. Heat the oil on high heat in a heavy Dutch oven. In a shallow dish, mix together the salt, pepper and flour. Roll the meat in the seasoned flour. Brown the meat in batches on all sides. Remove and reserve.

3. Add the onions and garlic to the remaining oil and cook, stirring, until softened, about 2 minutes. Pour in the beef stock, tomatoes, Worcestershire, vinegar, Tabasco and bay leaf. Bring to a boil, scraping up any bits from the bottom of the pan.

4. Return the meat to the pan, cover and bake in the oven for 1½ hours. Remove the bay leaf, add the remaining vegetables and cook for 45 to 60 minutes or until the vegetables are tender. Taste for seasoning, adding salt and pepper as needed.

Serves 6 to 8

Lemon Chicken in a Pot

A fabulous lemony, self-saucing chicken with a moist texture. Orange, lime or grapefruit slices can be substituted for the lemon. The pot-roasted chicken is started without any liquid, but will cook in its own juices as they accumulate.

1	3½-lb (1.75 kg) chicken	1
1 tbsp	butter	15 mL
1	carrot, thinly sliced	1
1	onion, thinly sliced	1
1 tsp	dried tarragon	5 mL
1	1-inch (2.5 cm) slice lemon rind	1
	Salt and freshly ground pepper to taste	
1½ cups	chicken stock, approx.	375 mL

1. Preheat the oven to 400 F (200 C).

2. Truss the chicken (see page 83). Melt the butter in an ovenproof casserole on medium heat. Brown the chicken slowly on all sides, starting with the breast side down. This will take about 10 minutes. When the chicken is browned, remove.

3. Add the carrot, onion, a pinch of tarragon and lemon rind to the casserole. Stir with the butter. Place the chicken on top and sprinkle with salt and pepper and the remaining tarragon.

4. Cover the casserole and bake for 1 hour. Baste occasionally.

5. Remove the chicken and reserve. Scrape the carrot, onion, lemon and any accumulated juices into a food processor or blender and puree. Stir in enough chicken stock to make a pouring sauce. Carve the chicken and serve with the sauce.

Serves 4

Lamb Curry

"A curry for people who aren't sure they like curry," says friend Jackie McCarten, who provided this recipe. Use a coffee grinder or blender to grind the spices (wash coffee grinder well afterwards to prevent "curried" coffee); a food processor will not grind the spices finely enough. Spice the curry up with extra chilies for a hotter taste. Serve with rice and spiced yogurt.

1 tbsp	cumin seeds	15 mL
1 tbsp	coriander seeds	15 mL
10	peppercorns	10
1	cinnamon stick, ¾ inch (2 cm) long	1
3	cloves	3
½ tsp	cayenne pepper	2 mL
2 tbsp	vegetable oil	25 mL
2	onions, finely chopped	2
1 lb	lean lamb, cubed	500 g
¾ cup	water	175 mL
⅔ cup	desiccated coconut	150 mL
½ tsp	turmeric	2 mL

1. In a small frying pan on low heat, cook the cumin, coriander, peppercorns, cinnamon, cloves and cayenne for 1 minute. Cool and grind. Reserve.

2. On medium-low heat, heat the oil in a large pot. Add the onions and cook, stirring, until lightly brown, about 10 minutes. Add the lamb and the water. Bring to a boil, cover and simmer for 20 minutes on top of the stove.

3. Preheat the oven to 325 F (160 C).

4. Add the reserved spices, coconut and turmeric to the pot. Cover and bake in the oven for 45 minutes, or until the lamb is tender.

Serves 4

Spiced Yogurt

1	English cucumber, unpeeled	1
2 cups	plain yogurt	500 mL
1 tbsp	ground cumin	15 mL
2 tbsp	chopped fresh coriander or parsley	25 mL
	Salt and freshly ground pepper to taste	

1. Grate the cucumber and mix with the yogurt in a bowl. Stir in the cumin, coriander, salt and pepper. Chill until serving time.

Makes 2½ cups (625 mL)

Braised Fish

Have the fish filleted but left whole with the head and tail attached. If you cannot buy a whole fish, use two fish fillets and put the stuffing in between. Serve with noodles or rice.

1	2-lb (1 kg) whitefish, filleted	1
2 tbsp	olive oil	25 mL
2	leeks, including 2 inches (5 cm) green, chopped	2
1 cup	whipping cream	250 mL
¼ tsp	salt	1 mL
pinch	freshly ground pepper	pinch
1 cup	fresh breadcrumbs	250 mL
	Grated rind of ½ lemon	
½	green pepper, chopped	½
½	red pepper, chopped	½
1 cup	canned tomatoes, drained and pureed	250 mL
¼ cup	finely chopped parsley	50 mL
1 tsp	dried basil	5 mL

1. Preheat the oven to 350 F (180 C). Open the fish butterfly fashion.

2. Heat 1 tbsp (15 mL) olive oil in a large frying pan on high heat. Add the leeks and cook, stirring, until softened. Add the cream and reduce on high heat until the cream thickens and binds the leeks together. Season well with salt and pepper.

3. Stir in the breadcrumbs and the lemon rind. Stuff the fish with the mixture. Skewer the cavity shut.

4. Brush an ovenproof gratin dish slightly larger than the fish with the remaining oil.

5. In a small bowl, combine the peppers, tomatoes, parsley and basil. Spoon all but 2 tbsp (25 mL) into the gratin dish. Top with the fish. Cover the fish with the remaining vegetables. Cover with foil.

6. Bake for 30 minutes, or until the fish juices are white.

Serves 4

When you are cooking a whole fish, leave the head on. It does help to keep the juices in. When the eyes turn milky white, the fish is cooked.

Ratatouille

This vegetable stew hails from the south of France. It can be served as a first course or a side dish with lamb or chicken. A true ratatouille stews the vegetables in oil, not in tomato liquid. The vegetables should hold their shape but have a meltingly tender texture and a background hint of olive oil, garlic and herbs. There is no standard recipe for ratatouille—it is a dish that varies from house to house and from restaurant to restaurant. The ingredients remain the same, but the quantities vary with what is on hand. Remember to cut all the vegetables the same size for even cooking. Use six fresh, ripe tomatoes when tomatoes are in season.

When refrigerating ratatouille, leave the accumulated olive oil on top of the dish—it will help to protect the food. Ratatouille also makes a good filling for omelets.

1	eggplant	1
1 tsp	salt	5 mL
½ cup	olive oil	125 mL
1	Spanish onion, sliced	1
1	green pepper, diced	1
2	zucchini, sliced	2
1	28-oz (796 mL) can tomatoes, drained	1
	Salt and freshly ground pepper to taste	
1 tbsp	finely chopped parsley	15 mL
2 tsp	dried marjoram	10 mL
2 tsp	dried basil	10 mL
2	cloves garlic, finely chopped	2

1. Slice the eggplant into ½-inch (1.25 cm) cubes and place in large colander. Lightly sprinkle with the salt and let stand for 1 hour.

2. Heat the oil in a large frying pan on high heat. Add the onion and cook, stirring, until transparent, about 2 min-utes. Add the green pepper and the eggplant and cook, stirring occasionally for 5 minutes. Add the zucchini, toss in the oil then stir in the tomatoes. Cover the pan, turn heat down to low and simmer gently for 20 minutes.

3. Add salt and pepper to taste. Stir in the parsley, marjoram, basil and garlic. Simmer, uncovered, for 15 minutes. If any liquid remains, boil until thickened. Serve hot or cold.

Serves 6 to 8

·5·
Cooking with Fat

Fat—butter, vegetable oil, olive oil, margarine or animal fat—is a common cooking medium. When food is cooked in fat on a high heat, the fat seals in the juices. Recipes frequently ask you to sauté in butter or stir-fry in oil, but what do these terms mean, and how do they affect a dish?

Sautéing

Sautéing is a basic technique common to all the world's cuisines. Sautéing in French cooking becomes stir-frying in Chinese cooking. The pans and ingredients may be different, but the technique is essentially the same.

The French word *sauté* means "to jump." When applied to cooking, it describes the technique of quickly flipping and turning food in a frying pan. Food can be cooked completely by sautéing, but it can also be the preliminary stage of browning before finishing the cooking in liquid.

The sautéing technique is ideal for the person who wants to produce fresh food quickly. Heat a little oil in a frying pan, toss in some thinly sliced meat, poultry or fish, add a few vegetables, season well, and you'll have a meal in minutes.

Equipment
• Use a high-sided frying pan with a lid, or invest in a sauté pan—a deep frying pan with a tight-fitting lid.

• A wooden spoon to toss ingredients around; metal spoons will burn your hands.

SAUTÉING TIPS

• Food to be sautéed should be uniform in size to cook evenly. Often the pieces are diced or cut in strips.

• Use room temperature ingredients to avoid lowering the heat in the pan.

• Make sure the food is dry before sautéing, or moisture will accumulate in the pan, causing the food to steam.

• Use very hot fat and a high heat—oil, clarified butter or a combination of butter and oil work best. Butter alone will burn before it is hot enough. The combination of oil and butter, usually 1 tbsp (15 mL) oil to 2 tbsp (25 mL) butter, raises the temperature of the butter to allow sautéing. Use this combination when you want to give a buttery taste to the dish.

• Keep the pan on high heat during the sautéing process. If the fat is not hot enough, the juices will not be sealed in and will run into the pan, causing steam. Don't crowd the pan, because this will lower the temperature and cause the juices to run out.

• Add the ingredients to hot oil and toss quickly. Sautéing involves constant stirring and tossing.

Clarified Butter

Clarified butter is sensational for sautéing, because the milk solids have been removed but the butter taste remains. It is the milk solids that cause the butter to burn. Try it as a dip for seafood. Use unsalted butter, which has more solid butter and less water per pound. Clarified butter keeps for months in the refrigerator, covered, so make a large amount.

1 lb	butter	500 g

1. Heat the butter slowly in a small pot. When it has melted, and the bubbles and sediment have risen to the top, remove the pot from the heat and let the butter settle for a few minutes.

2. Pour gently through a strainer lined with cheesecloth. The sediment will stay behind and the butter will drip through into the bowl. The butter in the bowl is now clarified.

3. When the butter has cooled, store, covered, in the refrigerator.

Makes about 12 oz (375 g)

Sautéing
In a frying pan, toss the food with a wooden spoon to cook but not brown.

Clarified butter is a boon to people who are lactose intolerant, because the milk solids have been removed.

Sautéed Chicken with Ginger

Monda Rosenberg, Food Editor of Cha-telaine magazine, demonstrated this delectable dish at the 1986 Ontario Science Centre Food Show.
This recipe illustrates the technique of sautéing and finishing a dish quickly in a liquid.

4	single chicken breasts, skinned and boned	4
¼ cup	all-purpose flour	50 mL
1 tbsp	vegetable or olive oil	15 mL
2 tbsp	butter	25 mL
¼ cup	chicken stock	50 mL
2 tbsp	syrup drained from preserved ginger	25 mL
2 tbsp	lime juice	25 mL
¼ cup	slivered preserved ginger	50 mL
	Salt and freshly ground pepper to taste	
2	green onions, sliced	2
	Grated rind of 1 lime	

1. Lightly coat the chicken with the flour, shaking off the excess.

2. Melt the oil and butter in a large frying pan. Add the chicken breasts and sauté over high heat for about 10 minutes, turning twice, until golden-brown.

3. Add the chicken stock to the pan along with the ginger syrup and 1 tbsp (15 mL) lime juice. Cover tightly and simmer for 5 minutes.

4. Remove the chicken to a serving platter and cover to keep warm. Stir the slivered ginger and remaining lime juice into the sauce. Turn the heat to high and boil vigorously until thickened, about 2 minutes. Taste for seasoning, adding salt and pepper as needed.

5. Pour the sauce over the chicken and garnish with the sliced green onion and grated lime rind.

Serves 4

Sautéed Mushrooms

Mushrooms are magnificent sautéed and scented with a touch of lemon. They make a great side dish for steaks or chicken. Don't cook the mushrooms until they are all dried out—a common mistake. They should be juicy. They are ready as soon as the juice starts to leak out.

1 tbsp	vegetable oil	15 mL
1 tbsp	butter	15 mL
8 oz	mushrooms, sliced	250 g
1 tbsp	lemon juice	15 mL
	Salt and freshly ground pepper to taste	

1. Heat the oil and butter in a frying pan on high heat until very hot.

2. Toss in the mushrooms. Sauté until glistening, about 2 minutes. When the juices start to leak out, remove the pan from the heat and add the lemon juice, salt and pepper.

Serves 2

Mushrooms should never be washed because they absorb water. Wipe them clean with a damp cloth or scrub them gently with a nail brush.

Sautéed Shrimps with Chili and Garlic

This recipe takes about 10 minutes to prepare, so it's perfect for a fast dinner. You can also use it as an appetizer for a dinner party.

Fresh chilies come in different sizes and colors. As they mature, the skin changes color from green to red. Their flavor varies in heat from mild to incendiary, and you often don't know how hot they are until you taste one. My rule of thumb is the smaller the chili, the more lethal the effect. Be careful when preparing chilies. If you have sensitive skin, use rubber gloves because the oil they release can burn. Remove the seeds and ribs, which are the hottest parts. If you don't like too hot a taste, use only half the quantity.

2 tbsp	olive oil	25 mL
1	fresh green chili pepper, seeded and chopped	1
4	cloves garlic, sliced	4
1 lb	large shrimps, peeled	500 g
1 tbsp	lemon juice	15 mL
2 tbsp	finely chopped parsley	25 mL
	Salt and freshly ground pepper to taste	

1. Add the olive oil, chili and garlic slices to a heavy frying pan. Simmer on low heat for 2 minutes to flavor the oil.

2. Turn the heat to high. Add the shrimp and sauté for 2 minutes, or until the shrimp is pink and curled.

3. Sprinkle with the lemon juice and parsley. Season to taste with salt and pepper. Serve at once.

Serves 6 as an appetizer, 4 as a main course

Stir-Frying

In stir-frying, small pieces of evenly cut food are tossed quickly in oil. Chinese stir-frying is similar to sautéing, but a wok and two utensils are used to toss the food quickly.

Equipment

• A carbon steel wok is an efficient cooking utensil for stir-frying. Its conical shape and high sides mean that heat is distributed evenly and the food will not fly out when tossed. Stainless-steel woks do not work as efficiently because stainless steel is not a porous metal. A frying pan can be used instead of a wok.

• A large scoop spoon and slotted spoon or skimming spoon are the most efficient utensils for tossing food, although you could use two wooden spoons or chopsticks. The Chinese skimming spoon is made with copper-wire mesh and is used to remove ingredients from the deep-frying oil, but I simply use a slotted spoon.

STIR-FRYING TIPS

• Have all the meat and vegetables cut the same size and same shape for even cooking and eye appeal.

• Use the highest heat to cook quickly without burning. Heat the wok, then add the oil. This prevents the food from sticking. Heat the oil until it is smoking to sear meat and poultry. The heat should always remain on the highest temperature.

• Season the oil with ginger, garlic and/or green onion. Cook the seasonings only until they sizzle.

• Stir-fry the meat first. Remove it from the wok as it cooks, so as not to overcook the meat or crowd the wok. Stir-fry the vegetables, then return the meat and add the final seasoning sauce.

• The final seasoning sauce is always added last for flavor. Thicken it with a cornstarch paste made of equal amounts of cornstarch and water combined together until smooth. (Give the paste a quick final stir before using, as the cornstarch tends to separate.)

A CHINESE INGREDIENT PRIMER

Black Beans
Salted, fermented black soy beans that are used as a seasoning. Rinse them with cold water, drain and mash lightly with the back of a spoon. Store in a cupboard.

Chinese Chili Sauce or Paste
It's hot and zingy, and made from fresh chili peppers. Use it as a flavoring or dip. Store in a cupboard.

Chinese Noodles
Fresh egg noodles in various thicknesses can be purchased in Chinese stores, but you can use dried Italian egg noodles instead. Rice sticks are noodles made with rice flour and water. They are either deep-fried or soaked in hot water before using. Cellophane noodles are made with powdered mung beans

and are considered a vegetable. They are soaked before using.

Ginger
Buy smooth fresh ginger, peel it and finely chop for maximum flavor. To store ginger, either cover the peeled ginger with wine and refrigerate (it should keep indefinitely), or leave the unpeeled ginger in a drawer or on the counter (not the refrigerator). The cut end will dry out, but simply slice it off before using. Do not substitute powdered ginger for fresh ginger.

Hoisin Sauce
A pungent, spicy/sweet bean sauce used to flavor a final seasoning sauce or as a dip. Store it in the refrigerator.

Oyster Sauce
A thick, rich brown sauce made from ground oysters; it is used as a flavoring for meat and noodles. Store it in a cupboard.

Rice Vinegar
Chinese rice vinegar is black or red in color and has a wonderful mellow flavor. Substitute a mild red or white wine vinegar if you can't find it.

Sesame Oil
An aromatic oil made from toasted sesame seeds. It is used for adding flavor to a dish, never for cooking. Store it in a cupboard.

Soy Sauce
There are two kinds of soy sauce, light and dark. Dark soy sauce is used for marinating meats and for giving color to rice or noodles. Light is used for a finishing sauce, as a condiment and for marinating poultry and fish. Dark soy sauce has a dark, thick look. Light soy sauce is lighter in color and flavor. Use all-purpose, medium-colored Japanese soy sauce as a substitute for both light and dark. Store it in a cupboard.

Don't use an electric wok, because the temperature fluctuations don't allow it to retain its heat.

Although stir-fried food should be eaten immediately for the freshest flavor and texture, all dishes can be reheated, uncovered, in a 400 F (200 C) oven until hot.

Chicken with Cashews

The key to successful stir-frying is organization. Measure out all the marinades and final seasoning sauces before cooking. If you cook some of the ingredients ahead of time, finishing the dish will only take 5 minutes.

This recipe is a typical stir-fried dish. Change the vegetables and nuts if you wish.

1	egg white	1
1 tbsp	cornstarch	15 mL
1 tbsp	water	15 mL
1 tbsp	soy sauce	15 mL
3	single boneless chicken breasts, cut into 1-inch (2.5 cm) cubes	3
⅔ cup	cashews	150 mL

Seasoning Sauce:

1 tbsp	dry white wine	15 mL
2 tbsp	rice vinegar	25 mL
¼ tsp	salt	1 mL
1 tsp	granulated sugar	5 mL
2 tbsp	soy sauce	5 mL
1 tsp	cornstarch	5 mL

To Finish:

⅓ cup	vegetable oil	75 mL
3	slices ginger, each the size of a quarter, finely chopped	3
3	green onions, cut into ½-inch (1.25 cm) pieces	3
1	green pepper, diced	1
1	red pepper, diced	1

The comma-shaped cashew is the seed of the cashew pear. They are usually sold roasted and salted and are good in stir-fried dishes because they retain their crispness when cooked quickly. Unfortunately, they go soft in baking.

1. Preheat the oven to 350 F (180 C).

2. In a medium bowl, mix together the egg white, cornstarch, water and soy sauce. Add the chicken and marinate for 30 minutes.

3. On a cookie sheet, toast the cashews in the oven for 10 minutes, or until brown. Stir occasionally. Reserve.

4. In a small bowl, combine all the ingredients for the seasoning sauce. Reserve.

5. Heat the oil in a wok until very hot. Remove the chicken from the marinade. Add one-third of the chicken and stir-fry until whitened. Remove and reserve. Repeat with the remaining chicken, one-third at a time. Drain all but 2 tbsp (25 mL) oil from the wok.

6. Stir in the ginger, green onions, red and green peppers. Stir-fry for 30 seconds.

7. Return the chicken to the wok and stir together. Add the final seasoning sauce. Bring to boil, stirring.

8. Add the cashews, stir together and serve.

Serves 4

Stir-Fried Pork with Chili Sauce

A spicy stir-fry from Sichuan, the province that serves some of the hottest food in China. More chili sauce will give more zing. Substitute beef or chicken for the pork, if desired.

8 oz	pork tenderloin	250 g
1 tbsp	soy sauce	15 mL
1 tbsp	cornstarch	15 mL
1 tbsp	cold water	15 mL
6	canned water chestnuts	6
1	large carrot	1

Seasoning Sauce:

1 tbsp	slivered green onion	15 mL
1 tbsp	soy sauce	15 mL
1 tbsp	rice vinegar	15 mL
1 tsp	Chinese chili sauce	5 mL
2 tsp	dry white wine	10 mL
1 tsp	granulated sugar	5 mL
1 tsp	water	5 mL
1 tsp	cornstarch	5 mL
1 tsp	sesame oil	5 mL
¼ tsp	freshly ground pepper	1 mL

To Finish:

2 tbsp	vegetable oil	25 mL
1 tbsp	chopped fresh ginger	15 mL
1	clove garlic, chopped	1

1. Cut the pork into slivers.

2. In a medium bowl, mix together the soy sauce, cornstarch and water. Add the pork and marinate for 15 minutes.

3. Slice the water chestnuts and carrot into slivers.

4. In a small bowl, combine all the ingredients for the seasoning sauce.

5. Heat the oil in a wok on high heat. Add the ginger and garlic. Stir-fry for 30 seconds, then add the pork. Stir-fry for 1 minute, or until no longer pink. Remove with a slotted spoon and reserve.

6. Add the water chestnuts and carrot to the wok. Stir-fry for 1 minute. Add the reserved meat and final seasoning sauce. Bring to boil, stirring until thickened. Serve immediately.

Serves 2 as a main dish, or 4 as part of a Chinese meal

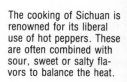

The cooking of Sichuan is renowned for its liberal use of hot peppers. These are often combined with sour, sweet or salty flavors to balance the heat.

Stir-Fried Beef with Black Beans and Noodles

Add other vegetables such as spinach, Chinese cabbage, zucchini or carrots if desired. Use the thin egg noodles. To remove the strings from snow peas, grasp the little fiber at the end of the curved section and pull. Use sliced broccoli stems if snow peas are unavailable.

Chili peppers come in different colors and sizes. Green poblano chilies are large and mild and are usually used in Mexican cooking for dishes such as stuffed peppers. The yellow banana peppers range in heat from mild to fiery; taste one before using them in a dish. The shiny, hot, dark-green jalapeños are frequently available, both fresh and canned. They are used in both Mexican and Chinese cooking. The true oriental chili is small and can be either green or red; they can bring tears to your eyes!

8 oz	fresh egg noodles	250 g
2 tbsp	vegetable oil	25 mL
8 oz	flank steak	250 g
1 tsp	granulated sugar	5 mL
2 tsp	cornstarch	10 mL
1 tbsp	dark soy sauce	15 mL
1 tsp	sesame oil	5 mL
1 tbsp	water	15 mL

Seasoning Sauce:

1½ cups	chicken stock	375 mL
1 tsp	granulated sugar	5 mL
2 tbsp	soy sauce	25 mL
2 tbsp	cornstarch	25 mL
1 tsp	sesame oil	5 mL

To Finish:

½ cup	vegetable oil, approx.	125 mL
1	small chili pepper, chopped	1
1 tbsp	finely chopped ginger	15 mL
1 tbsp	finely chopped garlic	15 mL
3 tbsp	salted black beans, rinsed and mashed	45 mL
1 cup	snow peas, strings removed	250 mL
1	red pepper, thinly sliced	1
1	onion, thinly sliced	1

1. Bring a large pot of water to a boil. Add the noodles and boil on high heat for about 1 minute, or until tender. Drain well and mix with 2 tbsp (25 mL) oil. Reserve.

2. Slice the flank steak against the grain into thin slices.

3. In a medium bowl, combine 1 tsp (5 mL) sugar, 2 tsp (10 mL) cornstarch, 1 tbsp (15 mL) soy sauce and 1 tsp (5 mL) sesame oil. Add the meat and marinate for 30 minutes.

4. In a small bowl, combine all the ingredients for seasoning sauce.

5. Heat the wok over medium heat. Add 2 tbsp (25 mL) oil. Cook the noodles until golden-brown on one side, about 5 minutes. Turn over, adding more oil if needed, and cook on the other side until golden-brown. Remove from the wok and keep warm on a serving platter in 300 F (150 C) oven.

6. Heat the wok over high heat. Add 2 tbsp (25 mL) oil. Drain the meat from the marinade and stir-fry until it loses its pinkness. Remove with a slotted spoon and reserve.

7. Add the remaining oil and stir in the chili pepper, ginger, garlic and black beans. Add the vegetables. Stir-fry until the red pepper softens slightly, about 1 minute.

8. Stir together the seasoning sauce, and pour into the wok. Bring to boil, stirring. Return the meat and juice. Mix well. Pour the contents of the wok on top of the noodles.

Serves 3 to 4 as a main course, or 6 as part of a Chinese meal.

Deep-Frying

Deep-frying is a cooking technique that is common to many cultures. In India and China, deep-frying carts on the streets provide on-the-spot, crisp pastries and dumplings. I have seen canoe-sized boats in Hong Kong harbor with built-in woks heated by blazing gas jets, deep-frying your chosen fish as you sail by. In Britain, fish and chips remain the fast food of choice. In Canada we eat French fries, doughnuts, onion rings, battered vegetables and chicken nuggets, all deliciously deep-fried.

Unfortunately, the technique of home deep-frying has lost favor. Fear of frying at high temperatures causes people to use lower than optimum heat. This leaves food soggy and greasy, increases the calorie count and diminishes the actual taste of the food. If food is deep-fried at the proper temperature, only a minuscule amount of oil is absorbed, leaving the food virtually fat-free. The method is fast, and the food—crisp on the outside and steamed in its own juices inside—retains its flavor and crunchy, light texture.

Don't be afraid of deep-frying properly. Using the right techniques, the proper oil and the right pan will prevent high calorie intake and flash fires, and will result in wonderfully crisp and exciting food.

Equipment
• Use a deep, heavy pan. A wok sitting on a wok ring is the best because its conical shape will prevent hot oil spillovers. The shape also decreases the amount of oil needed. The ring prevents the wok from tipping over. A deep-frying pan works with smaller-sized ingredients, but is not high sided enough for chicken. Although electric deep-fryers are acceptable, their thermostats are not always a reliable guide to the oil temperature, and their built-in temperature control means that the heat doesn't go back on until the oil falls below a certain temperature, which is in fact not hot enough for deep-frying.

• A slotted metal spoon for removing food from the pan.

• Long-handled metal tongs are necessary for turning food. Two spatulas help to turn over large pieces of food efficiently.

DEEP-FRYING TIPS
• Use vegetable or peanut oil for deep-frying. They have a higher flash point than other oils, and are therefore less likely to catch fire.

• Meat, poultry, fish, vegetables and fruit can all be successfully deep-fried.

• Oil should be heated to 375 F (190 C). Too low a temperature means the food will absorb oil. At the optimum temperature, food will brown and be grease-free. The best way to test for the right temperature is to use a deep-fat frying thermometer, available at kitchen stores. A less reliable method is to drop a bread cube into the oil. If it bubbles but does not brown, the temperature is too low; if it browns within 15 seconds, the oil is ready.

• Use enough oil to prevent food from sitting on the bottom of the pan, but remember that hot oil bubbles up when ingredients are first added. Fill a pot or wok half full, which will allow plenty of room for bubbling up.

• Food to be deep-fried must be thoroughly dried first, or the oil will spit.

• Before deep-frying, many foods are batter-coated or floured to form a crust that minimizes oil absorption. More delicate foods, such as fish or fruit, are always coated with batter, because they will

To clean the oil you use for deep-frying, sprinkle it with 2 tbsp (25 mL) cornstarch while it is still hot. Remove from the heat and allow the cornstarch to settle while the oil cools. Strain. The cornstarch will remove odors and tastes and allow you to use the oil longer.

break up in the hot oil without some form of protection.

• Add room temperature food to the oil; refrigerated food will make the oil temperature drop too much.

• Using tongs or a metal spatula, slide the food down the side of the deep-fryer into the oil to prevent splashing.

• Don't add too much food at once; this causes the temperature to lower and the food will become soggy.

• If the food has to be turned in the oil, use two utensils such as a slotted spoon and spatula to turn and lower the food gently back into the oil. This prevents splashing. Don't use tongs on large fragile pieces of food, because they cause breakage.

• Properly fried food will be a crisp golden-brown, with no sign of sogginess.

• Depending on size of the food, use a slotted spoon or tongs to remove the food from the oil. Shake the food over the pan to remove any surface oil.

Do not leave breadcrumb-coated food in the refrigerator before frying, because the refrigerator dampness will be absorbed into the breadcrumbs, and they will fall off when immersed in oil.

• Drain large pieces of food on a rack placed on a cookie sheet. Use paper towels for smaller pieces of food such as French fries, or for ingredients that appear, through too low an oil temperature, to have absorbed a lot of oil. Keep changing paper towels as they become greasy, otherwise the food is sitting in its own fat.

• To reheat deep-fried food and retain its crispness, place on a rack to allow air circulation and reheat in 400 F (200 C) oven for 5 to 10 minutes.

• To save the oil, let it cool, then strain through cheesecloth, a double wire mesh strainer, or a coffee filter to remove sediment. Oil can then be stored in a cool place and reused—about 10 times, or until the flavor of another food such as fish permeates it.

• Keep a box of baking soda handy should you have an oil fire. Liberally sprinkle the soda on the fire, and it will douse at once.

• Don't leave hot oil unattended, or allow young children near deep-frying.

Bistro French Fries

There is nothing finer than a good French fry. Both thick British chips doused with vinegar or skinny French frites sprinkled with salt have their devotees. For those brought up on frozen fries or who consider McDonald's the supreme, try making your own— they're a real treat.

The best French fries are cooked on two heats. The lower heat cooks the potatoes through; the high heat crisps them. Baking potatoes work best because of their floury texture. Cut the potatoes the same size—thick or thin —for even frying.

4	baking potatoes, peeled	4
	Salt	
	Oil for deep-frying	

1. Slice the potatoes into strips about ¼ inch (5 mm) thick.

2. Heat the oil to about 325 F (160 C). (When the oil is hot enough, a cube of bread will take 30 seconds to brown.) Slide the potatoes into the oil in batches; fry for about 5 minutes, or until limp and cooked through but not colored. Drain on paper towels.

3. Reheat the oil to 375 F (190 C), or until a bread cube browns in 15 seconds. Refry the potatoes in two or three batches until golden, about 3 minutes. Drain well in a strainer placed over a bowl or on paper towels. Add salt and serve at once.

Serves 4

BATTERED FOODS

Coating certain wet foods with batter prevents the food from disintegrating in the oil. For example, if fish is added directly into oil it breaks up, and its juices cause the oil to spit and overflow. Coating the food with batter or egg and breadcrumbs prevents this.

Egg and Breadcrumb Batter

Make sure that the food is absolutely dry before being breaded.

Season flour with salt and pepper. Sprinkle on a chopping board or plate. In a shallow dish, combine a beaten egg with 1 tbsp (15 mL) vegetable oil. (The oil prevents the crumbs from browning too fast in the deep-frying oil.) Sprinkle the breadcrumbs on a cookie sheet. Dip the food first into the flour, then the egg and finally the breadcrumbs. The mixture must be floured before being dipped in the egg to make sure the batter adheres.

Southern Fried Chicken

This chicken reheats well in a 400 F (200 C) oven for 15 minutes; it can also be successfully frozen. Reheat from the frozen state in a 350 F (180 C) oven for about 30 minutes, or until heated through. Try it cold for picnics, served with aoili (see page 55). Use this flour and buttermilk coating for the finest onion rings and deep-fried shrimp.

1 cup	all-purpose flour	250 mL
1 tsp	dried marjoram	5 mL
1 tsp	dried thyme	5 mL
1 tsp	paprika	5 mL
1 tsp	salt	5 mL
½ tsp	freshly ground pepper	2 mL
1	4-lb (2 kg) chicken, cut into 10 pieces	1
1 cup	buttermilk	250 mL
	Oil for deep-frying	

1. In a large bowl, combine the flour and seasonings.

2. Dip the chicken in the buttermilk, then roll in the seasoned flour. Set aside on a cookie sheet.

3. Add oil to come halfway up a wok. Heat to 375 F (190 C), or until a cube of bread turns brown in 15 seconds.

4. Add the chicken pieces to the hot oil a few at a time. When the coating is a rich brown color, turn the heat down to medium-high. Deep-fry for 12 to 15 minutes, or until the chicken juices run clear, turning occasionally. Keep warm in a 250 F (120 C) oven while frying the remainder. (Remember to raise temperature again before frying the second batch.)

Serves 6

Homemade Breadcrumbs

Use two-day-old bread with crusts, cut into even-sized pieces. Place in a food processor or blender and process until fine crumbs appear. If drier crumbs are needed, bake at 200 F (90 C) until dried, about 20 minutes. Store in plastic bags in the freezer. (They do not need to be defrosted before being used.)

Deep-Fried Camembert with Cumberland Sauce

This dish is particularly good if your Camembert is unripe; canned Camembert works well. Once deep-fried, the hot runny cheese oozes out of a crisp, almond-flavored coating. Instead of Cumberland sauce, try chutney, or use jam as the Danish do. Brie can be substituted for the Camembert. Serve this as a first course.

1 lb	Camembert, well chilled	500 g
2 tbsp	all-purpose flour	25 mL
½ cup	dry breadcrumbs	125 mL
½ cup	ground almonds	125 mL
1	egg	1
	Oil for deep-frying	
	Parsley sprigs for garnish	

1. Cut the Camembert into 1½-inch (3.75 cm) even-sized wedges. Lightly flour each wedge on all sides.

2. On a plate, combine the breadcrumbs and almonds. Beat the egg in a shallow dish.

3. Dip each wedge into the beaten egg, then roll in the almond-breadcrumb mixture. Be sure to coat the cheese wedges thoroughly, leaving no exposed cheese, or the cheese will leak out during frying. Coat again with the egg and breadcrumbs if necessary, so that the cheese is completely covered.

4. Heat the oil in a wok or deep-fryer to 375 F (190 C). Fry the cheese wedges, turning occasionally until golden-brown on all sides, about 3 minutes. Serve immediately on a small plate with a pool of Cumberland sauce. Garnish with parsley.

Serves 4

Dishes without batters can be reheated in a microwave. Dishes with batters need the dry heat of the oven.

Cumberland Sauce

Serve this tangy condiment with the deep-fried cheese or with roast lamb instead of mint sauce. A dab on a slice of pâté balances the richness.

2	oranges	2
1	lemon	1
1 tbsp	dry mustard	15 mL
1 tsp	ground ginger	5 mL
2 tbsp	vinegar	25 mL
1 cup	red currant jelly	250 mL
2 tbsp	finely chopped onion	25 mL
¼ cup	dry red wine or port	50 mL
	Salt and freshly ground pepper to taste	

1. Grate the rind from the oranges and lemon and reserve. Squeeze out the juices, mix together and reserve.

2. In a small bowl or cup, combine the mustard, ginger and vinegar.

3. In a small pot, heat the jelly on low heat. Add the reserved juices, grated rind, mustard paste, onion and wine. Stir to blend.

4. Simmer for 20 minutes. Season to taste. Cool before serving.

Makes about 1½ cups (375 mL)

Fried Eggplant with Ginger Salsa

Beer batter is a crisp, all-purpose batter that lightly coats vegetables, fish, seafood or fruit. The beer gives the batter its crisp texture.

This interesting appetizer can be reheated in a 400 F (200 C) oven for 2 minutes. It will lose its straight-from-the-oil crispness, but is still excellent.

Salsa is the Spanish word for sauce, often uncooked and always full of flavor. If fresh coriander is unavailable, use parsley. Try mushrooms or zucchini instead of the eggplant.

Beer Batter:

½ cup	all-purpose flour	125 mL
1	egg	1
1 tbsp	butter, melted	15 mL
¼ tsp	salt	1 mL
pinch	freshly ground pepper	pinch
½ cup	beer	125 mL
1	large eggplant	1
	Oil for deep frying	

Ginger Salsa:

1	14-oz (398 mL) can tomatoes, undrained	1
1 tbsp	finely chopped onion	15 mL
1 tbsp	finely chopped fresh ginger	15 mL
1 tsp	finely chopped garlic	5 mL
2 tbsp	lime juice	25 mL
2 tsp	granulated sugar	10 mL
1 tsp	hot pepper flakes	5 mL
2 tbsp	finely chopped fresh coriander	25 mL
½ tsp	salt	2 mL
¼ tsp	freshly ground pepper	1 mL

1. In a medium bowl, beat together the flour, egg, butter, salt, pepper and beer until the batter is smooth. Refrigerate until ready to use, up to 24 hours.

2. Cut the green stem from the eggplant. Slice the eggplant into fingers about ½ inch (1.25 cm) thick.

3. Combine all the ingredients for the salsa and process in a food processor, blender or by hand. The salsa should have a sharp taste. Taste for seasoning, adding more salt, pepper or lime juice as needed. Reserve.

4. Heat the oil in a wok or deep-fryer to 375 F (190 C), or until a cube of bread turns brown within 15 seconds.

5. Dip the eggplant slices into the batter. Drain off the excess. Deep-fry until golden, about 2 minutes, turning for even browning. Drain on paper towels. Serve with the salsa.

Serves 4 to 6

The sexuality of eggplants is a hot discussion point among gourmands. It is alleged that female eggplants have more seeds but are sweeter than male eggplants. To identify the sex, check the round blossom end— if the scar is round, the eggplant is male; if it is oval, the eggplant is female. (There are more male eggplants than females!)

·6·
Cooking with Dry Heat

Roasting

Roasting is a dry heat technique where meat or vegetables are cooked by the heat of the oven.

Nothing beats the mouth-watering smell of a succulent, juicy roast. Roasts are symbols of celebrations. What would Thanksgiving or Christmas be without roast turkey, or Easter without roast lamb? My family, beef-eaters no matter what the occasion, likes to celebrate birthdays with a traditional roast beef and Yorkshire pudding dinner. However, tastes are changing in these nutrition-conscious times. Many people, concerned about fat and cholesterol content, are replacing their traditional red meat dinner with chicken or turkey. Whatever roast makes it onto your table, there are basic cooking techniques that are crucial for good results.

I believe the best results are obtained with high-heat 400 F (200 C) roasting. Although meat shrinks more when cooked this way, its flavor, texture and juiciness are unsurpassed. Tender cuts of beef such as sirloin, prime rib, rolled rib and filet can all be cooked by this method.

Low heat 325 F (160 C) is suitable when roasting pork and less tender cuts of beef, but it robs flavor from the more tender cuts. The low-heat method dates back to the time when meat and poultry were less well bred and tougher, and the low heat was gentle on the fibers. Today, however, animals are more tender and need a different approach in the oven.

I have also never believed in the wonders of the meat thermometer. I think that poking a hole in the meat and allowing the juices to run out after you've worked so hard to keep them in does not make much sense. As well, unless you have a clear idea of how long a piece of meat will take to cook, you can end up with meat ready an hour before or after you expect it. If you must use a meat thermometer, an instant reading type that plugs in near the end of the roasting time does the least damage.

To help you gauge roasting times, I have compiled the following chart that over the years has produced roast meat and poultry exactly the way I like it. This chart can be used for roasts weighing less than 10 lb (5 kg)—beef rib and sirloin roasts, lamb leg, rack, crown and shoulder, and all poultry.

ROASTING CHART

Rare
Roast at 400 F (200 C) for 15 minutes per pound (500 g), plus 15 minutes extra cooking time.

Medium-rare
Roast at 400 F (200 C) for 18 minutes per pound (500 g), plus 18 minutes extra cooking time.

Medium
Roast at 400 F (200 C) for 20 minutes per pound (500 g), plus 20 minutes extra cooking time.

Well done
Roast at 400 F (200 C) for 25 minutes per pound (500 g), plus 25 minutes extra cooking time.

Larger roasts weighing more than 10 lb (5 kg) start to cook more quickly because they are cooking from both the inside and the outside. When timing them, roast as if cooking a 10-lb (5 kg) roast, but do not include the final extra roasting time. Then lower heat to 375 F (190 C) and roast for 7 minutes per each additional pound (500 g). For example, a 15-lb (7.5 kg) rare roast beef will cook for 150 minutes for the first 10 lb (5 kg), then for 35 minutes at 375 F (190 C) for the last 5 lb (2.5 kg), giving a total roasting time of just over 3 hours.

Equipment
• A roasting pan made of stainless steel or heavy aluminum.

• A metal roasting rack to fit the pan.

• A long-handled metal spoon for basting.

BASIC ROASTING TIPS
• Always roast meat on a rack placed in a roasting pan. This allows the heat to circulate more efficiently and will brown the underside of the meat without requiring turning.

• Never salt meat before roasting. It draws the juices out. Salt the meat about 10 minutes before the end of roasting time, or after the meat is taken out of the oven. (Poultry can be salted before roasting, because the skin protects the meat.)

• Never cover the meat or the poultry with a lid or foil when roasting. It will produce steam and the meat will be an anemic color and taste dull and stringy.

• When you roast boneless beef roasts such as filets, the method of timing is different. Filet, rolled rib and rib eye roasts are tender, tubular pieces which cook in a flash. Because of their shape, the thickness of the meat determines the cooking time, not the weight. Measure the meat vertically at its thickest point and roast at 425 F (220 C) for 15 minutes per inch (2.5 cm) for rare; 20 minutes per inch (2.5 cm) for medium-rare; 25 minutes per inch (2.5 cm) for medium to well done.

• Let the meat sit loosely covered with a dish towel for 10 minutes before carving, to let the juices retract. The roast will be easier to carve.

• If your roast is underdone, slice it up and slip the underdone slices into the gravy while it is simmering on the stove.

Check your oven to make sure it heats to the right temperature. An oven thermometer will give you an accurate reading.

BEEF

• The best beef cuts for roasting are prime rib, filet, rolled rib and porterhouse roasts.

• Buy beef that is a darkish-red color with firm, cream-colored fat.

• Look for meat that is well marbled, i.e. has ribbons of fat running through it. This has a self-basting effect on roasts during cooking.

• Prime ribs are cut from the first through seventh ribs of the rib section. The best proportion of tender meat to the top flap of coarser brisket comes from the first ribs. When ordering, ask for the first cut (the roast starts at the first rib); it's a better buy.

• If you want to roast sirloin tip or rump, use a 325 F (160 C) oven and roast for 25 minutes per pound (500 g) for rare, 30 minutes for medium-rare. (Always serve these roasts rare or medium-rare, otherwise the meat will be tough.) Lean cuts like round roasts are best braised rather than roasted, because they are tougher.

• Buy 12 oz (375 g) meat per person on the bone; 8 oz (250 g) per person off the bone. This will allow some leftovers for sandwiches.

• The best seasonings for beef are Dijon mustard, garlic, thyme, curry powder and cayenne pepper.

• Classic accompaniments are Yorkshire pudding and horseradish sauce.

Buy 12 oz (375 g) meat per person on the bone; 8 oz (250 g) per person off the bone. This will allow some leftovers for sandwiches.

Roast Prime Rib of Beef with Pan Gravy

This classic English dish is traditionally served with Yorkshire pudding. The best roast is a prime rib. Remember to ask for it from the first cut; you will have more of the central eye of the meat and less of the tougher top cover.

1	clove garlic, finely chopped	1
1	7- to 8-lb (3.5 to 4 kg) rib roast Freshly ground pepper	1
2 tbsp	all-purpose flour	25 mL
1/4 cup	dry red wine	50 mL
1 1/2 cups	beef stock	375 mL
1 tsp	tomato paste	5 mL

1. Preheat the oven to 400 F (200 C).

2. Rub the garlic over the meat, then sprinkle with pepper. Place the meat on a rack in a roasting pan.

3. Turn on the broiler. Place the roast 3 inches (7.5 cm) from broiler rack and broil for 5 minutes. (This helps to give the meat a crispy fat layer).

4. Turn the oven heat to 400 F (200 C) and roast the meat for 15 minutes per pound plus 15 minutes for rare; 20 minutes per pound plus 20 minutes for medium.

5. Remove the roast from the pan and let it sit for 10 minutes.

6. Drain the fat from the pan, leaving 2 tbsp (25 mL).

7. Over medium heat, add the flour to the fat and stir well. Cook until the flour is browned, about 2 minutes. Add the wine and stock. Scrape up any bits from the bottom of the pan. Bring to the boil, stirring. Add the tomato paste. Simmer for 2 minutes.

Serves 8

Roast Filet of Beef

Beef filet is an exceptionally tender, non-fatty roast that has a delicate melt-in-your-mouth taste. Try marinating it to enhance the flavor. Serve it with sautéed potatoes and green beans or asparagus.

Shallots are from the onion family but have a milder, more subtle flavor. They look like large brown garlic cloves.

1	4 lb (2 kg) filet roast	1

Marinade:

3 tbsp	Dijon mustard	45 mL
1 tbsp	soy sauce	15 mL
1 tsp	Worcestershire sauce	5 mL
1	clove garlic, finely chopped	1
pinch	cayenne pepper	pinch

Sauce:

3	shallots or green onions, finely chopped	3
¼ cup	dry red wine	50 mL
2 cups	beef stock	500 mL
1 tbsp	brandy	15 mL
2 tbsp	butter, at room temperature	25 mL

1. Measure the beef filet at its thickest part to determine the roasting time.

2. In a small bowl, whisk together the marinade ingredients. Brush all over the filet. Marinate for 2 hours at room temperature.

3. Preheat the oven to 425 F (220 C).

4. Place the meat on a rack in a roasting pan. Roast for 15 minutes per inch (2.5 cm) for rare, or to the desired degree of doneness.

5. Remove the roast from the roasting pan. Cover with a tea towel and let rest while making the sauce.

6. Skim off any fat (but not the juices) in the roasting pan. Add the shallots and, on medium heat, cook, stirring, until softened, about 2 minutes.

7. Pour in the wine and reduce until 1 tbsp (15 mL) remains. Add the stock and reduce by half. Stir in the brandy. Turn the heat to low and whisk in the butter.

8. Slice the roast into ½ inch (1.25 cm) slices and serve topped with the sauce.

Serves 8 to 10

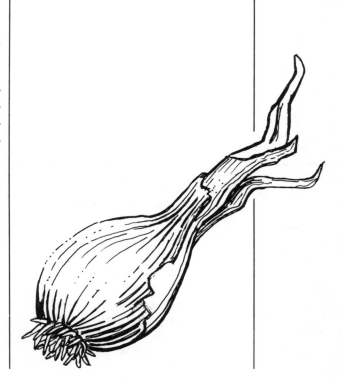

Carving a Leg of Lamb

1 Holding the lamb firmly with the back of a carving fork, and starting at the narrow shank end, carve ½-inch (1.25 cm) slices through to the bone.

2 Lay the knife parallel to the bone and carve through horizontally, releasing the slices.

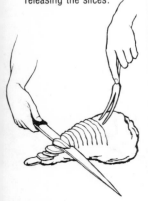

Many people consider lamb fatty, but it generally has a lower fat content and fewer calories than beef. One problem with lamb is that the fat congeals at a lower temperature than beef fat, often making fatty puddles on the plate and giving people the impression that lamb is fatty. The solution is to heat the plates before serving.

LAMB

• Lamb is succulent and mildly flavored; it should be served pink or medium-rare for the best taste.

• The best cuts for roasting are leg, loin and racks, although boned shoulder is tasty if a little fatty.

• Look for smaller legs that come from younger animals. They are tender and mild in flavor.

• Frozen New Zealand lamb is a good, reasonably priced alternative to the more expensive Canadian lamb. Defrost it in the refrigerator to maintain the juicy texture. If you defrost at room temperature, the juices leak out. Legs take about 24 hours to thaw; racks about 12 hours.

• Cut away most of the fat and the tough outer skin (known as the fell) before cooking.

• Garlic, rosemary, lemon and Dijon mustard have a great affinity for lamb; the classic accompaniment is mint sauce or jelly.

Roast Leg of Lamb

The classic roast lamb should be cooked rare or medium-rare. The red currant jelly in the sauce adds a sweetness that brings out the delicate flavor of the lamb.

1	5-lb (2.5 kg) leg of lamb	1
¼ cup	butter, at room temperature	50 mL
1 tbsp	dried rosemary	15 mL
	Grated rind of 1 lemon	
2	cloves garlic, finely chopped	2

Pan Gravy:

1 tbsp	all-purpose flour	15 mL
1 ½ cups	beef stock	375 mL
1 tbsp	tomato paste	15 mL
2 tbsp	red currant jelly	25 mL
	Salt and freshly ground pepper to taste	

1. Preheat the oven to 400 F (200 C).

2. Trim the tough outer skin and some of the fat from the lamb.

3. In a small bowl, blend together the butter, rosemary, lemon rind and garlic.

4. At frequent intervals, make ¼-inch (5 mm) slits in the lamb fat. Fill the slits with the butter mixture.

5. Place the lamb on a rack in a roasting pan and roast for 1½ hours. Remove the lamb to a platter, reserving 2 tbsp (25 mL) fat and juices in the pan. Keep the lamb warm in a 200 F (90 C) oven.

6. In the roasting pan on medium heat, whisk the flour into the accumulated fat and juices. Cook slowly until the flour turns light brown, about 2 minutes.

7. Whisk in the stock, tomato paste and red currant jelly. Bring to boil, stirring, then turn the heat down to low and simmer for 5 minutes. Season to taste with salt and pepper. If the sauce is too thick, thin it with some water or stock. Serve with the lamb.

Serves 6 to 8

PORK

Today, pork is much leaner than it was some decades ago, and there is less fat or marbling. The main thing to remember is not to overcook it. With new methods of raising pigs, pork no longer has to be cooked well done. It should be cooked just until the juices run clear or a medium doneness is reached. (Even if the juices still run pink, there is absolutely no health hazard.)

• The best cuts for roasting are loins and legs. Crown roast is a special cut from the rib end of the loin, and makes a spectacular presentation.

• Pork is roasted at 325 F (160 C) for 30 minutes per pound (500 g) for medium; 40 minutes per pound (500 g) for well done.

• Pork has an affinity for sage, rosemary, Dijon mustard and soy sauce.

• The best accompaniments are fruit stuffings of apricots, plums and raisins, or applesauce.

Crown Roast Pork

A crown roast of pork is a pork rib roast. To serve, carve the roast vertically into chops. There will be about six chops in one 3-lb (1.5 kg) crown roast.

Some butchers clean the ends of the bones for you, but if not, scrape off about 2 inches (5 cm) meat and fat from the bones. When roasted, the bones become a rich brown color and look impressive. If a crown roast is unavailable, substitute a loin of pork.

1 tsp	dried rosemary	5 mL
3 tbsp	Dijon mustard	45 mL
1	3-lb (1.5 kg) crown roast of pork	1
½ tsp	freshly ground pepper	2 mL

1. In a small bowl, combine the rosemary and mustard. Using a knife, spread on all sides of the roast. Place the roast on a rack in a roasting pan and marinate at room temperature for 2 hours.

2. Preheat the oven to 325 F (160 C).

3. Roast the pork for 1½ hours or until the juices run clear. Serve with applesauce.
Serves 4 to 6

VEAL

• Roast veal has become an elegant substitute for beef at weddings, banquets and on the home table. It has a lower fat content and fewer calories than beef, as well as a mild flavor and a fork-tender texture.

• The best cuts for dry roasting are rack and filet. Rack of veal, the veal version of a prime rib roast, is expensive but exceptional. It can be roasted following the instructions for roast beef. Serve it medium-rare for the best flavor. Veal filets roast well, too, but they are often unavailable. Other cuts of veal become dry when roasted. Unless you are willing to insert strips of fat into the meat, they are best pot roasted to help retain the juices.

• In pot roasting, meat is cooked slowly in a heavy pot on top of the stove with a small amount of liquid. Pot roasting works well for dry but tender cuts of meat such as veal and pork.

• The best veal cuts for pot roasting are leg, sirloin and shoulder.

• The best seasonings for veal are rosemary, basil and lemon. Classic accompaniments are mushrooms, spinach and prunes.

Applesauce
To make a simple applesauce, use any quantity of tart apples (Spys are my favorite), using the basic formula of 1 tbsp (15 mL) water and 1 tsp (5 mL) sugar to each apple.
Peel and core the apples. In a medium pot, combine the apples, water, sugar and cinnamon. Bring to a boil, reduce the heat and simmer for 10 to 15 minutes, or until the apples are tender. Using the back of a fork, lightly mash the apples.

Peel and core the apples. In a medium pot, combine the apples, water and sugar. Bring to a boil, reduce the heat and simmer for 10 to 15 minutes, or until the apples are tender. Using the back of a fork, lightly mash the apples.

Pot-Roasted Veal with Rosemary and Balsamic Vinegar

This superb recipe was demonstrated by an American journalist and cooking teacher, Lynn Kaspar, when she taught at The Cooking School. She used veal shoulder, and the students said they had never eaten more tender or more tasty veal. If you do not have balsamic vinegar, use cider vinegar.

1	4-lb (2 kg) boneless veal roast, cut from the leg or shoulder, tied with butcher twine	1
1	clove garlic, split	1
½ tsp	freshly ground pepper	2 mL
2 tbsp	olive oil	25 mL
1 tbsp	butter	15 mL
1	3-inch (7.5 cm) sprig fresh rosemary, or 2 tsp (10 mL) dried	1
1	small onion, finely chopped	1
1 tsp	finely chopped Italian parsley	5 mL
2 tbsp	dry red wine	25 mL
1½ cups	chicken stock	375 mL
½ cup	balsamic vinegar	125 mL

1. Rub the veal with the split garlic clove. Reserve the garlic. Sprinkle the veal with pepper.

2. On medium heat, heat the oil and butter in a heavy casserole large enough to hold the veal snugly. Slowly brown the veal on all sides. This will take about 20 minutes. Once the veal is browned, remove it from the pot.

3. Pour off all but 2 tbsp (25 mL) fat. Add the rosemary, onion and parsley and cook, stirring, for 1 minute.

4. Add the garlic and wine to the pan. Cook, scraping up all the bits on the bottom of the pan, until the wine has evaporated.

5. Return the meat to the pot. Add about ¼ cup (50 mL) stock. Bring to a gentle simmer, put the lid on the pot, leaving about 2 inches (5 cm) uncovered, and cook, basting veal occasionally with the pan liquid, until the liquid has evaporated.

6. In a small bowl, combine the remaining stock and vinegar. Keep cooking the roast, adding the stock and vinegar as needed. Baste the veal every 20 minutes. It should be kept moist but not wet. Turn the veal occasionally. Cook for about 1½ to 2 hours, or until the veal is very tender and juices run clear.

7. Remove the meat from the pan. Skim the fat from the liquid. If the sauce is watery, boil down until rich in flavor. Slice the veal thinly and moisten with the pan sauce.

Serves 10

POULTRY

Juicy, crisp-skinned roast poultry has no equal for taste and texture. Unfortunately, many cooks overcook their poultry because of outdated ideas about roasting times. This results in dry Christmas turkey or roast chicken that has to be chewed instead of savored. But my method of roasting poultry always works. Try roasting at high heat to seal in the juices, and you'll be assured of success every time.

• Those white, battery-raised supermarket chickens and turkeys don't deliver the flavor of the barn-bred species. Unfortunately, it's hard to find free-range birds today. Settle for the superior taste of yellow-skinned poultry usually available at butcher shops.

• Roast all poultry at 400 F (200 C) for 15 minutes per pound (500 g) plus 15 minutes extra cooking time. If the poultry is stuffed, count the stuffing as an additional pound.

• When roasting turkey, remember that any bird weighing more than 10 lb (5 kg) cooks from the inside as well as the outside, so the total cooking time is calculated differently. After 10 lb (5 kg), reduce the heat to 375 F (190 C) and cook for 7 minutes per pound (500 g). For example, a 14 lb (7 kg) turkey will cook for 150 minutes for the first 10 lb (5 kg) and 28 minutes for the last 4 lb (2 kg), giving a total cooking time of about 3 hours.

• If any pin feathers remain on the bird, remove them with tweezers.

• Remember to remove the giblets from the cavity of the bird. The heart and gizzard can be used for stock, but the liver will turn stock bitter. Quickly sauté it for a snack, chop it up and stir it into the stuffing, or give it to the cat.

• To keep the skin crisp and the meat moist, poultry should be basted with the fat that accumulates under the roast. Use a long-handled spoon to pour the fat over the breast meat.

• Let the roast rest for 10 minutes before carving to let the juices retract.

• The best seasonings for poultry are tarragon, orange, lemon, paprika and ginger.

• Traditional poultry accompaniments are cranberry sauce or applesauce, and stuffing.

• Stuffings for poultry can be as simple as bread soaked with water, onions and herbs, such as sage, or as exotic as dried fruits and nuts bound together with breadcrumbs and seasoned with cinnamon and tarragon.

• When storing leftover poultry and stuffing, remove the stuffing from the cavity and store separately. This avoids problems with bacteria growth.

How to Truss Poultry

Trussing poultry before roasting helps the bird roast more evenly by protecting the breast. It also preserves the shape of the chicken after cooking and prevents the stuffing from falling out.

To truss, cut a piece of string four times as long as the length of the bird. Place the string under the back and wing section, bringing both ends up to breast level. Draw along the body and hook under the drumstick. Pull the string up over the legs, cross over and bring each end around the tail. Pull up to the cavity and tie in a bow around the legs for easier removal after roasting. If the bird is stuffed, use a metal skewer to close the cavity.

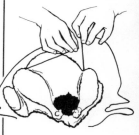

1 Place the string under the wings and back. Bring both ends up to breast level.

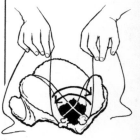

2 Cross the string over the breast cavity and hook under the legs.

3 Cross the string and hook around the tail. Bring the ends up and tie around the legs.

How to Carve Poultry

• Hold the chicken firmly with the back of a carving fork. With a sharp knife, slice through the thigh bone attached to the body. To make this easier, press the thigh down and away from the body until the joint appears. Cut through the joint and remove the thigh and leg. Cut in two through the bone joint. Repeat on the other side.

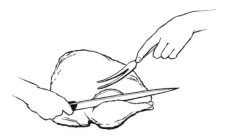

• Slice through the wing joint and remove. Repeat with other wing.

• In a small chicken remove the breast meat whole and serve it. For a larger bird, neatly slice the breast meat in two or three slices, making sure each slice has a piece of skin attached.

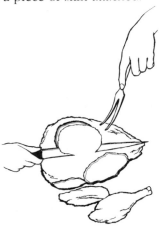

• Remove the little oysters of meat from the backbone and save for the chef. (They are the most tender parts of the bird!)

The Ultimate Roast Chicken

Alex, my stepson, always picks this when it is his turn to choose dinner. He loves the crisp skin and the moist juicy meat underneath.

1	4-lb (2 kg) chicken	1
2 tbsp	butter, at room temperature	25 mL
2 tsp	dried tarragon Salt and freshly ground pepper	10 mL
1 tbsp	all-purpose flour	15 mL
1½ cups	chicken stock	375 mL
1 tsp	dried tarragon, optional	5 mL

1. Preheat the oven to 400 F (200 C).

2. Trim the wing tips from the chicken.

3. In a small bowl, combine the butter and 2 tsp (10 mL) tarragon. Spread over the chicken skin and place the remainder in the body cavity. Season lightly with salt and pepper.

4. In a roasting pan, place the chicken on a rack, breast side up. Roast for 75 minutes, basting every 20 minutes. Remove from the oven and let the chicken rest for 10 minutes.

5. Meanwhile, discard all but 2 tbsp (25 mL) fat from the roasting pan. On medium heat, heat the fat. Sprinkle in the flour. Stir until the flour turns golden-brown, about 1 minute.

6. Pour in the stock. Bring to a boil, scraping up the bits from the bottom of the roasting pan. Add any accumulated juices from the chicken. Sprinkle in the tarragon and season with salt and pepper to taste.

7. Carve the chicken and serve with the gravy.

Serves 4 to 6

VEGETABLES

• Use baking potatoes for roasting. Quarter or halve them, allowing two halves per person. Peel the potatoes, place in a pot of cold water, bring to a boil on high heat and boil for 7 minutes. Drain well, then dry thoroughly in the pot over turned-off heat. Heavily score the surface of the potatoes with a fork. Place them in the hot fat around the roast, or in a separate pan containing ½ cup (125 mL) hot fat or olive oil. Baste well. Bake at 400 F (200 C) for 1 hour.

• Root vegetables are also sensational when roasted. Roasted turnips, parsnips, sweet potatoes and carrots have crisp outer skins and sweet, mellow centers. They go particularly well with roast meats.

• To prepare root vegetables for roasting, slice the vegetables into even-sized pieces. Place in a pot of cold water, bring to a boil on high heat and boil for 5 minutes. Drain well. Place in the roasting pan under the roast, or in a separate pan basted with ¼ cup (50 mL) olive oil or fat from the roast. Bake at 400 F (200 C) for 1 hour, turning occasionally.

• Roast potatoes are a favorite accompaniment to all roast meats. Roast some unpeeled garlic cloves alongside them for added flavor, then squeeze the creamy cloves out of the skins and eat them with the potatoes. If the potatoes still look pale when the meat comes out, turn the oven to broil, but be sure to watch for burning!

Broiling

Broiling is a method of cooking which produces tasty results and uses very little fat. I find I turn more and more to broiling as a quick and easy cooking technique.

Broiling is a dry heat technique where the intense heat of a broiler or barbecue sears the outer surface of the food, locking in flavor and texture. However, because the heat blasts the outside of the food so intensely, it is easy to end up with a charred outside and a raw middle. By following proper broiling procedures, you can avoid these problems.

Equipment

• Tongs to turn the meat over without piercing.

• A broiler pan with a rack usually comes as part of the oven equipment.

• Use a brush to brush on marinades.

BASIC BROILING TIPS

• Tender pieces of beef (such as rib or sirloin steak), lamb chops and poultry pieces are excellent broiled. Choose firm-textured fish such as grouper, mackerel and salmon, because they do not fall apart.

The placement of the oven racks is important when broiling. The rack should be placed close enough to the broiler so that when the meat is placed on the rack, there is a 3-inch (7.5 cm) space between the meat surface and the broiler element.

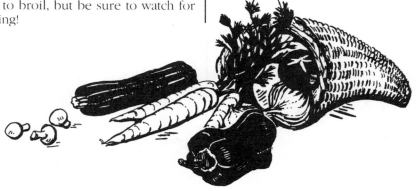

• Tender dry meats such as veal and pork are not recommended for broiling, except as chops, because they dry out.

• Because it is easy to blacken the outside of meat without cooking the inside, don't use pieces of meat thicker than 1½ inches (4 cm) unless you can turn the heat down after the first intense searing, or move the oven rack lower.

• Use room temperature meats for even cooking. Preheat the broiler and then heat the broiler pan and rack. This method will sear the underside of the meat and help seal in the juices.

• Brush the meat with oil or butter. Season with pepper, herbs and spices. Do not use salt, as this prevents browning and causes the outside of the meat to harden.

• Place the meat on the rack in the broiler pan and position about 3 inches (7.5 cm) from the broiler. Do not close the oven door, otherwise the element will turn off and on. Broil until the surface of the meat is brown. Turn over with tongs to prevent piercing the meat, causing juices to leak out. Broil the second side. Do not turn the meat again.

• Delicate fish that will break if turned over is placed on a hot rack and broiled on one side only.

• It is not necessary to marinate all foods before broiling, but marinating does add to the flavor and tenderizes the meat.

Multi-Purpose Marinade

This marinade works with all cuts of meat and poultry, and it keeps indefinitely in the refrigerator. Make a large quantity and have it on hand for instant marinating. Use ½ cup (125 mL) marinade for each pound (500 g) of meat. (Pour the amount you will need into a separate dish before using, so that any raw meat juice will not taint the rest of the marinade.)

I prefer to marinate meat for a few hours at room temperature. If you do marinate in the refrigerator, leave the meat as long as possible—overnight or all day.

For flavor variations, try adding 1 tbsp (15 mL) Dijon mustard, 2 tbsp (25 mL) soy sauce, or three chopped tomatoes to the basic recipe.

¾ cup	vegetable or olive oil	175 mL
¼ cup	wine vinegar or lemon juice	50 mL
2	cloves garlic, finely chopped	2
3 tbsp	chopped fresh tarragon, thyme or basil, or 1 tbsp (15 mL) dried	45 mL
1 tsp	freshly ground pepper	5 mL

1. In a medium bowl, whisk together all the ingredients.

2. To marinate meat, film the bottom of a stainless-steel, enamel or china dish with the marinade. Place the meat on top. Brush the top of the meat with the marinade. Turn the meat occasionally.

Makes about 1 cup (250 mL)

Broiled Calves Liver

Broiled liver is tender, juicy and flavorful. I prefer calves' liver for texture and flavor, but beef or lamb liver will also work well. Try serving liver with sausages and lamb chops as part of a mixed grill, or serve it with Orange Butter (see page 88).

½ cup	Multi-Purpose Marinade (see page 86)	125 mL
1 tbsp	grated orange rind	15 mL
6	slices calves' liver	6

1. In a medium bowl, combine the marinade and the orange rind. Add the calves' liver, toss gently, and marinate for 30 minutes at room temperature.

2. Preheat the broiler. Remove the liver from the marinade and place on a broiler rack about 3 inches (7.5 cm) from the element. Broil for 2 to 3 minutes on each side, or until pink juices begin to come to the surface. (Liver is best served pink.)

Serves 6

Broiled Hamburgers

Use meat that has about 20 percent fat; it will produce a juicier hamburger. Ground chuck works very well. Handle the patties lightly; overhandling results in dry burgers. Before seasoning, spread the meat on a board so that the seasoning penetrates all the hamburger. (If this is done in a bowl, it is a hit and miss effort.) Use 6 oz (180 g) meat per adult; 4 oz (125 g) for kids. The burgers should be about 1 inch (2.5 cm) thick for even cooking.

Be creative with hamburgers. Top them with different mixtures such as chili, avocado or ratatouille, and try different kinds of bread, such as garlic bread, sesame buns or pita.

1 ½ lb	ground chuck	750 g
¼ cup	finely chopped onion	50 mL
1 tsp	salt	5 mL
1 tsp	freshly ground pepper	5 mL
	Vegetable oil for brushing	

1. Spread the meat on a board, and combine with the onion, salt and pepper. Mix lightly together and divide into four patties.

2. Preheat the broiler. Brush the rack with oil to prevent the hamburgers from sticking. Brush the patties with oil.

3. Cook the burgers 3 inches (7.5 cm) from the broiler element for 3 minutes. Turn over and cook for 4 minutes. (This produces rare hamburgers; cook for a further 2 to 3 minutes for medium.)

Makes 4 hamburger patties

Before seasoning hamburger, spread the meat on a board so that the seasoning penetrates all the meat. If this is done in a bowl, it is hit and miss effort.

Flavored Butters

Flavored butters are great with broiled foods. Place a dollop on hot food, and it will melt immediately, creating a sauce. Make up several kinds of butters and freeze for future use.

Garlic Butter

Combine ½ cup (125 mL) butter with 1 finely chopped clove garlic, 1 tsp (5 mL) lemon juice and 1 tbsp (15 mL) each chopped parsley and chives. Use on hamburgers or as a spread for garlic bread.

Orange Butter

Combine 1 cup (250 mL) butter with the grated rind and juice of 1 orange. Beat in 3 chopped shallots and season to taste with salt and pepper. Excellent on chicken, liver and fish.

Mustard Butter

Combine ½ cup (125 mL) butter with 2 tbsp (25 mL) Dijon mustard, 1 chopped green onion and 1 tbsp (15 mL) each chopped parsley and chives. Serve with steaks, hamburgers or lamb chops.

Teriyaki Salmon

Use salmon steaks that are 1 inch (2.5 cm) thick and serve with cucumber salad and rice. The salmon has a subtle oriental flavor. If you use salmon fillets, broil them skin side down and do not turn them over, or the fish will break apart.

4	salmon steaks	4

Marinade:

½ cup	teriyaki sauce	125 mL
1 tsp	honey	5 mL
1 tsp	lemon juice	5 mL
1	clove garlic, finely chopped	1
1 tbsp	finely chopped fresh ginger	15 mL
¼ tsp	freshly ground pepper	1 mL

1. Place the salmon steaks in a large shallow dish or bowl.

2. In a small bowl, mix together the marinade ingredients. Pour the marinade over the steaks and marinate at room temperature for 2 hours, turning occasionally.

3. Preheat the broiler. Remove the salmon steaks from the marinade and broil 3 inches (7.5 cm) from the element for 4 minutes per side, brushing occasionally with the marinade. When white juices rise to the surface, the salmon is ready.

Serves 4

Broiled Eggplant Salad

Eggplant is wonderful when broiled because all the flavor is locked in and the texture can stand up to the intense heat. Serve this with or without the dressing. Salt the eggplant before cooking to draw out the bitter juices. If you use this method when preparing eggplant for moussaka, rather than frying it, you'll avoid ending up with oil-soaked eggplant slices.

1	eggplant	1
2 tsp	salt	10 mL
¼ cup	olive oil	50 mL

Dressing:

½ cup	olive oil	125 mL
2	cloves garlic, finely chopped	2
1	red chili pepper, seeded and chopped	1
2 tbsp	lemon juice	25 mL

1. Slice the eggplant into ¼-inch (5 mm) slices. Sprinkle with salt and let stand in a colander for 30 minutes to drain off the bitter juices. Pat dry with a paper towel.

2. Preheat the broiler. Brush the eggplant slices with oil and place on a broiler rack about 3 inches (7.5 cm) from the element. Broil for about 2 minutes on each side, or until cooked through and browned.

3. Whisk together the dressing ingredients and pour over the broiled eggplant. Serve hot or cold.

Serves 4

Part 3

Techniques of Baking

·7·
Pastry

Pastry is one of life's little mysteries. While some people's pastry is crisp and flaky, others can produce tasteless cardboard from the same recipe.

The first rule in pastry-making is, don't be nervous. The hands of nervous pastry-makers start to get warm and sweaty, and heat, to which the gluten in the flour reacts, is the bane of perfect pastry dough. The second rule is handle the dough lightly so as not to overwork the gluten. Gluten is a chemical element in flour which develops as the dough is worked. If pastry is overworked or if heat is introduced, the gluten expands too much, and the dough becomes tough and elastic. Flours with a low gluten content make the best pastry.

There are three basic ingredients in pastry: flour, fat and liquid.

Flour
• Use all-purpose flour or cake and pastry flour. My recipes call for all-purpose flour, although cake and pastry flour, if you have it, has a lower gluten content, which produces a good, tender crust. It is not always readily available, however. To substitute cake and pastry flour for all-purpose, use an extra tablespoon (15 mL) cake and pastry flour per cup (250 mL).

• Whole wheat flour is more nutritious than white flour because the outer bran layer has not been removed, but I think it makes a leaden pastry.

Fat
• Butter makes the best-tasting pastry, but it doesn't give you that flaky, melt-in-your-mouth texture. Vegetable shortening makes flaky pastry, but it is pasty white and has no taste. For a pastry that is both flaky and buttery, I like to use 75 percent butter and 25 percent shortening.

• Good-quality hard corn oil margarine makes a flaky crust with lower cholesterol (but not fewer calories) than a butter crust. The flavor and color are better than shortening, but it lacks a bit of butter's taste.

• Lard makes a tasty pastry with the best texture, but it has fallen into disfavor because it is animal fat. It has a slightly stronger flavor than the other fats, and I prefer it for meat pies.

• In general, the higher the proportion of fat used, the crisper and tastier the pastry, but the more difficult the pastry will be to roll out. Pastry with a high fat content can be patted out instead of rolled.

Liquid
• The liquid binds the flour and fat together. The liquid can be water, wine, citrus juice, beaten egg or a combination. The most important point to remember is to use ice-cold liquid so it doesn't expand the gluten. The acid in a tablespoon (15 mL) of white vinegar or lemon juice mixed with the water makes a flakier dough.

• Too much liquid makes a tough crust; too little won't hold it together, and the dough will crack when rolled out. With practice you will begin to feel the right texture.

Equipment
• Use a rolling pin that is at least 16 inches (40 cm) long, so that you can roll out large pieces of pastry. Little rolling pins are useless. Pins that are one long cylinder of wood give good results because they are easy to control and are long enough to roll a large piece of pastry. Rolling pins with handles are effective for heavier doughs such as puff pastry but, again, look for large ones. Marble pins are lovely to look at, but I find them too heavy for pastry work. I use them for rolling pasta. Although rolling pins

that you fill with ice would seem perfect for the job, because they keep the pastry chilled, in reality they can leak over your pastry and ruin it. Some cooks like to use special pastry cloths or rolling-pin covers to prevent sticking. However, I think dusting the countertop and rolling pin with flour is much simpler and works just as well.

• Flan or tart pans are fluted metal rings with loose removable bottoms. When the flan is baked, you slip off the sides, leaving the pie sitting on the base. To do this, place the flan pan over a jar or glass. The sides will fall away. It is a much more attractive presentation than a tart served in an ordinary pie plate. Pyrex and other pie plates work efficiently, but the pie is more difficult to remove and does not look as spectacular. Black metal pie plates absorb the heat most efficiently, and therefore produce the crispest crust.

• A pastry blender for cutting the fat into the flour.

• A pastry brush for brushing on glazes.

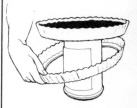

To remove the rim of a flan pan, place the flan pan on top of a jar or can. The rim will slip off.

MAKING PASTRY

• Make sure all the ingredients are cold.

• Always handle the pastry gently to avoid overworking the gluten. If you are right-handed and inclined to be nervous or heavy handed, use your left hand when handling the pastry—you will have a lighter touch.

• Although prepackaged flour has usually been "presifted," it never hurts to sift it again in case there are coarse granules in the flour. Always measure before sifting, since sifting adds air to the flour and increases the volume.

• Unless you are using a food processor, the fat should be cold but not too hard, or it will not blend properly with the flour. Remove the fat from the refrigerator about an hour before using. (For food processor recipes, the fat should be very cold—straight out of the refrigerator.) Cut the fat into about ½-inch (1.25 cm) pieces.

• With a pastry cutter, two knives or your fingertips, cut the fat into the flour until the mixture resembles coarse breadcrumbs. (I prefer to rub the fat and flour together using my fingers, because I feel I have more control over the consistency.)

• Add the liquid, sprinkling it over the fat/flour mixture. The liquid should be very cold. Use only enough liquid to hold the pastry together. Start with a small amount, adding more as needed.

• Gather the pastry into a ball with your fingertips. It should hold together but not feel sticky. If your pastry becomes too elastic and difficult to roll, cover it with plastic wrap and refrigerate for 30 minutes to relax the gluten.

ROLLING PASTRY

• Cut the dough into two pieces.

• Lightly flour a large area of the counter or pastry board and the rolling pin. Flatten the dough a little by pressing with the rolling pin.

• Starting in the center, roll gently to the edges of the pastry, using light but firm strokes. Whatever direction you are rolling, always start from the center. Occasionally turn the pastry in a circular motion to keep it from sticking. Dust the counter with more flour only when the pastry is close to sticking. Roll the dough about ⅛ inch (3 mm) thick and large enough to fit your pan. Allow at least a ½ inch (1.25 cm) overhang.

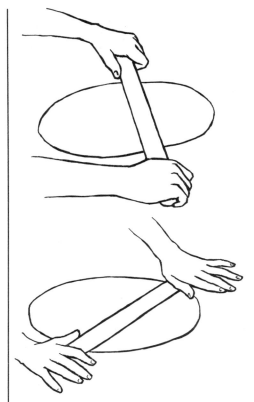

• To place the dough in the pan, dust the pin lightly with flour, then roll the dough gently around the rolling pin starting at the edge closest to you. Place the pin over the top edge of the pie plate and unroll the pastry gently.

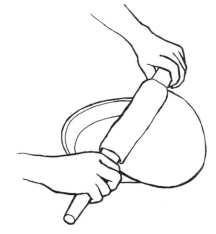

• Pinch off a little piece of excess pastry and use it to ease the dough into place. (Using a piece of dough means your hands touch the pastry as little as possible.) Press the dough gently into the base and sides of the pan. Make sure the dough reaches into all corners of the pan and up the sides to prevent shrinkage. If the pastry tears or you have gaps, moisten the spot with a drop of water and patch with some extra pastry.

• Cut away the excess pastry, leaving a ½-inch (1.25 cm) overhang. Chill the bottom crust in the refrigerator until the filling and top crust are ready.

• Roll out the top crust, but make it a little thinner than the bottom crust, if possible.

• Place the filling in the chilled bottom crust.

• Gently roll the top crust around the rolling pin. Lift, place over the filling and unroll. Make steam vents by cutting slits or a design into the dough with a knife.

• Moisten the outer edges of the bottom crust with cold water, then seal the bottom and top crusts by pinching, fluting or pressing the edges together. Trim off the excess pastry.

• If you are making a single-crust pie such as a quiche, roll your rolling pin across the top of the pie plate to cut away the excess pastry before adding the filling. You don't need an overhang.

• For a shiny crust, brush the top of the pie with milk or cream or an egg yolk beaten with 1 tbsp (15 mL) cold water.

• Always bake the pie in the lower third of the oven to make sure the bottom crust is properly cooked.

BAKING BLIND

Baking blind means to pre-bake the bottom crust to prevent the filling from making the crust soggy. Baking blind also stops the dough from shrinking down the sides of the pie plate. Even when recipes don't call for it, I usually pre-bake a pie shell for a few minutes to prevent soggy crusts and leaky fillings.

• Preheat the oven to 425 F (220 C).

• Cut a piece of parchment, foil or waxed paper to fit inside the pastry shell. The paper should extend about 1 inch (2.5 cm) beyond the rim of the pan. Place the paper on the pastry.

• Fill the paper to the top with dried beans or peas, making sure the corners and sides are supported by beans. They are used to weight down the crust.

• Bake for 15 minutes.

• Lift out the paper and the beans. Store the beans in a container to reuse for baking blind. (Julia Child says she has used the same beans for 25 years!) You now have a partially baked pie shell that can be used for quiches or any liquid fillings.

• For a fully baked pie shell, turn the oven heat down to 375 F (190 C) and return the partially baked shell to the oven. Bake for 10 minutes, or until the bottom is crisp and pale-gold. Use for open-faced fruit flans.

A foolproof method for rolling pastry: place the pastry in the center of a large square of plastic wrap. Cover with a second sheet of plastic wrap. Roll the pastry out; the plastic wrap will stop the pastry from sticking. When the pastry is rolled out, remove the top sheet of wrap and reverse the pastry into a pie plate.

Basic Shortcrust Pastry

This easy, no-fail, flaky all-purpose pastry can be made by hand or in the food processor. The proportion of butter and shortening gives the pastry a perfect flavor and texture. Use this pastry for quiches and fruit or meat pies.

3 cups	all-purpose flour	750 mL
1 tsp	salt	5 mL
¾ cup	butter	175 mL
¼ cup	shortening	50 mL
½ cup	cold water	125 mL
1 tbsp	white vinegar or lemon juice	15 mL

1. In a large bowl, sift together the flour and salt. Blend in the butter and shortening until the mixture resembles coarse breadcrumbs.

2. In a cup, combine the water and vinegar or lemon juice. Sprinkle the liquid over the flour mixture. Using your fingers, work the liquid in and gather the dough into a ball. Divide the dough into two equal pieces.

3. Roll out as needed or wrap the dough in plastic wrap and chill.

4. To partially bake the pastry, preheat the oven to 425 F (220 C). Cut a piece of parchment, foil or waxed paper to fit inside the pie plate (see page 93). Fill the paper with dried beans and bake for 15 minutes. Lift out the paper and beans and proceed with the rest of the recipe.

Makes enough pastry for one 9- or 10-inch (23 or 25 cm) double-crust pie

---

Food Processor Pastry

The food processor helps nervous people make better pastry, because their warm hands do not come in much contact with the dough. Make sure the butter is cold, and cut it into even pieces so that it processes evenly. Do not let the dough form a ball in the processor—this will toughen the pastry. Food processor pastry should be chilled before rolling, because it has been worked, and the gluten needs time to relax. The pastry can be partially baked before using (see page 93).

1½ cups	all-purpose flour	375 mL
pinch	salt	pinch
¾ cup	butter, chilled	175 mL
3 tbsp	ice water	45 mL

1. Place the flour and salt in a food processor fitted with the steel knife. Cut the butter into six pieces and distribute evenly over the flour. Turn the machine on and off until the mixture resembles coarse breadcrumbs.

2. With the machine running, gradually pour the water into the feed tube. Stop the machine as soon as all the water has been added. Scrape the contents onto a floured board.

3. Knead the dough together gently until the pastry holds together. Wrap in plastic wrap and refrigerate for 30 minutes before rolling and baking.

Makes enough pastry for one 9- or 10-inch (23 or 25 cm) single-crust pie

---

Cream Cheese Pastry

This is the perfect pastry for sweet and savory tartlets. Rich and buttery, the pastry is so easy that children can make it, but because of the high fat content, it can be difficult to roll out. Pat the pastry into tart tins instead. If you do not have a food processor, cut the butter and cream cheese in by hand until the mixture resembles coarse breadcrumbs, then gather into a ball.

2 cups	all-purpose flour	500 mL
¾ cup	cream cheese, chilled	175 mL
¾ cup	butter, chilled	175 mL

1. Place the flour in a food processor fitted with the steel knife. Cut the cream cheese and butter into 1-inch (2.5 cm) chunks. Distribute the chunks evenly over the flour.

2. Turning the machine on and off, combine until the mixture resembles coarse breadcrumbs.

3. Remove the dough from the processor and gather it into a ball. Wrap and chill for 30 minutes.

Makes enough pastry for thirty 2¾ × 1-inch (7 × 2.5 cm) tarts

---

Sweet Pastry

This recipe makes a pastry that is similar to shortbread. It is used for tart shells that are fully prebaked and then filled with fresh fruit and custard fillings. Because of the high fat content, this pastry can be difficult to roll out. If so, pat it into the pan with your fingertips. The high sugar content means the pastry is only baked until it turns a light golden color. If it is baked too long, the sugar will caramelize and the pastry will have a burnt taste.

½ cup	butter	125 mL
1½ cups	all-purpose flour	375 mL
3 tbsp	granulated sugar	45 mL
2	egg yolks	2
2 tbsp	lemon juice or water	25 mL

1. Preheat the oven to 375 F (190 C).

2. Cut the butter into ½-inch (1.25 cm) cubes.

3. In a bowl, combine the flour and sugar. Blend in the butter until the mixture resembles coarse crumbs.

4. In a small bowl or cup, combine the egg yolks and lemon juice. Blend into the flour mixture.

5. On a floured board, roll out the pastry until it is ⅛ inch (3 mm) thick and place in a 9- or 10-inch (23 or 25 cm) flan pan. (You can also pat the pastry directly into the pan.) Trim off the excess and prick the pastry with a fork.

6. Bake blind for 15 minutes in the lower third of the oven. Remove the beans. Bake for a further 5 minutes, or until the pastry is pale gold.

Makes enough pastry for one 9- or 10-inch (23 or 25 cm) single-crust pie

Sweet pie shells can be made up to three days ahead of time and refrigerated until needed. They also freeze well. However, do not refrigerate the shells after filling and glazing, because the glaze will absorb the refrigerator dampness and become runny.

Storing Egg Whites
Egg whites can be stored in the refrigerator for up to one week. The whites can also be frozen. Use them for meringues or soufflés.

Pearl's Meat Pie

This pastry recipe is a treasure that my mother has used for years. When she first came to Canada, she found that the flour worked differently here, so she could no longer make the wonderful light puff pastries she had made in Scotland. She fiddled and fiddled until she developed this pastry that follows no rules of pastry making. It bakes like a many-layered crisp pastry and is wonderful for meat pies and apple pies. It can also be frozen and then thawed before rolling and baking.

My mother always uses her hands for mixing this pastry, which may seem a little bizarre and messy, but it does work. (If you prefer, you can make this in a food processor.)

Fillings for meat pies should be quite highly seasoned; otherwise they may taste bland once they are encased by the pastry.

Pastry:

1 cup	hard corn oil margarine, at room temperature	250 mL
1	egg	1
1 ¾ cups	all-purpose flour	425 mL
pinch	salt	pinch

Filling:

2 lb	ground beef	1 kg
1 ½ cups	finely chopped onion	375 mL
½ cup	chopped carrot	125 mL
1	bay leaf	1
2 tbsp	rolled oats	25 mL
2 tsp	salt	10 mL
1 tsp	freshly ground pepper	5 mL
1 cup	beef stock	250 mL
2 tbsp	breadcrumbs	25 mL

1. In a cold stainless-steel bowl, blend together the margarine and egg with your hands until smooth.

2. In a separate bowl, mix together the flour and salt. Gradually add the dry ingredients to the egg mixture, ½ cup (125 mL) at a time, working in the flour until the dough forms a soft ball and no longer sticks to your fingers. Cover the dough and refrigerate overnight, or freeze for 30 minutes.

3. To make the filling, in heavy pot, brown the ground beef over high heat, stirring occasionally, until the pinkness disappears. Drain off the fat.

4. Stir in the onions, carrots, bay leaf, rolled oats, salt and pepper. Add enough stock just to cover the meat. Lower the heat to medium-low, cover and cook slowly for about 1 hour, or until the onions disintegrate. Stir after 30 minutes.

5. Preheat the oven to 450 F (230 C).

6. Flour the counter or pastry board heavily. With a floured rolling pin, roll the pastry out into a rectangle approximately 5 × 12 inches (13 × 30 cm). Flour the pastry and fold into thirds. Turn the dough so the open edges face you and roll out into a rectangle again. Repeat this procedure five more times. Divide the dough into two pieces.

7. Roll half the dough out into a circle and fit into a 9-inch (23 cm) flan pan. Sprinkle the breadcrumbs over the pastry base to absorb any fat. Fill the pastry shell with the meat mixture.

8. Roll out the remaining pastry and fit over the pie. Cut off the excess pastry and crimp the edges together. Make the steam vents in the top crust.

9. Pour 1 cup (250 mL) water over the finished pastry. Pour off the excess.

10. Bake for 15 minutes on the low shelf of the oven. Turn the oven down to 400 F (200 C) and bake for a further 15 to 20 minutes, or until the crust is golden.

Serves 6

·8·
Cakes and Cookies

S ometimes I think there are two types of cooks—those who love to bake, and those who love to cook. It seems to take different kinds of personalities to master the separate arts.

A person who cooks well likes to experiment, taste and create. Baking is a science; the baker is usually more obsessive, likes to measure accurately and keep things in order. Each personality can be good at the other processes, but it is unusual to find a person who is an outstanding cook and baker.

Although I am a good baker, it has never come as easily to me as cooking. Because of this, when I bake, I demand easy recipes that work beautifully every time. Here are not only my personal favorites, but the best recipes gleaned from friends and associates.

Baking for friends and family gives a great deal of pleasure to both the baker and the recipient. Home-baked goods, at least to me, always taste better than the store-bought variety, because you can control the sugar and flavorings to your own taste.

To turn yourself into a baker supreme, be organized. Read the recipe all the way through before you start! Have everything ready and measured, prepare your pans and preheat the oven—then start baking.

Equipment
• Two round cake pans, preferably 9 inches (23 cm) or 10 inches (25 cm) in diameter; an 8-inch (20 cm) square pan; an 11 × 7-inch (2 L) baking dish; a 13 × 9-inch (3.5 L) rectangular dish that can double as a lasagna pan.

• A 9- or 10-inch (23 or 25 cm) spring-form pan is necessary for deeper cakes and cheesecakes.

• A pastry brush for glazes; a rubber spatula for scraping out the last drops of batter; a sieve for sifting; a wooden spoon for mixing batters; a metal spatula for smoothing the tops of cakes and icing.

• Electric mixers are highly recommended if you do a lot of baking.

• Keep toothpicks or skewers on hand for cake testers.

Flour
• Use all-purpose flour for the recipes in this chapter. If you are substituting cake and pastry flour for all-purpose, use 1 tbsp (15 mL) more per cup (250 mL).

• Most flour is presifted. Sift the flour when you are combining it with other ingredients so they will be well mixed. Measure the flour before sifting.

• Measure the flour accurately. To do this, scoop the flour loosely into a dry measuring cup. Do not tap the cup. Draw a knife across top of the measuring cup to sweep off the excess flour.

Butter
• Nothing tastes better than butter in baking, but margarine can be substituted in all recipes. I always use unsalted butter in baking, since it contains less salt and less water.

• Use room-temperature butter for cake- and cookie-making, as it will cream more efficiently.

• When butter is creamed, air is beaten in; the air expands and acts as a leavening agent.

Sugar
• Sugar is primarily used as a sweetener. However, it also gives baked goods color as it caramelizes in the oven. Sugar retains moisture in baked goods and acts as a preservative, helping cakes to stay fresh longer. It tenderizes cakes by balancing flour and egg proteins.

• Brown sugar is refined white sugar with molasses added. When substituted for white sugar, it gives a butterscotch flavor, darkens the color and gives a chewier texture.

• Icing or confectioners' sugar is finely ground sugar that dissolves instantly. Use it for icings.

Eggs
• Eggs are used for flavor, richness, body, leavening, color and nutritive value. All the recipes in this book use large eggs.

• Although there are special gadgets for separating eggs, the easiest method is to use your hands. Crack the egg shell and break the egg into your hand. Place your hand over a bowl and open your fingers slightly. The white will drip through. A more traditional method requires you to crack the egg and then pass the yolk from one shell to the other, letting the white fall into a bowl. If some yolk drops in the bowl, the oil in it will prevent the egg whites from whipping. Remove it with the egg shell.

Leaveners
• Several different processes act as the raising agent for cakes and cookies. Air is trapped in batter by creaming butter and sugar together. Egg whites beaten stiff and folded into a batter also act as a leavener. When the egg whites are beaten, air is trapped in them. When heated in the oven, this air expands, and the cake rises. Another mechanical method is achieved by beating the eggs and sugar together until thick, as for a sponge cake, then folding in the flour.

• Baking powder and baking soda generate a chemical reaction, where gas is formed and causes the cake to rise. Baking soda is a form of sodium bicarbonate, but it must be combined with an acid to give off carbon dioxide. This expands and rises, making the cake rise with it.

Separating Eggs
Break the egg into your hand. Gently open your fingers slightly and let the egg white slip into a bowl.

Baking powder goes stale over time. To test for freshness, combine 1 tsp (5 mL) baking powder with 1/3 cup (75 mL) hot water. If the baking powder is fresh, it rapidly fizzes and bubbles.

• Baking powder is a combination of baking soda and an acid. Most baking powder is double-acting, which means that two acid salts have been added to the soda. One begins working when dry ingredients are combined with wet; the other begins to work only in the heat of the oven. Single-acting baking powder acts only when it meets the liquid, meaning you have to rush to finish the cake and get it in the oven before the action fizzles out.

Chocolate
• The better the chocolate tastes, the better it is for cooking. After all, a cake is only as good as its ingredients. I prefer to use good European chocolate instead of baking chocolate.

• **Unsweetened chocolate** is pure, hard chocolate liquor with no sugar or flavoring added. It gives a rich, chocolatey taste to cakes and is often combined with semisweet chocolate for a richer, more intense flavor.

• **Semisweet and bittersweet chocolate** are a blend of chocolate liquor, sugar, cocoa butter and vanilla. The percentage of sugar and chocolate varies according to brand. If a recipe calls for bittersweet chocolate and you only have unsweetened, add an extra tablespoon (15 mL) sugar per ounce (30 g) chocolate. I use semisweet and bittersweet chocolate interchangeably.

• **Milk chocolate** contains milk solids. Don't use milk chocolate in a recipe unless specified.

• **White chocolate** is not really chocolate but a mixture of sugar, cocoa butter, milk solids and vanilla. Some varieties contain vegetable shortening, not cocoa butter. Brands using vegetable shortening give a bland, boring taste to cakes.

• **Coating chocolate or couverture** is semisweet chocolate with extra cocoa butter added for high gloss. It is used by professional chocolate-makers for a finer finish to chocolate and cakes.

Cooking with Chocolate
• Chocolate is temperamental. Melt it over low heat in a double boiler or heavy pot, because high heat will make it granular. Once it turns granular there is nothing you can do to return it to its proper state. Chocolate can also be melted in a microwave on Medium-Low (30%) for 2 to 3 minutes.

• Keep liquid away from chocolate when melting. One drop will make it stiffen. To correct this, beat in some vegetable oil to help the chocolate release.

• Chop chocolate uniformly for even melting.

• Always pour melted chocolate into cream or custards, not vice versa, for easier mixing.

Cakes

There are different types of cakes, which use different methods of preparation. Butter cakes are made with a base of creamed butter and sugar. They depend on baking powder or baking soda for leavening and are heavier and denser than batter cakes. Batter cakes, such as sponge or angel food cakes, are made without fat. The eggs and sugar are beaten together until thick, making a light, airy, foamy cake.

Cakes such as genoise (French sponge cake) and chiffon combine the properties of both butter and batter cakes. Although the cakes are made by the sponge method, melted butter is folded into the batter before baking.

CAKE-BAKING TIPS
• Unless otherwise specified, work with room temperature ingredients.

Chocolate does not react well to changes in humidity. It should be wrapped in foil and plastic wrap, then stored in a cupboard. If moisture reacts with chocolate, a white "bloom" develops on it. This whiteness shouldn't affect the taste.

How to Whip Cream

It is important that the cream, bowl and whisk be very cold. Add the cream to the bowl and whip with a large whisk, hand-beaters or an electric mixer until the cream stands in soft peaks. If you are adding a flavoring such as vanilla, brandy or sugar, beat it in at this point. Do not over-beat; over-beating leads to butter. If you over-beat, add some extra cream and beat it in.

• Prepare the baking pans before baking. For cakes made by the butter creaming method, use butter to grease the baking pan. Then sprinkle flour over the pan and shake gently to distribute evenly. Shake off the excess flour. For sponge cakes, line the pan with parchment paper or oiled foil or waxed paper. Grease and lightly flour the sides of the pan. Shake off the excess flour.

• The most important step in making a butter cake is the proper creaming of the butter and sugar. Use an electric mixer if you have one; if not, use a wooden spoon. Soften the butter to room temperature by allowing it to stand at room temperature for 1 hour, or process in a food processor for 3 to 5 seconds. Never melt to soften, because this will change the texture of the butter, and air will not be beaten into it successfully. The softened butter is then beaten until it is light, soft and airy. Sugar is added a few spoonfuls at a time, beating after each addition, until the mixture is very light and fluffy and no grains of sugar are visible.

• Add the eggs one at a time and beat each in thoroughly before adding the next.

• Add the liquid and dry ingredients alternately to butter/sugar/egg mixture, making three dry additions and two liquid additions. After each addition, stir to combine, beat well for a few seconds, then scrape down the sides of the bowl and beaters with a rubber spatula.

• Pour or spoon the batter into the prepared cake pan, then spread evenly in the pan with a rubber spatula.

• After the batter has been poured into the cake pan, tap the pan lightly on the counter to release the air bubbles. Bake immediately. (If there are beaten egg whites in the batter, do not tap the pan, because it will break down the air.)

• Cake pans and cookie sheets should be placed on the middle rack of the oven and should be at least 1 inch (2.5 cm) from each other and the sides of oven to allow heat to circulate evenly. If you are using more than one rack, stagger the pans.

• Cakes must be baked in a dry atmosphere; do not bake them in the oven with foods that might produce steam.

• Resist the temptation to peak in the oven until three-quarters of the cooking time has passed. Don't bang the oven door.

• A cake is done when the edges have pulled away slightly from the sides of the pan, and the top of the cake springs back lightly when touched, or when a toothpick inserted in the center of the cake comes out clean.

• Cool cakes on wire racks in the cake pan for 10 minutes. Slide a spatula around the sides, then invert onto a wire rack to cool completely. Cakes are best eaten within one to two days. Cakes without fat, such as sponge and angel cakes, should be cooled upside down to keep them from falling.

• Wait until the cake has cooled completely before icing.

• Store cakes wrapped in foil in an airtight container. If they are filled with whipping cream, refrigerate them. If the cake has been cut, cover the cut edges with plastic wrap to prevent drying out.

• Cakes can be successfully frozen. For the best results, defrost them overnight in the refrigerator.

Egg Whites

• Egg whites are used to help a cake rise. Ideally, egg whites should be beaten in a copper bowl, because copper reacts with egg whites, producing a lighter, higher mixture. However, if you add cream of tartar to whites beaten with an electric mixer, or if you whisk them in a stainless-steel bowl, you will get the same effect.

• To beat egg whites, place them in a large copper or stainless-steel bowl. Tilt the bowl with one hand. With a large wire whisk, whisk slowly with a circular motion until the egg whites froth. Whisk more quickly and continue to whisk until the egg whites form peaks that hold their shape when the whisk is lifted out. I prefer using a whisk to an electric beater because I have better control.

• If your beaten egg whites look dry and flaky, they have probably been over-beaten. They will have lost their elasticity and won't hold as much air. The remedy is to add another white and continue beating until the mixture is creamy, glossy and holds stiff peaks.

• Folding is the process of gently combining a lighter ingredient with a heavier ingredient so as not to dislodge any air. Folding beaten egg whites must be done carefully and quickly, or the mixture will deflate. First stir one-quarter of the egg whites into the mixture to lighten it. Then spoon the remaining egg whites on top of the heavier mixture. Using the largest metal spoon or spatula you have, cut down the center to the bottom of the bowl. Turn the spoon parallel to the surface of the bowl and bring it up along the side, turning the bowl slightly as you work. Continue lifting a layer of heavy mixture over the lighter one, using as few strokes as possible, until almost evenly combined.

• Leftover egg yolks can be stored, covered, in the refrigerator for five days. Use them to make Hollandaise sauce (see page 51). Leftover egg whites can be refrigerated for five days or frozen.

TROUBLE-SHOOTING

Heavy damp cake with sunken top:
—baking pan too small
—oven temperature too low
—baking time too short
—a sudden draft caused by opening the oven door before cake has set

Cake surface is badly cracked:
—baking pan too small
—temperature too high
—oven racks too high

Cake texture is too coarse:
—under-beating of eggs and sugar
—oven temperature too low

Pale surface:
—under-baking
—overcrowded oven, preventing proper heat circulation

Cake top too brown and base burned:
—incorrect lining of pan
—oven racks too low
—baking pan too large, causing mixture to be too shallow
—oven temperature too high

Curdling of butter and egg mixture:
—butter and egg *not* at room temperature
—butter and egg not creamed well enough
Remedy: Stand the mixing bowl in a little hot water and beat vigorously. If there is more egg to add, stir in 1 tbsp (15 mL) of the sifted flour from the recipe with each further addition of egg. Then, using a metal spoon, stir in the remaining flour and any liquid.

Speckled cake surface:
—insufficient beating of sugar, leaving sugar crystals on the sides of the bowl

Folding Beaten Egg Whites

With a large metal spoon, cut down the center of the beaten egg whites to the bottom of the bowl. Turn the spoon parallel to the surface of the bowl and sweep it up along the side, turning the bowl slightly with your other hand as you work.

Mrs. Reid's Plain Cake

Mrs. Jean Cunningham, a grand-mother from Arnprior, Ontario, has baked this cake for years. She doesn't know who Mrs. Reid was, but the recipe was passed on to her from an aunt. This is an excellent, buttery plain cake which should be in everyone's repertoire. Serve it with strawberries and ice cream, or cut it into layers and sandwich with whipped cream and fruit. Double the recipe to make a two-layer birthday cake.

½ cup	butter, at room temperature	125 mL
1 cup	granulated sugar	250 mL
2	eggs, beaten	2
1 tsp	vanilla extract	5 mL
1½ cups	all-purpose flour	375 mL
1½ tsp	baking powder	7 mL
½ tsp	salt	2 mL
½ cup	milk	125 mL

1. Preheat the oven to 375 F (190 C). Butter an 8-inch (20 cm) square or round cake pan.

2. In a large bowl, with an electric mixer or by hand, cream together the butter and sugar until light and fluffy. Beat in the eggs one at a time. Stir in the vanilla. Reserve.

3. In a separate bowl, sift together the flour, baking powder and salt. Mix the dry ingredients into the creamed mixture alternately with the milk.

4. Spoon the batter into the cake pan. Bake for 35 minutes, or until a toothpick inserted comes out clean.

Makes one 9-inch (23 cm) cake

Chocolate Cake
For a simple chocolate cake, add ⅓ cup (75 mL) cocoa to the dry ingredients in plain cake recipe and reduce the flour by ⅓ cup (75 mL). Omit the vanilla.

To make cupcakes, pour the plain cake batter into large muffin pans and bake for 12 minutes. Makes about 20 cupcakes.

Sponge Cake

A sponge cake is very versatile. Split it and fill with jam, lemon curd, or sliced strawberries and whipped cream. Hollow out the center and fill it with fresh berries. For a moister cake, add 2 tbsp (25 mL) melted butter when folding in the flour. Sugaring the cake pan gives a crust to the sponge cake.

For a lighter cake, use the hot water method described below to warm the eggs and sugar. Use a hand beater to whip the eggs and sugar. If you have a table model electric mixer, heat the bowl and beaters with boiling water before beating the eggs. This cake freezes well.

3	eggs	3
½ cup	granulated sugar	125 mL
½ cup	all-purpose flour	125 mL
pinch	salt	pinch

1. Preheat the oven to 375 F (190 C). Butter, flour and sugar two 8-inch (20 cm) round cake pans.

2. Half fill a large bowl with hot water. Place the eggs and sugar in a second bowl inside the large one.

3. Hold the second bowl steady while whisking the eggs and sugar. Whisk until thick, white-colored and triple in volume.

4. Sift the flour and salt into the egg mixture and gently fold in.

5. Pour the batter into the prepared cake pans and bake for 20 minutes, or until the cake springs back when lightly touched.

Makes two 8-inch (20 cm) cakes

Grandma's Chocolate Cake

This recipe comes from my friend Sandy Druckman's grandmother and was originally cooked in a wood stove. This is a moist but firm cake good for icing. Use a Dutch cocoa in the cake and icing—chocolate cake is only as good as the chocolate you use in it. Sour the milk with 1 tsp (5 mL) lemon juice. It can be used within minutes.

½ cup	butter	125 mL
2 cups	brown sugar	500 mL
2	eggs	2
½ cup	cocoa	125 mL
½ cup	boiling water	125 mL
½ cup	sour milk	125 mL
1 ½ cups	all-purpose flour	375 mL
1 tsp	baking soda	5 mL
½ tsp	salt	2 mL
1 tsp	vanilla extract	5 mL

1. Preheat the oven to 325 F (160 C). Butter and flour two 8-inch (20 cm) round cake pans.

2. In a large bowl, cream the butter and sugar. Add the eggs one at a time, beating after each addition.

3. In a small bowl, dissolve the cocoa in the boiling water. Stir in the sour milk.

4. In a separate bowl, sift together the flour, baking soda and salt.

5. Add the sifted dry ingredients to the butter-sugar mixture alternately with the cocoa mixture, blending lightly after each addition. Stir in the vanilla.

6. Bake for 45 to 50 minutes, or until the top of the cake springs back when lightly touched, or a toothpick inserted comes out clean.

7. Cool for 5 minutes in the pans, then turn out onto racks. Cool completely before icing. Fill with Quick Chocolate Frosting (see page 104) and ice with Chocolate Icing.

Serves 8

Chocolate Butter Icing

Use a good semisweet or bittersweet chocolate. The rule of thumb is 1 tbsp (15 mL) butter to 1 oz (30 g) chocolate. If the icing hardens before use, it may be softened by stirring over hot water. This icing is used for the top of a cake.

6 oz	semisweet or bittersweet chocolate	180 g
⅓ cup	butter	75 mL

1. Break up the chocolate and place in a heavy pot on low heat. When melted, remove from the heat.

2. Add the butter 1 tbsp (15 mL) at a time and whisk into the chocolate. The icing will thicken instantly, but then will thin out. Allow to cool to spreading consistency.

3. With a metal spatula, spread the icing over the top and sides of the cake. The icing will harden further when cold.

Makes about 1 ¼ cup (300 mL)

When icing a cake, keep the spatula clean to prevent cake crumbs from speckling the icing.

Before icing a cake, cut four strips of waxed paper or foil and lay them on the edges of the serving platter in a rectangular shape. Place the cake on top. After the cake is iced, pull out the paper. This will keep your cake platter icing-free.

Vanilla Icing

Simple vanilla icing can be flavored in many different ways. However, it sets very quickly, so have everything ready before you start. Decorations should be assembled ahead of time so that they can be applied immediately to the wet icing.

Have a cup of hot water on hand as you ice the cake. Dip the spatula in the water to prevent the icing from sticking.

2 cups	icing sugar, sifted	500 mL
¼ cup	boiling water	50 mL
¼ tsp	vanilla extract	1 mL

1. Sift the sugar into a small bowl. Make a well in middle, using a wooden spoon.

2. Combine the water and vanilla in a cup. Slowly add to the sugar, stirring constantly. Avoid adding too much liquid at once, because the icing may become too runny. It should be thick and smooth.

3. Using a spatula, smooth the icing from the middle to the edges of the cake. Do not rework the surface, as this icing sets very rapidly. Coat the sides of the cake with the remaining icing. Decorate immediately.

Makes about 2 cups (500 mL)

Vanilla Icing Variations

Orange Icing

Instead of ¼ cup (50 mL) boiling water, use 1 tbsp (15 mL) orange juice concentrate and 3 tbsp (45 mL) boiling water.

Lemon Icing

Substitute ¼ cup (50 mL) lemon juice for the boiling water.

Coffee Icing

Add 1 tbsp (15 mL) instant coffee powder to the boiling water.

Chocolate Icing

Add 2 tsp (10 mL) cocoa powder and 1 tsp (5 mL) instant coffee powder to the boiling water.

Quick Chocolate Frosting

Frostings are slightly thicker and fluffier than icings, and are often used to sandwich layer cakes together. Although frostings can be more complicated— either custard-based or cooked, this simple one is quick and delicious. Change the flavor by omitting the cocoa and Kahlua and substituting 2 tbsp (25 mL) lemon or orange juice and 1 tsp (5 mL) grated rind.

2 tbsp	butter, at room temperature	25 mL
1 cup	icing sugar	250 mL
2 tbsp	cocoa	25 mL
2 tbsp	Kahlua or milk	25 mL

1. In a bowl, beat together the butter and icing sugar until light and fluffy. Beat in the cocoa and Kahlua. Use to fill cakes or ice cookies.

Makes about 1¼ cups (300 mL)

Cookies and Bars

It is every mother's fantasy that she will bake cookies and have them in the cookie jar for the kids. If you are like me, often the thought is there but not the time, so kids are brought up on store-bought brands. But cookie-making is easy if you follow the rules; a batch can be whipped up in 10 minutes. If you have children, let them help you bake. It's one of the best ways to introduce them to the kitchen.

• **Drop cookies** are made by dropping spoonfuls of dough onto cookie sheets. The cookies will be evenly baked if you attempt to make the size and shape uniform. Drop cookies spread as they bake, so leave about 2 inches (5 cm) between them. Remove the baked cookies from the cookie sheets as soon as they are removed from the oven, or they will continue to bake. Allow the cookies to cool in a single layer on wire racks.

• **Rolled cookies** are made by rolling the dough out on a floured, smooth surface. The dough is then cut into shapes with a cookie cutter or knife before being baked. The cookies do not spread when cooking, so you can place them close together. Shortbread cookies are a good example of a rolled cookie.

• **Bar cookies** have a shortbread or Graham cracker base that is pressed into a baking dish. Then a batter mixture is poured over it. After baking, it is cut into bars or squares. Bar cookies are usually rich and moist and are quick and easy to make—a boon for busy people and those who don't like baking.

Equipment
• Two heavy cookie sheets. I prefer rimmed cookie sheets because they can be used as jelly roll pans. They also tend to buckle less than rimless sheets.

• Two wire racks.

• Metal cookie cutters for rolled cookies and a rolling pin to roll them out.

• A square or rectangular baking dish for bar cookies.

• A long spatula for removing cookies from the cookie sheet.

• A food processor or electric mixer for mixing cookies is a benefit if you bake frequently; otherwise a large bowl and wooden spoon will do.

COOKIE-BAKING TIPS

• Place the cookie sheet on the middle rack of the oven for even baking. If using more than one cookie sheet on two racks, reverse the positions after they have baked for half the baking time.

• Use two cookie sheets together to protect the bottom of delicate cookies from burning, or if the cookie sheets are not heavy.

• Grease cookie sheets lightly with oil or use parchment paper for easy cleanup. Non-stick coatings can be sprayed on sheets, too.

• Don't bother regreasing cookie sheets between batches; just wipe off any crumbs with a paper towel.

• Cookies will become crisper if they are removed from the cookie sheets and cooled on racks. If they cool directly on the sheets, they will be chewier. Shortbread and delicate cookies must be left on the cookie sheets until cool, otherwise they will break.

Non-stick parchment paper is a valuable kitchen tool. It stops cakes and cookies from sticking to the base of baking pans, and it saves in cleanup.

Cool cookies completely before storing, or they will become soggy.

Chocoholic Chunk Cookies

This is a good example of a drop cookie, as well as being the definitive chocolate monster chunk cookie—with chocolate in the dough and chocolate chunks distributed throughout the cookie.

Store crisp drop or rolled cookies in a cookie jar or in a tin with a loose-fitting lid; store soft cookies in a container with a tight-fitting lid.

½ cup	butter	125 mL
2 oz	unsweetened chocolate	60 g
10 oz	semisweet chocolate, cut into chunks	300 g
1½ cups	all-purpose flour	375 mL
½ tsp	baking powder	2 mL
½ tsp	salt	2 mL
2	eggs	2
1½ cups	granulated sugar	375 mL
2 tsp	vanilla extract	10 mL

1. Preheat the oven to 350 F (180 C).

2. Line cookie sheets with parchment paper or foil.

3. In a heavy pot on low heat, melt the butter, unsweetened chocolate and 2 oz (60 g) semisweet chocolate, stirring until smooth. Remove from the heat. Cool slightly.

4. In a medium bowl, combine the flour, baking powder and salt.

5. In a large bowl, combine the eggs, sugar and vanilla. Blend in the chocolate mixture and the flour mixture. Stir in the remaining chocolate chunks.

6. Place the dough on the cookie sheet in mounds of approximately 2 tbsp (25 mL), about 2 inches (5 cm) apart.

7. Bake for 12 to 15 minutes, or until the cookies are glossy and cracked on the surface and soft inside. Do not overbake. Allow the cookies to set on the cookie sheet for 5 minutes. Remove the cookies from cookie sheet and let them cool completely on a wire rack.

Makes about eighteen 3-inch (7.5 cm) cookies

Hazelnut Crescents

This is a typical rolled cookie. If you prefer, you can use pecans or almonds instead of hazelnuts, but buy the whole nut, toast it for 10 minutes in a 350 F (180 C) oven until browned, and then grind in a food processor or with a nut mill. Toasted nuts have more flavor. Do not overprocess, or you will have nut butter. After you roast whole hazelnuts, rub them in a tea towel, and the skins will flake off.

1 cup	butter, at room temperature	250 mL
1 cup	granulated sugar	250 mL
1	egg yolk	1
1 tsp	vanilla extract	5 mL
2¼ cups	all-purpose flour	550 mL
1 cup	ground hazelnuts	250 mL

1. Preheat the oven to 350 F (180 C). Grease the cookie sheets.

2. In a large bowl, cream the butter by hand or with an electric mixer until light. Beat in the sugar gradually until the mixture is light and fluffy.

3. In a small bowl or cup, whisk together the egg yolk and vanilla. Beat into the creamed mixture.

4. In a separate bowl, mix the flour with the nuts. Stir into the creamed mixture.

5. To shape the crescents, shape a heaping tablespoon of dough in your hands to form a thick roll about 2½ inches (6.5 cm) long. Place on the cookie sheet and turn in the ends to form a crescent shape.

6. Bake for 12 to 15 minutes, or until a light-brown color. Cool on a rack.

Makes about 3 dozen cookies

Lemon Squares

These are my daughter Emma's favorite bar cookies, because they are not too sweet or rich; she considers these bars the perfect breakfast food!

½ cup	butter, at room temperature	125 mL
¼ cup	icing sugar	50 mL
1 cup	all-purpose flour	250 mL
½ tsp	salt	2 mL
2	eggs, beaten	2
1 cup	granulated sugar	250 mL
2 tbsp	all-purpose flour	25 mL
	Grated rind and juice of 1 lemon	
1 tbsp	icing sugar	15 mL

1. Preheat the oven to 350 F (180 C).

2. In a bowl, blend together the butter, ¼ cup (50 mL) icing sugar, 1 cup (250 mL) flour and salt. Pat into a buttered 8-inch (2 L) square cake pan. Bake for 20 minutes, or until the pastry is a creamy color.

3. In a bowl, beat together the eggs, granulated sugar, 2 tbsp (25 mL) flour lemon juice and rind. Pour the topping mixture over the cooked base. Bake for 15 to 20 minutes, or until set. Dust with sifted icing sugar while still warm.

Makes about 24 squares

·9·
Bread

Making your own bread is easy, inexpensive, and very relaxing. And the smell of homebaked bread is irresistible—real estate agents say that the smell of bread baking will sell a house faster than anything else!

There are two kinds of breads: yeast breads, which are leavened with yeast, and quickbreads, which use baking powder or baking soda for the raising agent.

But bread-making creates problems for many people. Whether it is fear of the yeast, fear of kneading, time concerns or not knowing how much flour to add, most people don't make bread.

The good news is that bread reacts wonderfully to an unseasoned bread-maker, because it needs lots of handling, pushing and prodding to make the gluten work. Making bread is soothing to the spirit and gives you a tremendous sense of accomplishment.

Since science plays a large part in bread-making, understanding the ingredients and how they react with each other will make bread-making easier.

Yeast Breads

Flour
Use either high-protein all-purpose or bread flour. Bread flour contains more protein than all-purpose flour, but it isn't always available. It's the protein in the flour that produces the structure in bread. When mixed with a liquid, these proteins produce gluten, which gives the dough elasticity. Other flours such as whole wheat or rye, which have a lower protein content, are used in combination with all-purpose flour to produce

Most bread recipes give a quantity range for flour, because flour tends to dry out in winter and, as a result, less is needed; in the summer, flour picks up moisture from the air, so more is needed.

mixed-grain breads.

Never add the full amount of flour called for in a recipe. I usually hold back about 1 cup (250 mL) and add it if needed.

Yeast

Yeast is a tiny living organism that acts as the leavener to make dough rise. You can use either dried or fresh yeast. Dried yeast will keep in the refrigerator for several months, but fresh yeast only lasts for about 10 days.

To activate yeast, sprinkle a pinch of sugar onto warm water. The water should feel warm to the wrist—too much heat will kill the yeast. Stir in the yeast. The yeast will bubble and swell, reacting with the sugar to cause fermentation which produces carbon dioxide and alcohol. The gluten in the flour keeps this carbon dioxide trapped in the dough, causing the bread to rise. The alcohol evaporates. If the yeast does not bubble, it is inactive; you will have to start again.

Liquid

Liquids in bread-making dissolve and activate the yeast as well as dampening the flour to produce the glutens. Water produces a crisp outer crust and a dryish body. Milk makes dough rise more quickly than water and produces a sweeter, softer-crusted bread.

Fat

Fat makes bread softer and more delicate and produces a golden, firm crust. Butter, margarine, shortening and oil are interchangeable, but butter gives the best flavor and the best-looking crust. Olive oil makes the dough supple and easy to knead. It's perfect for pizza dough.

Eggs

Eggs give a fine golden color to bread. The interior is tender and the taste is richer. However, bread with eggs in it, such as challah, tends to go stale more quickly.

Salt

Salt gives flavor to bread.

Equipment

• Standard 9 × 5-inch (2 L) bread pans in a dark metal.

• Pastry brushes to brush on glazes.

BREAD-MAKING TIPS

Kneading

• Kneading means to mix the dough for a period of time to make the gluten elastic and give the bread form. Knead dough with floured hands by folding the dough toward you and then pushing it away. Turn the dough a quarter turn and repeat. You must knead until the dough is elastic and no longer sticky.

• Use only enough flour on the kneading board to prevent sticking. The kneading takes about 10 minutes.

• You can also knead in a food processor or in a large mixmaster with a dough hook, if you prefer. Both these methods are quicker but less satisfying than hand-kneading.

Rising

• Brush vegetable oil in a bowl. Place the dough in the bowl. (The oil will prevent a skin from forming on the dough.) Cover with plastic wrap and place the bowl in a warm place, about 70 F (19 C), away from drafts. Some ideal spots are the top of the refrigerator, on top of the stove, or near the central heating. When the dough has risen, it looks puffy and spongy and has doubled in bulk. Make an impression in the dough with your finger. If the impression remains and does not spring back, the gluten has stretched to its full elasticity, and the dough is ready to be formed into bread. This step will take about an hour and a half. If you want to delay the rising

Kneading Bread

1 Fold the dough over toward you.

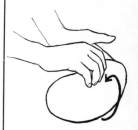

2 Push the dough away with the heel of your hand.

3 Turn the dough a quarter turn, then repeat.

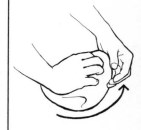

because you have run out of time, place the dough in a bowl that just fits. Cover with a heavy plate and refrigerate until needed. Remove the dough from the refrigerator and allow it to rise.

• Deflate the dough by punching it down with your hands to remove the air.

• Dough made from bread flour needs a second rising to fully work the gluten before being formed into loaves, but breads made in the home kitchen with all-purpose flour do not need this step. The second rising for home-baked breads takes place after the dough has been formed into loaves. Form the bread, lay on a greased cookie sheet and let rise again until double in bulk. The time is half the original rising time—usually about 45 minutes.

Shaping Loaves
• Loaves can be baked free-form on cookie sheets or in a variety of containers—coffee cans, molds or cake pans. Whatever you use, make sure the pans are one-half to two-thirds full. If the loaves are baked on a cookie sheet, they can be round, long, square or braided. Don't worry about perfect shapes; one of the advantages of home-baked bread is that it doesn't have to be flawless.

Glazing
• For a professional finish, apply one of the following mixtures with a pastry brush.

• Mix a whole egg with 1 tsp (5 mL) water, milk or cream. Apply before baking. It produces a shiny, brown crust.

• A leftover egg yolk mixed with 1 tsp (5 mL) water, milk or cream will give bread a rich, brown look.

• An egg white beaten with 1 tbsp (15 mL) cold water and applied 5 minutes before the baking time is finished gives a shiny, creamy look.

• Milk brushed on loaves gives you a soft, tender crust but a dull finish.

• For a sweet glaze, combine 1 cup sifted icing sugar with 2 tbsp (25 mL) water and ½ tsp (2 mL) vanilla extract. Spread over the loaves after they have been baked and are cool.

• Ten minutes before the bread has finished baking, sprinkle sesame seeds, caraway, oatmeal or poppy seeds on top of a glaze for an appetizing look.

Baking Bread
• Bake the bread on the lowest rack of a preheated oven, so the bottom will bake evenly.

• Perfectly baked bread will sound hollow when tapped, and will shrink away from the sides of the pan.

• Remove baked loaves from the cookie sheet or loaf pan immediately. Cool on racks for 2 to 3 hours before eating. Never eat bread fresh from the oven, no matter how appealing. The newly baked yeast can give you a stomach ache.

TROUBLE-SHOOTING

Sticky dough:
—underkneading or overkneading

Bread is too small:
—size of pan was too large for amount of dough
—dough was not left to rise long enough before baking

Bread is too large and poorly shaped:
—size of pan was too small for amount of dough
—dough was left to rise too long before baking
—too much yeast was used
—oven temperature was too low

Large air space beneath crust:
—dough was not left to rise long enough before baking
—dough was too stiff (too much flour)
—because dough was not covered during rising, it crusted
—dough was not left to rise long enough before baking
—bread was baked too long
—not enough fat

Crust too thick:
—dough crusted over during rising
—oven temperature was too low
—bread was baked too long

Crust cracked:
—dough crusted over during rising
—loaf cooled too quickly in a cold draft
—dough left to rise in a draft before baking

Bread crumbles easily:
—dough was not well mixed
—too much flour was added
—rising place was too warm
—dough left to rise too long before baking
—oven temperature was too low

Dough does not rise:
—too cool water temperature used for dissolving yeast
—too much flour causing too stiff a dough
—rising place was too cool

Bread has holes:
—air not completely pressed out of dough during shaping of loaves
—dough left to rise too long before baking

Bread has excessive break or slash on side:
—oven temperature was too high
—dough not left to rise long enough before baking
—improper shaping

Bread doesn't rise in oven:
—rising place was too warm
—old yeast
—dough left to rise too long before baking

Bread is heavy and compact:
—too much flour added
—dough not allowed to rise long enough before baking
—certain flours (whole wheat, rye) create heavier products than all white flour

Bread is wet inside and coarse grained:
—loaf underbaked
—dough not left to rise enough before baking

Bread is dry and has a coarse grain:
—too much flour added
—dough not kneaded enough
—dough left to rise too long before baking
—oven temperature was too low

Bread does not brown on sides:
—pans too bright and reflect heat away from sides
—placing too many pans in oven, creating an inconsistent heat flow

Basic White Bread

A faithful standby that always works and therefore is a good way to start your bread-baking career.

1½ cups	lukewarm water	375 mL
½ tsp	granulated sugar	2 mL
1	package active dry yeast, or 1 tbsp (15 mL)	
2 tsp	salt	10 mL
1 tsp	butter, at room temperature	5 mL
5 cups	all-purpose flour, approx.	1.25 L

Glaze:

1	egg white	1
1 tbsp	cold water	15 mL

1. Pour ¼ cup (50 mL) lukewarm water into a small bowl. Sprinkle the sugar over the water, stirring to dissolve. Add the yeast. Cover and leave until frothy, about 10 minutes.

2. Put the remaining water in a large bowl and stir in the yeast mixture. Stir in the salt and butter.

3. With a wooden spoon, beat in 2 cups (500 mL) flour until the batter is elastic. Then add more flour until the mixture is too stiff to beat.

4. Continue to add more flour, mixing with floured hands until the dough gathers in a ball and leaves the bowl clean. The amount of flour added will vary according to the humidity and the kinds of flour used.

5. Turn the dough onto a lightly floured board. Sprinkle some flour lightly on your hands and knead the dough. If the dough is too sticky, knead in more flour. Knead for 10 minutes, or until the dough is soft and silky.

If you are substituting fresh cake yeast for dry yeast, ⅗ oz cake yeast equals one package—1 tbsp (15 mL)—dry active yeast.

6. Place the dough in an oiled bowl. Brush the top of the dough with more oil. Cover and let rise in a warm place until doubled in bulk. This should take 1 to 1½ hours.

7. Turn the ball of dough onto a board and let it rest for 5 minutes, with a bowl upside down over the top. Knead for 1 minute, divide in two, then shape into two loaves and place in two oiled loaf pans. Set aside to rise in a warm place until doubled, about 45 minutes.

8. Preheat the oven to 450 F (230 C).

9. In a small bowl, beat together the egg white and water. Reserve.

10. Bake the bread for 20 minutes, then reduce the heat to 400 F (200 C) and bake for a further 15 minutes.

11. Remove the bread from the oven and brush on the glaze. Bake for a further 5 minutes, or until the bread sounds hollow when tapped.

Makes 2 loaves

Pizza Dough

This is a foolproof pizza dough. If you prefer a thin crust, roll it out as thinly as you can.

1 cup	warm water	250 mL
1	package active dry yeast, or 1 tbsp (15 mL)	1
1 tsp	granulated sugar	5 mL
2½ cups	all-purpose flour, approx.	625 mL
1 tsp	salt	5 mL
2 tbsp	olive oil	25 mL

1. In a small bowl, mix the warm water, yeast and sugar. Let stand for 5 minutes, or until frothy.

2. In a large bowl, combine 1½ cups (375 mL) flour with the salt. Pour the yeast mixture into the flour mixture. Using a wooden spoon, beat well. Add the oil and gradually incorporate the remaining flour to make a soft, slightly sticky dough.

3. On floured surface, knead the dough for 3 to 4 minutes, or until smooth and elastic.

4. Divide the dough into four portions. Each one is enough for one 9-inch (23 cm) pizza. On a floured surface, roll the dough to ⅛-inch (3 mm) thickness. Cut into 10-inch (25 cm) diameter and place on a cookie sheet. Fold in a ½-inch (1.25 cm) border and crimp. Spread on topping.

5. Preheat the oven to 450 F (230 C).

6. Bake the pizza for 10 minutes, or until the filling is bubbly.

Makes enough dough for four 9-inch (23 cm) pizzas

Spicy Italian Pizza Topping

1	spicy Italian sausage	1
1 cup	tomato sauce	250 mL
pinch	dried basil	pinch
½ cup	grated mozzarella cheese	125 mL

1. Prick the sausage and boil in a pot of water until partially cooked, about 5 minutes. Slice into ¼-inch (5 mm) pieces.

2. Spread the tomato sauce over the pizza base. Cover with the sausage slices, basil and cheese.

Makes enough for one 9-inch (23 cm) pizza

Mushroom Topping

1 tbsp	olive oil	15 mL
1 cup	thinly sliced mushrooms	250 mL
1	clove garlic, finely chopped	1
pinch	dried basil	pinch
pinch	dried tarragon	pinch
4 oz	Brie or Camembert (rind removed), chopped	125 g

1. In a frying pan, heat the oil over medium-high heat. Add the mushrooms and garlic. Sauté for 2 to 3 minutes, or until the mushrooms are slightly softened. Stir in the basil and tarragon.

2. Spoon the mushroom mixture over the pizza. Top with the Brie.

Makes enough for one 9-inch (23 cm) pizza

Quickbreads and Muffins

QUICKBREADS

Quickbreads taste good, are usually less fattening and rich than cakes, and don't crumble in lunch boxes. They are a cross between a bread and cake. In Great Britain, where teatime is a national institution, they are called tea breads. I like them because they are easy to make, don't need kneading or rising time, and often use up the extra bits and pieces residing in the refrigerator.

There are two categories of quickbreads—savory doughs such as soda bread, biscuits and scones, and batter-type sweet quickbreads usually containing fruit, vegetables or dried fruits. Both types of quickbreads rise with baking powder or baking soda, not yeast. Savory dough quickbreads have a dense texture. Batter quickbreads are cake-like. They are usually not frosted and toast well. Try slathering them with butter and jam!

Bake quickbreads in greased loaf pans or in large clean, greased juice cans for a spectacular presentation. Bake quickbreads in the lower third of the oven to ensure a cooked bottom and a top that is not over-browned.

To reheat muffins from the frozen state, place them in a paper bag. Run cold water over the bag until wet, then reheat in a 350 F (180 C) oven for 15 minutes. This method works well for stale rolls, too.

The easiest way to spoon muffin batter into muffin pans is to use an ice cream scoop.

MUFFINS

There are lots of fallacies about muffins. Somehow they have a healthy, low-calorie label. But muffins are not necessarily low calorie, nor are they particularly healthy with their high sugar content, but they are delicious and easy to make.

A good muffin has a dense, moist interior and is quite crumbly. To make the best muffins, make sure the dry ingredients are sifted together to incorporate them properly, then stir in the wet ingredients. The secret is not to overmix. Batter that is overmixed produces muffins with a dense, dry texture. Combine until the ingredients are just moistened, and don't worry about any lumps—they will disappear in the baking.

Bake muffins in well-greased muffin pans, or use paper baking cups. Fill two-thirds full to leave room for rising. If all the muffin cups are not filled, fill the empty ones halfway up with water to protect the pans and to help muffins bake more evenly.

Bake muffins in the center of the oven for even baking. After baking remove them from the muffin cups immediately and cool on a wire rack or serve warm. Store in plastic bags to help maintain moisture or freeze. Reheat from frozen state in a microwave or place in a paper bag. Run cold water over the bag until wet, then reheat in a 350 F (180 C) oven for 15 minutes. This method works well for stale rolls, too.

Equipment
• Muffin pans come in three sizes: mini, which are about 1 inch (2.5 cm) in diameter; standard, which are 2¾ inches (7 cm); and giant, which are about 4 inches (10 cm) across. The best material for muffin pans is darkened tin, which helps prevent burnt bottoms.

• Quickbreads are made in regular loaf pans.

Cream Wheat Scones

A rich whole wheat scone developed from a recipe at a cooking class given by Marion Cunningham, the "new" Fanny Farmer. Use with Southern-fried chicken, stews, or buttered with jam.

1 ½ cups	all-purpose flour	375 mL
½ cup	whole wheat flour	125 mL
1 tsp	salt	5 mL
1 tbsp	baking powder	15 mL
2 tsp	granulated sugar	10 mL
1 cup	whipping cream	250 mL
½ cup	butter, melted	125 mL

1. Preheat the oven to 425 F (220 C).

2. In a large bowl, combine the flours, salt, baking powder and sugar. Stir in enough cream for the dough to come together in a ball.

3. Turn the dough out onto a floured surface and knead for 1 minute. Pat to thickness of ½ inch (1.25 cm). Cut in squares and dip into the melted butter. Arrange on a baking sheet.

4. Bake for 15 to 18 minutes, or until pale gold and firm to the touch.

Makes 12 scones

Bruce's Bran Muffins

Although my husband, Bruce, has never made a muffin, after watching me trying to make the quintessential bran muffin, he went through the not-quite-perfect recipes and worked out a ratio of liquid to dry measures that would produce a moist, flavorful result. His background in chemistry obviously helped, because these muffins are the best!

1 cup	natural bran	250 mL
1 cup	bran buds	250 mL
2 cups	all-purpose flour	500 mL
1 cup	brown sugar	250 mL
2 tsp	baking soda	10 mL
½ tsp	salt	2 mL
2	eggs	2
2 cups	buttermilk	500 mL
⅔ cup	vegetable oil	150 mL
3 tbsp	molasses	45 mL
1 cup	raisins or chopped dates	250 mL

1. Preheat the oven to 400 F (200 C). Prepare 12 large muffin cups.

2. In a large bowl, combine the bran, bran buds, flour, brown sugar, baking soda and salt.

3. In a medium bowl, stir together the eggs, buttermilk, vegetable oil, molasses and raisins.

4. Stir the wet ingredients into the dry ingredients. Be careful not to overmix.

5. Fill the muffin cups three-quarters full. Bake for 15 to 18 minutes, or until a toothpick inserted comes out clean. Remove the muffins from the pans and cool on a wire rack.

Makes 12 large muffins

When measuring molasses, dip the measuring spoon into vegetable oil first; the molasses will slip off the spoon more easily.

Cornbread

This is a moist cornbread with the added spice of hot chilies. I sometimes use this recipe to top a ground meat casserole or shepherd's pie. Occasionally I add 1 cup (250 mL) corn niblets to the batter. If you prefer, you can omit the chilies and/or the cheese.

1 1/3 cups	all-purpose flour	325 mL
2/3 cup	cornmeal	150 mL
1/3 cup	granulated sugar	75 mL
2 tbsp	baking power	25 mL
1/2 tsp	salt	2 mL
1 1/3 cups	milk	325 mL
1/3 cup	butter, melted	75 mL
1	egg, beaten	1
1/2 cup	grated Cheddar cheese	125 mL
1	canned green chili, chopped	1

1. Preheat the oven to 375 F (190 C).

2. Combine the flour, cornmeal, sugar, baking powder and salt in a large bowl. Mix well to break up any lumps.

3. In a separate bowl, stir together the milk, butter and egg. Add to the dry ingredients.

4. Blend until mixed and large lumps are dissolved, but do not overbeat. Stir in the cheese and chili. Pour into a greased 8-inch (2 L) square cake pan. Bake for 30 minutes, or until skewer inserted comes out clean.

Serves 6

Chocolate Zucchini Bread

You can omit the chocolate and make plain zucchini bread, but I think the chocolate is better. The zucchini makes the bread moist and nutritious, and no one will recognize the secret ingredient.

4 oz	bittersweet chocolate	125 g
1 cup	all-purpose flour	250 mL
1/2 cup	whole wheat flour	125 mL
1/3 cup	quick-cooking rolled oats	75 mL
1 tsp	baking soda	5 mL
1/2 cup	butter, at room temperature	125 mL
1/2 cup	granulated sugar	125 mL
2	eggs	2
1/2 cup	plain yogurt	125 mL
1 tsp	vanilla	5 mL
1/2 tsp	grated lemon rind	2 mL
2 cups	finely shredded zucchini	500 mL
1/2 cup	chopped walnuts, optional	125 mL

1. In a small pot, melt the chocolate over low heat. Reserve.

2. Preheat the oven to 350 F (180 C).

3. In a medium bowl, combine the flours, oats and baking soda. Reserve.

4. In a large bowl, cream together the butter and sugar until fluffy. Add the eggs, yogurt, vanilla and lemon rind, beating well.

5. Stir in the zucchini. Add the flour mixture, a third at a time, until combined. Beat in the walnuts and chocolate.

6. Spread the batter in a greased 9 × 5-inch (2 L) loaf pan. Bake for 60 to 70 minutes, or until a toothpick inserted comes out clean. Cool on a wire rack, then turn out of the pan. Store overnight for easier slicing.

Makes 1 loaf

Part 4

Recipes

·10·
Appetizers and Soups

ONION TARTS

A rich and satisfying hors d'oeuvre that freezes well. Bake, cool, freeze on a cookie sheet, then place in freezer bags. To reheat, place the frozen tarts in a 350 F (180 C) oven for 10 minutes, or until heated through. Serve warm.

2 tbsp	butter	25 mL
1	large onion, finely chopped	1
1 cup	whipping cream	250 mL
2 tsp	Dijon mustard	10 mL
	Salt and freshly ground pepper to taste	
1	recipe Cream Cheese Pastry (see page 95)	1

1. In a frying pan, heat the butter on medium-high heat until sizzling. Stir in the onions and sauté until they are coated with butter. Turn the heat to low, cover the pan and cook slowly for 20 minutes, or until the onions are softened but not brown.

2. Add the whipping cream, turn the heat to high and boil down the cream until thickened, about 5 minutes. Stir in the mustard. Season well with salt and pepper.

3. Preheat the oven to 400 F (200 C).

4. Divide the pastry into thirty 1-inch (2.5 cm) balls. Pat into 1-inch (2.5 cm) small muffin cups or tartlet pans.

5. Spoon the onion mixture into the shells, filling almost full. Bake for 15 minutes, or until the pastry is golden. Cook on a rack. Remove the tarts from the pans when cool.

Makes thirty 2¾ × 1-inch (7 × 2.5 cm) tarts

SALMON QUICHE

This is a delightful luncheon or brunch dish. It is a traditional quiche with a custard filling. You can substitute equal amounts of other fresh fish or smoked fish for the salmon. Serve it with a green salad.

8 oz	fresh salmon	250 g
1	9-inch (23 cm) partially baked Food Processor Pastry pie shell (see page 94)	1
3	eggs	3
1 cup	milk or light cream	250 mL
½ tsp	salt	2 mL
¼ tsp	freshly ground pepper Few sprigs fresh dill	1 mL

1. Preheat the oven to 375 F (190 C).

2. Cut the salmon into ½-inch (1.25 cm) cubes. Arrange evenly over the base of the pastry.

3. In a medium bowl, beat together the eggs and milk. Season with salt and pepper and pour the mixture over the salmon. Tear the dill into bits and scatter over the top of the quiche.

4. Bake for 30 minutes, or until the filling is firm to the touch. Serve hot or cold.

Serves 6

SMOKED SALMON PÂTÉ

This smoked salmon pâté is a simple combination of cream cheese and smoked salmon—quickly made and elegant to serve, especially when garnished with salmon caviar.

4 oz	cream cheese, at room temperature	125 g
3 oz	smoked salmon, finely chopped	90 g
2 tbsp	finely chopped green onions	25 mL
pinch	cayenne pepper Salt to taste	pinch
4	lettuce leaves	4
1	small cucumber, sliced	1
2 oz	salmon caviar, optional	60 g

1. In a bowl, beat the cream cheese until light and creamy. Fold in the smoked salmon and green onions.

2. Season with cayenne and salt.

3. Serve the pâté spooned onto lettuce leaves on individual plates. Surround with cucumber slices and garnish with the salmon caviar. Or serve in a crock with hot buttered toast or crackers so guests can help themselves.

Serves 4

Salmon caviar is the roe of the female salmon; it is similar to black sturgeon caviar, but with larger eggs and less salt. It is a good, less expensive substitute for sturgeon caviar.

119

VEGETABLE CHEESE TART

Quiche usually contains a custardy filling and some vegetables or meat. This recipe features a vegetable-laden filling with a little custard.

1	10-oz (300 g) package fresh spinach	1
¼ cup	butter	50 mL
8 oz	mushrooms, sliced	250 g
1 tsp	lemon juice	5 mL
3	leeks, white part only, sliced	3
1 tsp	dried thyme	5 mL
1	partially baked 9-inch (23 cm) Basic Shortcrust Pastry shell (see page 94)	1
½ cup	grated Gruyère cheese	125 mL
2	eggs	2
¾ cup	whipping cream	175 mL
1 tsp	salt	5 mL
¼ tsp	freshly ground pepper	1 mL

1. Wash the spinach and remove the stems. Place in a pot with the water that clings to the leaves and steam on medium heat until wilted, about 5 minutes. Drain well and rinse with cold water. Squeeze out all liquid and chop coarsely.

2. In a frying pan, melt the butter over medium-high heat until sizzling. Stir in the mushrooms and sauté until softened, about 2 minutes.

3. With a slotted spoon, transfer the mushrooms to a side plate. Sprinkle with the lemon juice and reserve.

4. Preheat the oven to 350 F (180 C). In the same frying pan, sauté the leeks until softened, about 6 to 8 minutes. Sprinkle with the thyme. Reserve.

5. Layer the spinach, mushrooms and leeks in the partially baked pastry shell, sprinkling 2 tbsp (25 mL) cheese over each layer.

6. In a medium bowl, beat together the eggs and the cream. Season with salt and pepper. Pour over the vegetables. Top with the remaining cheese and bake for 30 to 35 minutes, or until hot and bubbly.

Serves 6 to 8

SAUTÉED ONIONS AND EGGS

One of the best ways to wake up a jaded palate is to sauté a large pan full of onions. Who can resist the aroma of mounds of brown, shimmering onions sizzling away and then bound together by the lightest scrambled eggs? Sunday mornings are made for this dish.

1	large Spanish onion	1
1 tbsp	vegetable oil	15 mL
1 tbsp	butter	15 mL
4	eggs	4
	Salt and freshly ground pepper to taste	

1. Cut the onion in half and slice thinly.

2. Heat the oil and butter in a large frying pan on high heat. When sizzling, add the onions and sauté until golden-brown, about 5 to 7 minutes.

3. Whisk the eggs together in a bowl. Turn the heat to low, add the eggs and stir together with the onions until the eggs are cooked through but not dry. Season with salt and pepper. Serve immediately.

Serves 2

Scrambled eggs should be slightly runny; they will continue to cook after they have been removed from the heat.

VEGETARIAN HASH

In this recipe the eggs are poached on top of a vegetable sauce. When eaten, the soft eggs mix with the spicy sauce to make a heavenly dish. Serve it for lunch or as a first course for dinner.

2 tbsp	olive oil	25 mL
1 tbsp	butter	15 mL
2	onions, chopped	2
1	red pepper, chopped	1
1	green pepper, chopped	1
2 tsp	ground coriander	10 mL
1 cup	canned tomatoes, undrained, chopped	250 mL
pinch	cayenne pepper	pinch
	Salt and freshly ground pepper to taste	
6	eggs	6
2 tbsp	finely chopped parsley	25 mL

1. In a heavy frying pan, heat the oil and butter on high heat. Add the onions and peppers. Cook for about 6 to 8 minutes, stirring occasionally, until the onions are transparent and the peppers are tender but crunchy. Stir in the coriander and cook for 30 seconds.

2. Add the tomatoes and cayenne and bring to a boil. Reduce the heat to medium-low and simmer for 5 minutes. Season with salt and pepper to taste.

3. Break the eggs on top of the tomato mixture. Cover and poach gently for 5 to 7 minutes, or until the eggs are set. Sprinkle parsley on top and serve.

Serves 6

ASPARAGUS WITH SOFT-BOILED EGGS

Ideally, asparagus should stand in the water when it is boiled, so that the stalks cook while the heads steam. If you do not have a narrow pot, tie the stalks in small bundles with string and cook, lying down, in a frying pan filled with boiling water.

1 lb	asparagus, peeled	500 g
4	eggs	4
¼ cup	butter, melted	50 mL

1. Choose the narrowest pot you have. Fill it with salted water and bring to a boil on high heat. Add the asparagus, return to a boil and boil until the stalks are crisp-tender. Cooking times vary according to the thickness of the stalk, but peeled asparagus should only take 5 minutes for stalks that are ½ inch (1.25 cm) thick.

2. Gently remove the stalks from the water, being careful not to break them. Drain well, and refresh by pouring cold water over to stop the cooking. Then lay on paper towels to dry.

3. Meanwhile, bring a pot of water to a boil on high heat. Add the eggs and boil for 3 minutes. Drain.

4. Serve the asparagus alongside a soft-boiled egg sitting in an egg cup, and a little pot of melted salted butter. Using your fingers (which is the correct way to eat asparagus), dip the asparagus into the egg, then into the butter.

Serves 4

Asparagus stalks have a hard outer skin that should be peeled off with a vegetable peeler. Without this layer, the asparagus will cook in half the time. Thin stalks do not need to be peeled.

CHEESE SCOTCH EGGS

These eggs are super served hot as an appetizer or accompanied by a salad for lunch or a light supper. The eggs may also be served cold, cut into wedges as an hors d'oeuvre. They are a lighter and more interesting version of sausage-wrapped Scotch eggs.

2 cups	fresh breadcrumbs	500 mL
½ tsp	salt	2 mL
½ tsp	freshly ground pepper	2 mL
3 cups	grated Cheddar cheese	750 mL
2	eggs	2
8	hard-boiled eggs (see page 26)	8
	Oil for deep frying	

Wash spinach in warm water. It will help loosen the dirt better than cold water.

1. In a small bowl, season the breadcrumbs with salt and pepper.

2. In a medium bowl, mix the cheese with 1 egg and about 1 cup (250 mL) breadcrumbs to make a pliable dough. Refrigerate for 30 minutes.

3. Divide the cheese mixture into eight portions; form around the hard-boiled eggs.

4. Beat the remaining egg in a shallow dish. Roll the wrapped eggs in the egg. Roll the eggs in the remaining breadcrumbs.

5. Heat the oil in a wok until 375 F (190 C), or until a bread cube turns brown in 15 seconds. Deep-fry the eggs until brown, about 2 minutes.

Serves 8

CREAM OF SPINACH SOUP

Shred some raw spinach and float it on top of this soup for a garnish. For a spicier flavor, sprinkle on cayenne just before serving.

2 lb	fresh spinach	1 kg
2 tbsp	butter	25 mL
1	onion, chopped	1
1	potato, peeled and chopped	1
3 cups	chicken stock	750 mL
½ cup	whipping cream	125 mL
2 tbsp	chopped fresh dill	25 mL
	Salt and freshly ground pepper to taste	

1. Strip the stems from the spinach, and wash the leaves well in warm water.

2. In a large heavy pot, melt the butter on medium-high heat. Add the onion and potato. Sauté until the vegetables are coated with the butter and slightly softened, about 2 minutes.

3. Add the spinach and stir together. Pour in the stock and bring to a boil. Reduce the heat to low and simmer, uncovered, for 20 minutes.

4. Puree in a blender or food processor. Return to the pot and add the cream and dill. Bring to a boil on medium heat, then simmer for 5 minutes. Season well with salt and pepper. Serve hot or cold.

Serves 6

BRAZILIAN BLACK BEAN SOUP

With the recent interest in the cooking of South America, black or turtle bean soups and side dishes are becoming increasingly popular. This is a spicy, hearty soup which needs only a good salad or sandwich to follow. Serve it in the winter to ward off the chills.

Black turtle beans are available at health food and bulk stores.

2 cups	dried black turtle beans	500 mL
2 tbsp	vegetable oil	25 mL
1	onion, chopped	1
4	cloves garlic, finely chopped	4
1	green pepper, chopped	1
1 tbsp	ground cumin	15 mL
1	fresh green chili, seeded and chopped	1
6 cups	chicken stock or water	1.5 L
1	bay leaf	1
1/4 cup	red wine vinegar	50 mL
	Salt and freshly ground pepper to taste	
4	green onions, finely chopped	4
1 cup	sour cream	250 mL

1. Cover the black beans with cold water and soak overnight. Drain.

2. Heat the oil in a stockpot on high heat. Add the onions and sauté until softened, about 5 minutes.

3. Stir in the garlic and green pepper. Sauté for 1 minute. Add the cumin and chili. Continue to sauté until you can smell the spices, about 30 seconds.

4. Add the beans and combine with the onion mixture. Pour in the stock, stir together, and add the bay leaf and vinegar. Bring to boil, lower the heat and simmer, covered, for 1 1/2 hours, or until the black beans are tender. If the soup is too thick, thin with some extra water. Season well with salt and pepper. Serve garnished with the green onions and a dollop of sour cream.

Serves 8 to 10

RUSSIAN CHICKEN GARLIC SOUP

If chicken soup soothes most ills, then chicken garlic soup must cure them. This Russian recipe comes from an artist friend, Marilyn Mandel. Passed down through her family, it is basically a chicken soup with a difference. The taste of the large quantity of garlic mellows in cooking, and the soup has a spectacular sharp-sweet quality.

1 1/2	heads garlic	1 1/2
5 cups	chicken stock	1.25 L
1 tbsp	white vinegar	15 mL
	Salt and freshly ground pepper to taste	
3	hard-boiled eggs, grated	3

1. Peel and finely chop the garlic.

2. In a large heavy pot, bring the stock to a boil on high heat. Add the garlic, reduce the heat to low and simmer, covered, for 40 minutes.

3. Add the vinegar and simmer for 20 minutes longer. Season with salt and pepper to taste.

4. Place 1 tbsp (15 mL) grated egg at the bottom of each soup bowl. Ladle the soup on top.

Serves 8

Bean soups tend to thicken on standing. To thin, add a little extra water before reheating.

A head of garlic is the full bulb, which is made up of ten to twelve cloves. If you don't want to peel all the garlic, simmer the unpeeled cloves for 10 minutes in the stock, then remove. The cloves will slip easily out of their skins.

CURRIED ZUCCHINI AND APPLE SOUP

This soup is only mildly spiced, but the curry livens up a bland vegetable like zucchini. The rice thickens the soup. Use a tart apple like Granny Smith or Spy for the freshest taste.

¼ cup	butter	50 mL
1	large onion, chopped	1
1	apple, peeled and diced	1
3 cups	chopped zucchini	750 mL
½ tsp	curry powder	2 mL
4 cups	chicken stock	1 L
¼ cup	long-grain rice	50 mL
1 cup	milk	250 mL
2 tbsp	chopped parsley	25 mL

1. In a pot, heat the butter on medium-high heat. Sauté the onion and apple until soft but not brown, about 5 minutes.

2. Stir in the zucchini and curry powder. Sauté 1 minute longer.

3. Stir in the chicken stock and rice and bring to a boil. Cover. Reduce the heat to low and simmer for 20 to 25 minutes, or until the zucchini is tender.

4. Cool slightly, then puree in batches in a food processor or blender. Return to the pot, add the milk and heat through but do not boil. Garnish with chopped parsley.

Serves 8

POTATO, ONION AND LEEK SOUP

Although this soup can be pureed, it is tasty left chunky. Try serving it chilled at a picnic. It also freezes well.

3	leeks	3
2 tbsp	butter	25 mL
1	onion, chopped	1
3	potatoes, peeled and cubed	3
4 cups	chicken stock	1 L
¼ tsp	nutmeg	1 mL
¼ cup	whipping cream, optional	50 mL
	Salt and freshly ground pepper to taste	
¼ cup	finely chopped chives or leek tops	50 mL

1. Trim the leeks and discard the tops, leaving about 2 inches (5 cm) of the dark-green leaves. Slice down the center to, but not through, the roots. Gently separate the leaves and wash thoroughly. Drain, then slice thinly.

2. In a large heavy pot, heat the butter on medium-high heat. Add the leeks and onion and cook gently, without browning, for about 5 minutes, or until the vegetables soften.

3. Add the potatoes and stir in the chicken stock and nutmeg. Bring to a boil on high heat. Turn the heat down to low and simmer gently, uncovered, for 30 minutes, or until the potatoes are tender.

4. Puree the soup in a food processor or blender. Return to the pot, stir in the cream, return to a boil and simmer for 5 minutes. Season to taste with salt and pepper. Serve garnished with a sprinkling of chives.

Serves 6

FISH CHOWDER

Adding the fish at the end of the cooking time prevents it from becoming overcooked in the soup. Use firm-fleshed fish that will not disintegrate easily when simmered. Halibut, monkfish, cod and grouper are good choices.

The soup base can be made a day or two ahead of time and refrigerated, or can be frozen for up to one month.

2 tbsp	olive oil	25 mL
1	Spanish onion, chopped	1
1	clove garlic, finely chopped	1
1	leek, white part only, chopped	1
1 tbsp	finely chopped parsley	15 mL
1	bay leaf	1
pinch	saffron, or 1 tsp (5 mL) turmeric	pinch
2	tomatoes, chopped	2
4 cups	fish stock or chicken stock	1 L
1 lb	mixed fish	500 g
	Salt and freshly ground pepper to taste	
1/2 cup	grated Swiss cheese	125 mL

1. In large heavy pot, heat the oil on high heat. Add the onion, garlic, leek, parsley, bay leaf and saffron. Sauté for about 4 minutes, or until everything is softened.
2. Add the tomatoes and the stock and bring to a boil. Turn the heat down to low and simmer, uncovered, or 20 minutes.
3. Cut the fish into cubes. Add the fish and simmer gently on low heat for a further 10 minutes. Season to taste with salt and pepper.
4. Remove the bay leaf and serve with the grated cheese on top.

Serves 6

TURKISH CUCUMBER SOUP

An interesting cold soup that is excellent served before a lamb main course. You can use crabmeat instead of shrimp, or omit the seafood altogether. If you use regular cucumbers, peel and seed them first.

1	English cucumber	1
1 cup	chicken stock	250 mL
1/2 cup	tomato juice	125 mL
2 cups	plain yogurt	500 mL
2	cloves garlic, finely chopped	2
1/2 cup	light cream	125 mL
2 tbsp	tarragon vinegar	25 mL
1 cup	chopped, cooked shrimp	250 mL
	Salt and freshly ground pepper to taste	
2	hard-boiled eggs, grated	2
1 tbsp	chopped fresh mint	15 mL

1. Grate the cucumber into a bowl.

2. In a large bowl, beat the chicken stock and tomato juice together. Beat in the yogurt. Add the cucumber, garlic, cream, vinegar, shrimp, salt and pepper. Chill for at least 2 hours.

3. Before serving, garnish with grated eggs and chopped mint.

Serves 8

The name chowder comes from the French "chaudière," the name of the cauldron sailors used for cooking their fish soups and stews.

·11·
Seafood and Poultry

SALMON AND VEGETABLE CASSEROLE

Serve this uncomplicated recipe in shallow soup bowls along with crusty bread to soak up the broth. Leona Chase demonstrated this dish at the 1986 Ontario Science Centre Food Show.

6	salmon steaks, 12 oz (375 g) each	6
	Juice of 1 lemon	
½ tsp	freshly ground pepper	2 mL
1	10 oz (300 g) package spinach, coarse stems removed	1
3	leeks, thinly sliced	3
2	stalks celery, thinly sliced	2
3 tbsp	chopped fresh dill	45 mL
1 cup	fish stock or chicken stock	250 mL
½ cup	dry white wine	125 mL
2 tbsp	butter	25 mL

1. Preheat the oven to 350 F (180 C).

2. Sprinkle the salmon with the lemon juice; season with the pepper.

3. Arrange the spinach, leeks and celery in the bottom of a buttered ovenproof gratin or baking dish that holds the salmon steaks in a single layer. Arrange the salmon steaks on top. Sprinkle with the dill. Add the fish stock and wine; dot with the butter. Cover tightly with foil.

4. Poach in the oven for 20 to 30 minutes, or until the fish is opaque. Serve from the gratin dish.

Serves 6

COD PIZZAIOLA

Carol Ferguson, food editor of Canadian Living, *demonstrated this dish
during Canadian week at the Ontario
Science Centre Food Show. It is a fresh-
tasting, low-calorie meal-in-one-dish.
Serve with linguine, if desired.*

*This poaching method can be used
with cod, haddock, sole or halibut. The
sauce is a simplified version of an Italian favorite; make it with fresh or
canned tomatoes, depending on the
season.*

2 lb	fish steaks or fillets	1 kg
¼ tsp	salt	1 mL
¼ tsp	freshly ground pepper	1 mL
4 cups	water	1 L
½ cup	dry white wine	125 mL
	Juice of 1 lemon	
2 tbsp	olive oil	25 mL
1	small onion, chopped	1
2	cloves garlic, finely chopped	2
2 cups	tomatoes, peeled, seeded and chopped	500 mL
1 tsp	chopped fresh basil, or ¼ tsp (1 mL) dried	5 mL
1 tsp	chopped fresh oregano, or ¼ tsp (1 mL) dried	5 mL
1	bay leaf	1
1 cup	sliced mushrooms	250 mL
1	small green pepper, cut into strips, optional	1
1	small zucchini, sliced, optional	1
	Salt and freshly ground pepper to taste	

1. Sprinkle the fish lightly with salt
and pepper.

2. In a large frying pan, combine the
water, wine and lemon juice. Bring
to a boil on high heat and reduce the
heat to a simmer. Add the fish and
simmer, covered, for about 5 minutes
per ½-inch (1.25 cm) thickness, or
just until the fish is opaque. Remove
the fish and keep warm. Discard the
liquid.

3. Add the oil to the same frying pan
and heat on high heat. Add the onion
and garlic and sauté until softened
but not brown, about 2 minutes.

4. Add the tomatoes, basil, oregano
and bay leaf. Turn the heat to low and
simmer for 5 minutes.

5. Add the mushrooms, green pepper
and zucchini. Simmer just until tender,
about 5 minutes. Add salt and pepper
to taste.

6. Return the fish to the sauce for 2
minutes to heat through. Remove the
bay leaf before serving.

Serves 4 to 6

SAVORY SHRIMPS

Make the sauce ahead of time, adding the shrimp just before serving to avoid overcooking. Serve with rice as a main course, or as an appetizer with garlic toast strips.

2 tbsp	olive oil	25 mL
1	onion, finely chopped	1
¼ cup	dry white wine	50 mL
1 cup	fish stock or chicken stock	250 mL
2	cloves garlic, finely chopped	2
2 tsp	tomato paste	10 mL
2	tomatoes, peeled, seeded and cut into strips, or 1 cup (250 mL) drained canned tomatoes, cut into strips	2
1 lb	large shrimp, peeled	500 g
	Salt and freshly ground pepper to taste	
2 tbsp	finely chopped parsley	25 mL

1. In a frying pan, heat the oil on high heat. Add the onion and sauté until softened, about 2 minutes. Add the wine and boil until reduced to 2 tbsp (25 mL).

2. Add the stock, garlic, tomato paste and tomatoes. Turn the heat down to medium-low and simmer for 20 to 25 minutes, or until reduced by half.

3. Add the shrimp to the sauce and poach gently for 3 to 4 minutes, until the shrimp are pink and slightly curled. Season with salt and pepper. Sprinkle with parsley before serving.

Serves 6 as an appetizer, 4 as a main course

CHICKEN BREASTS WITH PEARS

This easy, quick chicken dish can be prepared in less than 15 minutes. I used this recipe at the 1986 Ontario Science Centre Food Show to demonstrate how quickly a main course could be produced. If you make it ahead of time, reheat until just hot in a 350 F (180 C) oven to avoid overcooking the chicken. Substitute apples for the pears, if desired. Serve with linguine or rice.

½ cup	butter	125 mL
2	pears, peeled and sliced in eighths	2
2	boneless whole chicken breasts, split in half	2
	Salt and freshly ground pepper	
¼ cup	dry white wine	50 mL
½ cup	whipping cream	125 mL
2 tbsp	Poire William or brandy	25 mL

1. On medium heat, add ¼ cup (50 mL) butter to a large frying pan. Heat until sizzling. Sauté the pears until soft, about 3 minutes. Remove and keep warm.

2. Add the remaining butter to the pan. Season the chicken breasts with salt and pepper. Add the breasts to the frying pan and cook for 2 to 3 minutes, or until golden. Turn and cook on the second side for 2 to 3 minutes.

3. Add the wine and reduce until 1 tbsp (15 mL) remains, about 2 minutes. Add the cream and Poire William. Reduce the sauce until it thickens slightly, about 2 minutes. Scatter in the reserved pears.

Serves 4

CHICKEN BREASTS WITH TARRAGON SAUCE

As a student wife, this was my constant support as an entertaining dish. It always worked and tasted special. Even today I use it for family dinners or with boneless breasts as a buffet dish. If you use boneless chicken breasts, cook them for only 20 minutes.

1 tbsp	dried tarragon	15 mL
¼ cup	all-purpose flour	50 mL
½ tsp	salt	2 mL
¼ tsp	freshly ground pepper	1 mL
6	single chicken breasts	6
¼ cup	butter	50 mL
1	small onion, chopped	1
¼ cup	dry white wine	50 mL
½ cup	chicken stock	125 mL
¼ cup	whipping cream	50 mL

1. In a bowl, mix together the tarragon, flour, salt and pepper. Lightly coat the chicken with the flour mixture. Reserve the remaining flour mixture.

2. On medium heat, melt the butter in a large frying pan until sizzling. Brown the chicken breasts, skin side down first, on both sides, for about 5 minutes per side. Remove.

3. Sauté the onion in the remaining butter until softened, about 3 minutes. Add the wine and reduce to 1 tbsp (15 mL). Sprinkle in any reserved flour. Cook for 1 minute, stirring. Pour in the chicken stock and bring to a boil, stirring.

4. Return the chicken to the frying pan. Cover and cook for 25 to 35 minutes, or until tender. Remove the chicken breasts and keep warm.

5. Add the cream to the pan and bring to a boil. Adjust the seasonings, adding salt, pepper and tarragon as needed. Pour the sauce over the chicken.
Serves 6

LIME CHICKEN

The refreshing taste of this salad beats the heat on a hot day.

6 cups	chicken stock	1.5 L
4	whole chicken breasts, cut in half	4
½ cup	lime juice	125 mL
3	cloves garlic	3
2 tbsp	dried tarragon	25 mL
1 tbsp	fresh basil	15 mL
3	green onions	3
1 cup	olive oil	250 mL
	Salt and freshly ground pepper	
1	bunch watercress	1

1. In a medium pot, bring the chicken stock to a boil on high heat. Reduce the heat to low, add the chicken breasts, and poach for 15 minutes, or until the juices run clear. Remove from the heat and let cool in the stock. Remove the skin and bones from the chicken. Reserve the chicken stock for another use. Cut the chicken into slivers.

2. Place the remaining ingredients except for the watercress in a food processor and process until combined. Pour over the chicken, cover and refrigerate for 24 hours.

3. Remove the chicken from the marinade and place on a platter. Surround with watercress. Serve the marinade separately.

Serves 8

Cooling poached chicken in stock helps to maintain its texture and juiciness.

SOY SAUCE CHICKEN

A Chinese braised chicken with hints of licorice. The chicken is not covered for this dish, which is why it needs to be turned frequently. The sauce reduces down as it cooks, resulting in a superb taste. Make it with chicken pieces, breasts or wings if you do not have a whole chicken. Breasts take 30 minutes; wings, 20 minutes; chicken pieces about 45 minutes. Serve with steamed rice. The chicken can be served hot or cold and reheats well.

½ cup	water	125 mL
½ cup	soy sauce	125 mL
½ cup	granulated sugar	125 mL
2	slices fresh ginger, the size of a quarter	2
1	star anise, or 1 tsp (5 mL) fennel seeds	1
1	3-lb (1.5 kg) chicken	1
1	bunch green onions, root ends cut off	1

Star anise is a licorice-flavored, star-shaped Chinese spice. Use fennel seeds as a substitute.

1. Use a pot that holds the chicken snugly. Add the water, soy sauce, sugar, ginger and anise and bring to a boil on high heat.

2. Fill the cavity of the chicken with the onions. Place in the pot, breast side down. Simmer on medium heat, uncovered, making sure there are always bubbles around the chicken. Cook the chicken for 60 minutes, turning every 10 minutes. Remove from the heat and let the chicken cool in the liquid.

3. Cut up and serve with some sauce poured over.

Serves 4

POACHED CHICKEN WITH VEGETABLES

This is a homey one-dish meal. Serve the chicken and vegetables together with a little broth poured over, or use the broth to make a velouté sauce enriched with cream and herbs (see page 47). Add cabbage or turnip to change the flavor, depending on your taste.

1	4-lb (2 kg) chicken	1
1	bay leaf	1
1	sprig parsley	1
1 tsp	dried thyme	5 mL
6	small onions	6
2	carrots, thickly sliced	2
2	stalks celery, thickly sliced	2
2	parsnips, thickly sliced	2
2	zucchini, thickly sliced	2

1. Cut the chicken into 4 pieces. Lay in a large pot and cover with cold water. Add the bay leaf and parsley. Bring the water to boil on high heat and skim off the scum that comes to the top.

2. Turn the heat to low, cover and poach the chicken for 20 minutes. Add the thyme, onions, carrots, celery and parsnips. Continue to poach for 20 minutes. Add zucchini and cook for 10 minutes, or until the chicken juices run clear. Remove the chicken and continue to poach the vegetables if they are not tender. Remove the vegetables and bay leaf.

3. Skin the chicken. Cut it into serving pieces. Serve with the poached vegetables and a little broth.

Serves 4

COCONUT CHICKEN

A chicken recipe from the Philippines, from Toronto caterer Dinah Koo. Serve it with rice and stir-fried vegetables.

1	Spanish onion, thinly sliced	1
2	cloves garlic, finely chopped	2
1 cup	white wine vinegar	250 mL
¼ cup	soy sauce	50 mL
2 tbsp	oyster sauce, optional	25 mL
½ tsp	Tabasco sauce	2 mL
1 tsp	salt	5 mL
1 tbsp	freshly ground pepper	15 mL
1	3-lb (1.5 kg) chicken, cut into 8 pieces	1
¼ cup	vegetable oil	50 mL
3 cups	coconut milk	750 mL

1. In a large bowl, combine the onions, garlic, vinegar, soy sauce, oyster sauce, Tabasco, salt and pepper. Mix well. Add the chicken pieces, turning to coat all over. Cover and marinate in the refrigerator for 8 hours or overnight.

2. Remove the chicken pieces from the marinade, reserving the marinade. Pat dry with paper towels.

3. In a large Dutch oven, heat the oil on medium-high heat. Cook the chicken pieces in batches (skin side down first to render the fat) until browned all over, about 5 minutes per side. Remove the chicken from the Dutch oven and reserve.

4. Add the marinade, including the onions, to the pot. Increase the heat to high and boil rapidly until reduced by half, about 5 minutes.

5. Add the coconut milk and chicken pieces to the pot. Simmer, uncovered, over medium-low heat for 30 to 35 minutes, or until the chicken is cooked through.

6. Remove the chicken pieces. Bring the liquid to boil on high heat and reduce by half or until thickened. Return the chicken pieces to reheat before serving.

Serves 6

LEMON GRILLED CHICKEN LEGS

Serve this with steamed rice and a green salad for a light summer meal. Use chicken legs with the thighs attached.

¼ cup	dry white wine	50 mL
2	cloves garlic, finely chopped	2
	Grated rind and juice of 1 lemon	
1 tbsp	dried tarragon	15 mL
½ cup	olive oil	125 mL
pinch	cayenne pepper	pinch
½ tsp	salt	2 mL
½ tsp	freshly ground pepper	2 mL
6	chicken legs	6

1. In a bowl, combine the white wine, garlic, lemon rind, juice and tarragon. Whisk in the olive oil and season with cayenne, salt and pepper.

2. Place the chicken legs in a large dish. Pour over the marinade. Marinate for 2 hours in the refrigerator, turning occasionally.

3. Preheat the broiler. Broil the chicken legs 6 inches (15 cm) from the element for 10 minutes per side, basting occasionally with the marinade. Or, barbecue the chicken legs for 10 minutes per side, or until the juices run clear.

Serves 6

Canned coconut milk can be found in Chinese or specialty food stores. If it is unavailable, creamed coconut in a package can be substituted. Blend it with 2 cups (500 mL) water in a blender or food processor.

BRAISED CHICKEN PROVENÇAL

Serve this dish with French bread to mop up the sauce, and a green salad. In the summer, use six fresh peeled, seeded and chopped tomatoes instead of canned. Cooking the onion slowly in this recipe gives a more mellow flavor to the sauce.

3	slices bacon, diced	3
2 tbsp	olive oil	25 mL
1	4-lb (2 kg) chicken, cut into eight pieces	1
	Salt and freshly ground pepper to taste	
1	Spanish onion, chopped	1
4	cloves garlic, chopped	4
1 tsp	dried rosemary	5 mL
1 tsp	dried thyme	5 mL
½ cup	dry white wine	125 mL
1½ cups	canned tomatoes, undrained	375 mL

Garnish:

12	black olives, optional	12
¼ cup	finely chopped parsley	50 mL

Provençal usually denotes garlic, olive oil, olives and tomatoes—the products indigenous to the area of France called Provence.

1. Preheat the oven to 325 F (160 C).

2. In a large frying pan on medium heat, sauté the bacon in the olive oil for about 1 minute, or until limp.

3. Dry the chicken with paper towels. Add the chicken legs and thighs to the frying pan, skin side down. Brown slowly until golden-brown, about 5 to 8 minutes per side. Remove to a heavy ovenproof casserole. Add the breasts to the frying pan, skin side down, and continue to brown for about 7 minutes per side until well browned. Remove to the casserole.

4. Stir the onions into the pan and sauté until softened and slightly browned, about 10 minutes. Add the garlic and continue to cook until the garlic softens slightly, about 1 minute. Add the rosemary and thyme.

5. Stir in the white wine and tomatoes. Scrape up any bits off the bottom of the pan and bring to a boil. Pour the sauce over the chicken.

6. Bake, covered, for 40 to 50 minutes, or until the chicken juices run clear. Serve garnished with black olives and parsley.

Serves 6

SAUTÉED CHICKEN LIVERS

Chicken livers are a healthy, inexpensive food that have a bad reputation in some quarters due to poor preparation. Badly cooked, they become dried-up little pebbles on the plate. Well executed, they are exquisite and succulent. For the best flavor and texture, cook them just until they are slightly pink in the middle.

1 lb	chicken livers	500 g
¼ cup	butter	50 mL
1	small onion, chopped	1
1	clove garlic, finely chopped	1
1 tsp	dried rosemary	5 mL
¼ cup	rice vinegar	50 mL
⅓ cup	orange juice	75 mL

1. Cut the chicken livers in half. Remove any fat or sinew.

2. On medium-high heat, melt 2 tbsp (25 mL) butter in a frying pan. Sauté the onion and garlic until softened, about 2 minutes.

3. Add the rosemary and chicken livers and sauté until browned, about 2 minutes.

4. Add the vinegar and orange juice. Scrape up any bits on the bottom of the pan and reduce until ¼ cup (50 mL) remains. Remove from the heat and stir in the remaining butter. Serve at once.

Serves 4

PIQUANT CHICKEN WINGS

Chicken wings can be snacks, appetizers or casual main courses. Kids love them because they are tangy and crunchy, and you get to eat them with your hands! Serve with one or all the dips, or with barbecue sauce.

12	chicken wings	12
½ tsp	cayenne pepper	2 mL
1 tsp	dried thyme	5 mL
1 tsp	dried basil	5 mL
2	cloves garlic, finely chopped	2
1 tsp	paprika	5 mL
½ tsp	salt	2 mL
	Oil for deep-frying	

1. Cut off the wing tips, discard or save for stock. Cut each wing into two sections.

2. In a bowl, mix together the cayenne, thyme, basil, garlic, paprika and salt. Sprinkle the spices over the wings and let sit for 1 hour at room temperature.

3. Heat the oil in a wok to 375 F (190 C), or until bread cube turns brown in 15 seconds. Deep-fry the wings for 5 to 8 minutes, or until brown and crispy.

Serves 4

Garlic Dip

Combine ¼ cup (50 mL) mayonnaise, 2 finely chopped cloves garlic, 1 tbsp (15 mL) lemon juice and 1 tbsp (15 mL) sour cream. Leave to mellow for 1 hour.

Soy Ginger Dip

Combine 2 tbsp (25 mL) cider vinegar with 1 tbsp (15 mL) grated fresh ginger and 1 tbsp (15 mL) soy sauce.

Cucumber Dip

Combine ¼ cup (50 mL) mayonnaise with ⅓ cup (75 mL) plain yogurt, ½ cup (125 mL) grated cucumber and salt and freshly ground pepper to taste.

GRILLED CHINESE CHICKEN SALAD

This chicken salad has a light oriental flavor. It makes a marvelous buffet dish as well as a good summer brunch dish.

| 2 | whole boneless chicken breasts, skin removed | 2 |

Marinade:

1 tbsp	dry white wine	15 mL
1 tsp	vegetable oil	5 mL
1 tbsp	soy sauce	15 mL
1 tsp	finely chopped fresh ginger	5 mL

Salad:

2 tbsp	red wine vinegar	25 mL
1 tbsp	granulated sugar	15 mL
2 tbsp	sesame oil	25 mL
2 tbsp	vegetable oil	25 mL
2 tbsp	soy sauce	25 mL
1 tsp	finely chopped fresh ginger	5 mL
1 tsp	Dijon mustard	5 mL
2	carrots, shredded	2
1	cucumber, shredded	1
6	leaves Chinese cabbage, shredded	6
2	green onions, finely chopped	2

When broiling chicken breasts for dinner, cook a few extra and use them in chicken salad the following day.

1. Place the chicken in a shallow dish. In a small bowl, mix the marinade ingredients together and pour over the chicken breasts. Marinate at room temperature for 30 minutes.

2. Preheat the broiler. Place the chicken breasts on a broiler rack about 3 inches (7.5 cm) from the element. Broil for 4 minutes per side, or until no longer pink. Cool and shred with your fingers or a knife.

3. To make the vinaigrette, combine the vinegar, sugar, sesame oil, vegetable oil, soy sauce, ginger and mustard in a bowl and mix well.

4. Arrange the carrots, cucumber and cabbage on a serving plate. Place the shredded chicken on top. Pour over the vinaigrette just before serving. Toss together. Garnish with the green onions.

Serves 4 to 6

INCOMPARABLE ROAST DUCK WITH PIQUANT ORANGE SAUCE

When Julia Child was asked for her favorite menu, roast duck was her choice as the main course. It would be mine, too. Nothing is as luscious as a well-roasted, crisp-skinned duck with a zesty sauce to balance the rich taste. Leave the bird to marinate overnight, uncovered, to dry out the skin. This will result in an even crisper covering.

1	5-lb (2.5 kg) duck	1
2 tbsp	soy sauce	25 mL
1 tsp	ground ginger	5 mL
1	onion, cut in half	1
1	orange, cut in half	1

Sauce:

2 tbsp	cider vinegar	25 mL
1 tbsp	brown sugar	15 mL
1 tbsp	grated orange rind	15 mL
3 cups	beef stock or chicken stock	750 mL
1 tbsp	arrowroot or cornstarch	15 mL
1 tbsp	orange juice	15 mL
1 tbsp	Cointreau or orange liqueur	15 mL
	Salt and freshly ground pepper to taste	
2 tbsp	butter, at room temperature	25 mL

1. Remove any fat pockets from the duck cavity. Cut off the wing tips. Brush the duck all over with the soy sauce. Refrigerate on a rack on a cookie sheet for 24 hours.

2. Preheat the oven to 400 F (200 C).

3. Sprinkle the ginger over the onion and orange. Stuff into the cavity. Truss the duck (see page 83). Prick the skin with a fork to allow the fat to run out. Place on a rack in a roasting pan and roast for 15 minutes per pound, plus an extra 15 minutes. Prick the skin again after 20 minutes of roasting time.

4. While the duck is roasting, prepare the sauce. In a medium pot, combine the vinegar, sugar and orange rind. Bring to a boil on high heat, reduce the heat to low, then simmer for 2 minutes. Pour in the stock, return to high heat and reduce by one-third.

5. In a cup, stir together the arrowroot and orange juice. Whisk into the sauce and bring to a boil. Add the Cointreau and season with salt and pepper.

6. When the duck is cooked, let it sit for 10 minutes, then remove the string and cut into quarters with kitchen shears or a heavy knife. Any accumulated juices (but not fat) can be stirred into the sauce. Whisk the butter into the sauce on low heat. To preserve the crisp skin, pour the sauce on a plate and top with the duck. Serve remaining sauce separately.

Serves 4

Brushing soy sauce on the skin of a duck gives it a dark, succulent look.

·12·
Meat

SAUTÉED LAMB TENDERLOIN WITH PRUNES

This was the first dish I made when I went to the Cordon Bleu and didn't know the difference between sautéing and stewing. My tenderloin slices shrank to the size of quarters because of the length of time I thought was required for cooking. These morsels cook quickly, within 5 minutes.

Use frozen lamb tenderloin, defrosted overnight in the refrigerator, if fresh lamb is not available.

8	pitted prunes, halved	8
1 cup	dry red or white wine	250 mL
1 lb	lamb tenderloin	500 g
1/4 cup	all-purpose flour	50 mL
1 tsp	dried rosemary	5 mL
1/2 tsp	salt	2 mL
1/2 tsp	freshly ground pepper	2 mL
2 tbsp	olive oil	25 mL
1 tbsp	red currant jelly	15 mL
1/4 cup	whipping cream	50 mL

1. In a small pot, on medium heat, combine the prunes and wine. Bring to a boil and simmer until the prunes are soft, about 15 minutes.

2. Slice the lamb tenderloin into slices 1/2 inch (1.25 cm) thick.

3. In a small bowl, mix together the flour, rosemary, salt and pepper. Dust the lamb slices with the seasoned flour.

4. Heat the olive oil in a frying pan on high heat. Sauté the lamb until cooked through but still slightly pink, about 5 minutes in total. Remove the lamb. Turn the heat to low. Add the prune cooking juice, red currant jelly and cream. Cook together until thickened, about 2 minutes.

5. Add the lamb and prunes and reheat until hot.

Serves 4

LAMB NAVARIN

This is my mother's unbeatable recipe for a robust lamb stew with a touch of orange in the sauce. It is the best lamb stew I have ever had.

2 tbsp	vegetable oil	25 mL
2 lb	boneless stewing lamb, cut into 1-inch (2.5 cm) cubes	1 kg
1 tsp	salt	5 mL
½ tsp	freshly ground pepper	2 mL
1	Spanish onion, finely chopped	1
2	carrots, peeled and diced	2
2	large cloves garlic, finely chopped	2
1	2-inch (5 cm) piece orange rind	1
1 tsp	dried marjoram	5 mL
pinch	granulated sugar	pinch
1 cup	dry red wine	250 mL
1 cup	beef stock	250 mL
2 tbsp	finely chopped parsley	25 mL

1. Preheat the oven to 325 F (160 C).

2. Heat the oil in a Dutch oven on high heat. Brown the lamb on all sides. Season with salt and pepper. Remove the lamb and reserve.

3. Add the onion, carrots and garlic to the Dutch oven and sauté until softened, about 1 minute.

4. Stir in the orange rind, marjoram, sugar, wine and stock. Bring to a boil. Return the lamb and cover. Bake for 1½ hours, or until the meat is tender.

5. Remove the meat. Puree the liquid and any solid ingredients in a food processor or blender. Return the meat and sauce to the Dutch oven. Reheat on top of the stove. Sprinkle with parsley.

Serves 6

TEXAS CHILI

The best meat for chili is chuck, which gives the nicest texture. Buying a chuck steak and dicing the meat yourself is ideal, but it is time-consuming, so I settle for ground chuck.

Although true chili freaks will tell you not to add kidney beans, you could add a can 30 minutes before the chili is ready to serve.

½ cup	vegetable oil	125 mL
3	onions, chopped	3
4	cloves garlic, finely chopped	4
3 lb	ground chuck	1.5 kg
2 tsp	salt	10 mL
1 tsp	freshly ground pepper	5 mL
1	28-oz (796 mL) can tomatoes, pureed	1
3 tbsp	tomato paste	45 mL
¼ cup	chili powder	50 mL
1 tbsp	dried oregano	15 mL
1 tbsp	ground cumin	15 mL
1 tsp	cayenne pepper	5 mL
2 tbsp	cider vinegar	25 mL
2 cups	beef stock	500 mL
12 oz	beer	375 mL

1. In a large pot, heat the oil on high heat. Sauté the onions and garlic until transparent, about 2 minutes. Add the ground meat and cook until the pinkness disappears. Season with salt and pepper.

2. Add the tomatoes, tomato paste and all the seasonings. Stir thoroughly.

3. Add the vinegar, stock and beer. Bring to a boil, then reduce the heat to low and simmer, uncovered, for about 1½ hours, or until thick. Stir often to prevent sticking. Let cool for a few minutes, then skim the fat off the top. Taste for seasoning, adding more salt, pepper, chili powder or cayenne as needed.

Serves 10 to 12

Serve chili with sour cream, grated cheese, chopped onion and, for those who want a spicier blast, chopped fresh chili peppers.

BEEF IN BEER

A tasty, succulent dish that uses beer instead of wine. The stronger the beer the better the dish, so I use Guinness stout if it is available. This is a great dish for hungry skiers or students with leftover beer in the fridge. Serve it with mashed potatoes or fried bread.

1 tbsp	vegetable oil	15 mL
3	slices bacon, diced	3
2 lb	stewing beef, cut into 2-inch (5 cm) cubes	1 kg
1 tsp	salt	5 mL
½ tsp	freshly ground pepper	2 mL
1	onion, chopped	1
2	carrots, chopped	2
2 tbsp	all-purpose flour	25 mL
1 tbsp	Dijon mustard	15 mL
1	12-oz (341 mL) bottle beer	1
2 cups	beef stock	500 mL
1 tbsp	brown sugar	15 mL
1 tbsp	wine vinegar	15 mL
1 tsp	dried thyme	5 mL
2	bay leaves	2
¼ cup	finely chopped parsley	50 mL

1. Preheat the oven to 325 F (160 C).

2. Heat the oil on high heat in a large frying pan or ovenproof casserole. Add the bacon and sauté until crisp. Remove the bacon with a slotted spoon. Reserve.

3. Add the meat to the pan in batches and brown on all sides. Remove with a slotted spoon. Season with salt and pepper. Reserve.

4. Turn the heat down to medium. Add the onions and carrots to the pan and sauté until softened, about 2 minutes. Sprinkle in the flour and continue to cook, stirring occasionally, until the flour is a pale gold. Mix in the mustard, beer, stock, sugar, vinegar, thyme and bay leaves. Bring to a boil, stirring. Boil for 1 minute.

5. Return the meat and bacon to the casserole. If using a frying pan, transfer the meat and sauce to an ovenproof casserole. Cover tightly and bake for 1½ to 2 hours, or until the meat is tender. Taste for seasoning, adding salt and pepper as needed. Sprinkle with the parsley before serving.

Serves 6

CAJUN FLANK STEAK

Flank steak is an inexpensive, low-fat cut that needs to be carved against the grain for maximum tenderness. The longer you marinate the meat, the stronger the flavor. Use the Cajun seasoning on pork chops or chicken when you want a spicy blast.

2 tsp	dried basil	10 mL
1 tsp	salt	5 mL
1 tbsp	freshly ground pepper	15 mL
2 tsp	cayenne pepper	10 mL
2 tsp	dried thyme	10 mL
2 tsp	paprika	10 mL
2	garlic cloves, finely chopped	2
2 tbsp	vegetable oil	25 mL
1½ lb	flank steak	750 g

1. Whisk all the ingredients except the flank steak together in a small bowl. Brush over the steak. Marinate for 1 hour.

2. Broil or barbecue for 3 to 5 minutes per side, depending on the thickness of the steak. Slice against the grain into thin slices.

Serves 6

GLAZED MEAT LOAF

With the resurgence of fifties' diners and a new interest in home cooking, the much maligned meat loaf has found a new acceptance. It's now considered a scrumptious combination of meat and gravy, which tastes best with homemade mashed potatoes. You can use any combination of ground beef, veal or pork. Serve it with a rich brown sauce or chutney. Honey mustard has a sweet/tart taste. If it is unavailable, use Dijon mustard plus a pinch of sugar.

1 tbsp	vegetable oil	15 mL
1	onion, finely chopped	1
1 lb	ground beef	500 g
8 oz	ground veal	250 g
8 oz	ground pork	250 g
1 cup	rolled oats	250 mL
2	eggs, beaten	2
2 tbsp	finely chopped parsley	25 mL
1 tsp	salt	5 mL
¼ tsp	freshly ground pepper	1 mL
½ cup	beef stock	125 mL
¼ cup	ketchup	50 mL

Glaze:

2 tbsp	honey mustard	25 mL
2 tbsp	ketchup	25 mL
2 tbsp	soy sauce	25 mL

1. Preheat the oven to 350 F (180 C).

2. In a frying pan, heat the oil on high heat. Add the onion and sauté until slightly softened, about 2 minutes.

3. In a large bowl, combine the onion with the meat and the remaining loaf ingredients.

4. Press into a 9 × 5-inch (2 L) loaf pan. Score the top of the loaf with deep gashes.

5. In a small bowl or cup, combine the mustard, ketchup and soy sauce. Fill the deep scores with the glaze.

6. Cover with foil and bake for 30 minutes. Uncover and pour off any accumulated fat and juices. Brush any remaining glaze on the loaf. Bake, uncovered, for another 45 to 60 minutes, or until the juices run clear.

Serves 6

MENU

A DINER DINNER

Our House Salad
(page 56)

Glazed Meat Loaf
(page 139)

Canadian Apple Pie
(page 180)

VEAL SHANKS WITH ST. CLEMENTS' SAUCE

Veal shanks are the leg meat and bone. The old nursery rhyme ("oranges and lemons say the bells of St. Clements") gave this stew its name. Use veal stewing meat if shanks are unavailable. The sauce is made by pureeing the cooking liquid and onions. It gives a rich, clear taste to the sauce. Serve with risotto (see page 152) or fettuccine.

The soft marrow in veal shanks is a special treat. Dig it out with marrow spoons if you have them, and savor.

	Rind and juice of 1 lemon	
	Rind and juice of 2 oranges	
2 tbsp	dried basil	25 mL
1	bay leaf	1
4	whole cloves	4
1 tbsp	dried thyme	15 mL
1 tsp	salt	5 mL
½ tsp	freshly ground pepper	2 mL
6	veal shanks, about 6 oz (180 g) each	6
¼ cup	all-purpose flour	50 mL
1 tbsp	vegetable oil	15 mL
4	onions, chopped	4
3 cups	chicken stock	750 mL
¼ cup	finely chopped parsley	50 mL

1. In a large bowl, combine the lemon and orange rind and juices, basil, bay leaf, cloves, thyme, salt and pepper. Add the veal shanks and refrigerate for 12 hours or overnight.

2. Remove the veal from the marinade. Pat dry with a paper towel. Sprinkle the veal with flour. Reserve the marinade.

3. Preheat the oven to 325 F (160 C).

4. On high heat, heat the oil in a large frying pan until very hot. Sear the veal shanks on each side until brown. Remove and place in an ovenproof casserole.

5. Add the onions to the frying pan and sauté until softened, about 3 minutes. Pour in the marinade and stock. Bring to a boil, scraping up any bits from the bottom of the pan. Pour over the veal.

6. Bake, covered, for 1½ to 2 hours, or until the shanks are tender when pierced with a fork.

7. Remove the veal from the casserole. Pour the remaining casserole contents into a food processor or blender and blend until smooth.

8. Pour the sauce back into the casserole and bring to a boil on the stove, on high heat. Boil down until slightly thickened, about 5 to 8 minutes. Taste for seasoning, adding salt and pepper as needed. Return the shanks to the casserole.

9. Stir in the parsley. Serve one veal shank per person.

Serves 6

TOAD IN THE HOLE

Sarah Lipscombe, a native of York-shire, swears by this recipe—a com-bination of sausages and Yorkshire pudding. Serve it as a main course for a light supper. To make regular York-shire pudding to serve with roast beef, omit the sausages and continue with the recipe.

Don't open the oven during the first 12 minutes of cooking, otherwise the pudding will drop.

1 cup	all-purpose flour	250 mL
pinch	salt	pinch
3	eggs, beaten	3
¾ cup	milk	175 mL
¾ cup	water	175 mL
4	pork sausages, cut in half	4
	Dripping or vegetable oil	

1. Sift the flour and salt into a large bowl. Make a well in the center. Com-bine the eggs, milk and water and pour into the well. Beat together until large bubbles rise to surface. Let stand for 1 hour, covered, in the refrigerator.

2. In a frying pan on medium heat, cook the sausages until browned, about 5 minutes. Reserve.

3. Preheat the oven to 450 F (230 C).

4. Beat the batter again. Whisk in 1 tbsp (15 mL) cold water.

5. Put ¼-inch (5 mm) fat in a 13 × 9-inch (3.5 L) baking dish. Place the dish in the oven until hot. Scatter in the sausages. Pour the batter over.

6. Bake for 5 minutes, then reduce the heat to 400 F (200 C) and bake for 30 minutes more, or until the pudding is puffed and firm.

Serves 6

PORK CHOPS WITH MUSTARD SAUCE

Mustard sauces are wonderful with pork, veal or hamburgers. This dish makes a quick dinner when served with pasta or rice and green beans.

6	pork chops	6
2 tbsp	butter	25 mL
2 tbsp	all-purpose flour	25 mL
2 tbsp	Dijon mustard	25 mL
1 cup	beef stock or chicken stock	250 mL
¼ cup	whipping cream	50 mL
	Salt and freshly ground pepper to taste	
2 tbsp	finely chopped parsley	25 mL

1. Trim the fat off the chops.

2. Preheat the oven to 350 F (180 C).

3. In a large frying pan, heat the butter on medium-high heat until sizzling. Brown the chops in two batches until colored, about 5 minutes on each side. Remove from the frying pan and place in an ovenproof casserole.

4. Turn the heat down to medium. Stir the flour into the fat in the frying pan. Cook, stirring, until lightly col-ored, about 2 minutes.

5. Whisk in the mustard and stock. Bring to a boil. Add the cream and turn the heat to low. Season with salt and pepper to taste. Pour the accumulated juices from chops into the sauce. Pour the sauce over the chops and cover with foil.

6. Bake for about 1 hour, or until tender. Sprinkle with parsley before serving.

Serves 6

Traditionally, Yorkshire pudding is served as a first course with a thin slice of onion marinated in vinegar and pepper. Gravy is poured into the well on top.

ORANGE PORK CASSEROLE

The orange-vermouth combination produces a subtle bittersweet sauce that intensifies the mild pork flavor. This stew is made with one large piece of meat, not smaller sections.

3 lb	boned loin of pork	1.5 kg
1	clove garlic, cut in half	1
	Grated rind of 1 small orange	
½ tsp	ground allspice	2 mL
1 tbsp	dried rosemary	15 mL
1 tsp	salt	5 mL
½ tsp	freshly ground pepper	2 mL
4	large oranges	4
2 tbsp	butter	25 mL
1 cup	red vermouth	250 mL
¼ cup	orange juice	50 mL
1 tbsp	cornstarch	15 mL
1 tbsp	water	15 mL

1. Preheat the oven to 325 F (160 C).

2. Unroll and flatten the pork. Rub both sides with the garlic, orange rind, allspice and rosemary. Sprinkle with the salt and pepper.

3. Roll up the roast and tie at 2-inch (5 cm) intervals with string.

4. Peel the oranges and remove the white pith and rind. Slice thinly.

5. On medium heat, melt the butter in an ovenproof casserole just slightly larger than the pork. Slowly brown the pork on all sides. Remove to a platter.

6. Add the vermouth and orange juice to the casserole and scrape up any bits from the bottom.

7. Return the pork to the casserole. Cover the top with the orange slices and bake, covered, for 2 hours.

8. Remove the roast, reserving the orange slices.

9. Skim the fat from the roasting liquid and strain the liquid into a pot.

10. In a cup, dissolve the cornstarch in the water. Add to the strained liquid. Simmer, stirring, until thickened, about 1 minute.

11. Slice the pork into thin slices. Coat with the sauce and garnish with the orange slices.

Serves 6

·13·
Salads

ESTELLE'S STRAWBERRY SALAD

My friend Estelle Steinhauer served this popular and pretty salad at her daughter's wedding. The dressing will keep for up to two weeks in the refrigerator. Other fruits in season can be used; try blueberries, melon or mango.

1	head Romaine lettuce	1
½	English cucumber, diced	½
4 cups	strawberries, hulled and halved	1 L
⅓ cup	white vinegar	75 mL
¾ cup	granulated sugar	175 mL
1 tsp	salt	5 mL
1 tsp	dry mustard	5 mL
1 tsp	paprika	5 mL
2 tsp	celery seed	10 mL
⅔ cup	vegetable oil	150 mL

1. Tear the lettuce into bite-sized pieces. Place in a large salad bowl.

2. Lightly salt the diced cucumber; leave to drain in a colander for 30 minutes so the juices will drip out. Dry with paper towels.

3. Toss the cucumber with the strawberries and the lettuce.

4. In a small pot, bring the vinegar, sugar, salt, mustard, paprika and celery seed to a boil on high heat. Boil for 1 minute. Remove from the heat.

5. Place in a food processor or blender. With the machine running, slowly pour the oil down the feed tube. Process until well combined. Chill. Pour over the salad just before serving.

Serves 10

CLASSIC CAESAR SALAD

The classic Caesar salad was actually invented in Tijuana, Mexico, not the United States, as many people claim. Don't be tempted to leave the anchovies out of this scrumptious dressing; they provide the necessary salt and only a slight background taste.

1	egg yolk	1
1	clove garlic, finely chopped	1
2	anchovy fillets, chopped	2
½ tsp	Worcestershire sauce	2 mL
¼ cup	lemon juice	50 mL
¾ cup	olive oil	175 mL
⅓ cup	grated Parmesan cheese	75 mL
	Freshly ground pepper to taste	
1	head Romaine lettuce	1
1 cup	croutons (see page 56)	250 mL

1. In a large bowl, whisk together the egg yolk, garlic, anchovy fillets and Worcestershire sauce. Beat in the lemon juice.

2. Whisking constantly, slowly add the olive oil. The mixture will thicken. Stir in half the Parmesan cheese. Season with pepper.

3. Wash and dry the Romaine. Tear into bite-sized pieces. Toss with the dressing. Add the croutons and remaining Parmesan. Toss again.

Serves 4 to 6

TOMATO AND MOZZARELLA SALAD

Because tomatoes are quite acidic, you don't usually need vinegar in tomato salads. In this recipe, however, vinegar is added because of the cheese. Cutting the cheese in rounds makes an attractive presentation.

1	head Boston lettuce	1
8	slices mozzarella cheese	8
3	large beefsteak tomatoes	3
1	red onion, chopped	1
1 tbsp	white wine vinegar	15 mL
¼ cup	chopped fresh basil	50 mL
	Salt and freshly ground pepper to taste	
⅓ cup	olive oil	75 mL

1. Arrange the Boston lettuce on a serving platter.

2. With a round cookie cutter, cut the mozzarella into circles. Slice the tomatoes thinly. Overlap the tomato and mozzarella slices on the lettuce.

3. Sprinkle the red onion over the salad.

4. In a small bowl, whisk together the vinegar, basil, salt and pepper. Slowly whisk in the oil. Pour over the salad and serve at once.

Serves 4

MARINATED MUSHROOMS

These mushrooms have been a family favorite for years. My mother used them in her cooking school, and I use them in mine. Serve them as a first course on a bed of lettuce, or as an hors d'oeuvre to eat with your fingers. These keep for up to three weeks in the refrigerator.

1 lb	mushrooms	500 g
2 cups	water	500 mL
1 tsp	salt	5 mL
	Juice of 1 lemon	
¼ cup	butter	50 mL
¼ cup	olive oil	50 mL
¼	Spanish onion, finely sliced	¼
2	pimientos, sliced	2
4	tomatoes, fresh or canned, skinned and chopped	4
2	cloves garlic, finely chopped	2
¼ cup	finely chopped parsley	50 mL
1	bay leaf	1
¾ cup	dry white wine	175 mL
3 tbsp	wine vinegar	45 mL

1. If the mushrooms are large, halve or quarter them.

2. In a pot, bring the water, salt and lemon juice to a boil on high heat. Add the mushrooms and butter. Return to a rapid boil and boil for 4 minutes. Drain. Place the mushrooms in a shallow dish.

3. To make the marinade, heat the oil in a frying pan on medium heat and sauté the onions until translucent, about 5 minutes.

4. Add the pimiento, tomatoes, garlic, parsley and bay leaf. Cover and cook for 5 minutes. Pour in the wine and vinegar, bring to a boil and simmer gently, uncovered, for 10 minutes.

5. Remove the bay leaf. Pour the marinade over the mushrooms and leave for 24 hours in the refrigerator before serving.

Serves 8

TOMATO AND ONION SALAD

The time to make this salad is during the short summer season, when the juicy, fragrant, intensely flavored beefsteak tomatoes are available. True tomato lovers will struggle to have this salad at other times of the year, but unless you can find the high-quality Israeli tomatoes, it will never taste the same. Use extra-virgin olive oil if possible, because its fruity flavor enhances the tomatoes.

3	large beefsteak tomatoes, thinly sliced	3
1	red onion, thinly sliced	1
¼ cup	extra-virgin olive oil	50 mL
2 tbsp	chopped fresh basil	25 mL
	Salt and freshly ground pepper to taste	

1. Lay the tomatoes on a platter. Top with the onions. Drizzle on the olive oil. Sprinkle with the basil. Season with salt and pepper and serve immediately.

Serves 6

MIMOSA POTATO SALAD

Potato salad can be served with a main course, or as part of a buffet. If this salad is served on a dinner plate, place it on a bed of spinach leaves for color. Mimosa refers to the grated egg yolk scattered over the salad.

2 lb	small new potatoes, unpeeled	1 kg
1 tbsp	white vinegar	15 mL
1/4 tsp	salt	1 mL
1/4 tsp	freshly ground pepper	1 mL
2 tbsp	olive oil	25 mL
1	apple, peeled and sliced	1
2 tbsp	wine vinegar	25 mL
1 tsp	granulated sugar	5 mL
1/4	Spanish onion, sliced	1/4
2 tbsp	finely chopped parsley	25 mL
2	stalks celery, finely chopped	2
1/2 cup	mayonnaise (see page 55)	125 mL
2	hard-boiled egg yolks, grated	2

1. Place the potatoes in a pot of cold salted water with the white vinegar. Bring to a boil on high heat and cook until tender, about 10 minutes. Drain and dry.

2. Peel the potatoes while still warm. Cut in slices and place in a large bowl. Season with salt and pepper. Pour over the olive oil. Toss and leave to cool.

3. In a small bowl, combine the apple slices, wine vinegar and sugar.

4. When the potatoes are cold, add the onion, parsley, celery, apple mixture and mayonnaise. Combine carefully. Taste for seasoning, adding more salt and pepper as needed. Sprinkle with the grated egg yolks.

Serves 6

The secret to a good potato salad is to dress the potatoes while they are still hot, so that the vinaigrette seeps into the flesh.

COLE SLAW

There are Southern cole slaws made with mayonnaise, and sweeter cole slaws made with vinegar. This is a true Southern version. The red and green cabbage make an outstanding color combination, but all green cabbage can be used instead. Cole slaw can be made ahead of time and will keep in the refrigerator for up to three days.

3 cups	shredded red cabbage	750 mL
3 cups	shredded green cabbage	750 mL
6	green onions, chopped	6
1/2 cup	sour cream	125 mL
1/4 cup	mayonnaise	50 mL
2 tbsp	plain yogurt	25 mL
2 tbsp	lemon juice	25 mL
1 tsp	paprika	5 mL
	Salt and freshly ground pepper to taste	

1. Toss the red cabbage, green cabbage and green onions in a large bowl.

2. In a small bowl, whisk together the sour cream, mayonnaise, yogurt, lemon juice, paprika, salt and pepper. Pour over the cabbage and toss together.

Serves 6

ASPARAGUS SALAD

Asparagus makes an attractive salad during the spring. Remember to pour on the vinaigrette while the asparagus is still warm; the asparagus will absorb the flavors better. If the stalks are thick, peel them, otherwise the vegetable will not cook evenly. If they are thin, leave them, but either way, break or cut off ½ inch (1.25 cm) of the bottom woody stem.

2 lb	asparagus	1 kg
2 tbsp	white wine vinegar	25 mL
1 tsp	Dijon mustard	5 mL
1 tbsp	whipping cream	15 mL
⅓ cup	olive oil	75 mL
	Salt and freshly ground pepper to taste	
2	green onions, chopped	2

1. Bring a narrow pot of water to boil. Stand the asparagus stalks in the pot so the heads are above the water line. Boil for 3 minutes, or until crisp-tender. Drain and refresh under cold water.

2. In a small bowl, whisk together the vinegar, mustard and whipping cream. Slowly whisk in the olive oil. Season well with salt and pepper.

3. Pour the dressing over the asparagus while still warm, then chill for 1 hour, turning occasionally.

4. Sprinkle the green onions over the asparagus before serving.

Serves 6

SPINACH SALAD

Spinach makes an interesting change from regular lettuce salads. Make sure it is well washed, because grit tends to cling to the leaves. Remove the stalks for a better appearance. This classic spinach salad features a spicy dressing. Add beansprouts, cheese or sliced mushrooms, if desired.

½ cup	mayonnaise (see page 55)	125 mL
1 tbsp	white wine vinegar	15 mL
1	anchovy, chopped	1
1	clove garlic, finely chopped	1
1 tsp	Worcestershire sauce	5 tsp
2 tbsp	water	25 mL
1	10-oz (300 g) package spinach	1
4	green onions, chopped	4
4	slices bacon, diced and cooked	4
1 cup	croutons (see page 56)	250 mL
¼ cup	toasted pine nuts	50 mL
2	hard-boiled eggs, sliced, optional	2

1. In a bowl, whisk together the mayonnaise, vinegar, anchovy, garlic and Worcestershire sauce. Thin with water to a coating consistency.

2. Remove the stems from the spinach and rinse the spinach leaves in warm water. Dry well. Tear into small pieces and place in a salad bowl. Sprinkle with green onions, bacon, croutons, pine nuts and egg.

3. Just before serving, toss with the dressing.

Serves 4

Asparagus used to be considered a cure for heart trouble, toothaches and bee stings! White asparagus is asparagus that has never seen the light; it spends its life buried under the earth.

TRI-COLOR PASTA SALAD

Pasta salad dressings should be strong to balance the bland taste of the pasta. Fusilli, the twisted spiral pasta, is good for pasta salads because it is easy to handle with a fork and it holds the dressing well.

1 lb	fusilli	500 g
2 tbsp	olive oil	25 mL
1	egg	1
2 tbsp	white wine vinegar	25 mL
2 tbsp	lemon juice	25 mL
½ cup	olive oil	125 mL
6	green onions, white part only, finely chopped	6
1 tbsp	chopped fresh basil, or 1 tsp (5 mL) dried	15 mL
	Salt and freshly ground pepper to taste	
1	red onion, diced	1
1	red pepper, diced	1
1	green pepper, diced	1
8 oz	baby shrimp, cooked, optional	250 g

Pasta salads should have the vinaigrette poured over them while the pasta is still warm, so it will absorb the flavor of the dressing.

1. Bring a large pot of salted water to a boil on high heat. Add the fusilli, return to a boil, and cook until the pasta is *al dente*, about 10 minutes. Drain.

2. In a large bowl, toss the pasta with 2 tbsp (25 mL) olive oil.

3. In a small bowl, whisk together the egg, wine vinegar and lemon juice. Slowly whisk in ½ cup (125 mL) olive oil. Stir in the green onions, basil, and salt and pepper to taste. Pour over the pasta while still warm and let marinate for at least 2 hours.

4. Combine with the remaining salad ingredients before serving.

Serves 8

PEAR GINGER WALDORF SALAD

Update the classic Waldorf salad—a combination of apples, walnuts, celery and raisins—by using firm ripe pears, stem ginger and pecans. Serve this salad at a brunch or on a buffet table, or serve it as an interesting first course before lamb or pork.

2 cups	chopped pears	500 mL
1 cup	chopped celery	250 mL
½ cup	chopped pecans	125 mL
½ cup	raisins	125 mL
½ cup	mayonnaise (see page 55)	125 mL
3 tbsp	lemon juice	45 mL
¼ cup	finely chopped stem ginger	50 mL
	Salt and freshly ground pepper to taste	

1. In a salad bowl, combine the pears, celery, pecans and raisins.

2. In a small bowl, combine the mayonnaise, lemon juice and ginger. Season with salt and pepper to taste. Pour over the salad, toss well and serve.

Serves 4 to 6

SALADE NIÇOISE

The classic salad from the south of France is a visually attractive feast. Serve it as a first course or with good French bread as a main course at lunch.

8 oz	green beans, topped and tailed	250 g
16	small new potatoes, unpeeled	16
4	hard-boiled eggs, sliced	4
1	7-oz (184 g) can flaked white tuna, drained	1
3	tomatoes, cut in wedges	3
½ tsp	Dijon mustard	2 mL
1	clove garlic, finely chopped	1
2 tbsp	red wine vinegar	25 mL
½ cup	olive oil	125 mL
1 tbsp	finely chopped parsley	15 mL
1 tbsp	finely chopped chives	15 mL
	Salt and freshly ground pepper to taste	
8	anchovy fillets, optional	8
16	black olives	16

1. To a large pot of boiling salted water, add the green beans and boil until crisp-tender, about 2 to 3 minutes. Refresh with cold water until cold. Drain and dry.

2. In a large pot of salted water, bring the potatoes to a boil. Cook until just tender, about 8 minutes.

3. On a plate, heap the green beans, potatoes, eggs, tuna and tomatoes in separate piles.

4. In a small bowl, whisk together the mustard, garlic and vinegar. Whisk in oil gradually, then add the parsley and chives. Season with salt and pepper and pour over ingredients. Top with anchovy fillets and olives.

Serves 8

BASQUE BEEF SALAD

A great way to use leftover roast beef or barbecued flank steak. Serve it as a main course with garlic bread.

2 tsp	Dijon mustard	10 mL
2 tbsp	tarragon vinegar	25 mL
½ cup	olive oil	125 mL
1 tsp	capers, chopped	5 mL
3 tbsp	finely chopped parsley	45 mL
8 oz	roast beef, thinly sliced	250 g
2	dill pickles, chopped	2
1	Spanish onion, chopped	1
2	tomatoes, chopped	2

1. In a small bowl, whisk together the mustard and vinegar. Slowly whisk in the olive oil until the mixture thickens. Stir in the capers and parsley.

2. On a flat dish, layer half the meat, pickles, onion and tomatoes. Pour over half the vinaigrette. Repeat the layers and pour over the remaining vinaigrette.

Serves 4 to 6

Salad niçoise can be served on a platter with the ingredients in individual mounds, or the ingredients can be layered in a salad bowl; traditionally, this salad is never tossed.

PEANUT CHILI NOODLES

The peanut flavor mingled with the soy sauce and chili becomes an exotic salad dressing for this Chinese-inspired salad. Omit the chicken breast and ham, use water instead of stock, and it becomes a vegetarian delight. Use other vegetables as well as those suggested.

Serve this as a main course with Soy Sauce Chicken (see page 130) or Piquant Chicken Wings (see page 133).

Sauce:

¼ cup	peanut butter	50 mL
2 tsp	Chinese chili paste	10 mL
1 tbsp	sesame oil	15 mL
1 tbsp	granulated sugar	15 mL
2 tbsp	soy sauce	25 mL
1 cup	chicken stock	250 mL
2	cloves garlic, finely chopped	2
1	green onion, finely chopped	1

Salad:

1 lb	thin fresh egg noodles	500 g
1 tbsp	vegetable oil	15 mL
1 tbsp	sesame oil	15 mL
1	whole boned chicken breast, cooked and shredded	1
2 oz	ham, cut in thin strips	60 g
8 oz	beansprouts	250 g
½	cucumber, shredded	½
2	zucchini, shredded, or 2 carrots, shredded	2
3	green onions, finely chopped	3
2 tbsp	chopped fresh coriander	25 mL

Coriander, otherwise known as Chinese parsley or cilantro, is a fresh green herb with a fragrant flavor that permeates dishes from Southeast Asia and the Orient. If fresh coriander is unavailable, ground coriander seeds are not an acceptable substitute; use fresh parsley or watercress instead.

1. In a small bowl, mix the sauce ingredients together. Reserve.

2. Bring a large pot of salted water to a boil. Add the noodles, return to a boil and cook until tender, about 1 minute. Drain and toss with 1 tbsp (15 mL) vegetable oil and 1 tbsp (15 mL) sesame oil. Pile onto a serving dish. Coat with half the sauce and chill.

3. Place the chicken on top of the noodles, garnish with the ham and vegetables and sprinkle with the coriander. Pour some of the remaining sauce over the salad just before serving. Serve the rest separately.

Serves 6

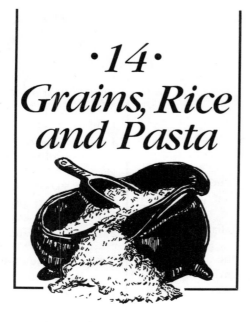

·14·
Grains, Rice and Pasta

OVEN-COOKED RICE

Because the dish holds its heat, the rice will stay hot, but not continue cooking, if it is left on the counter, covered, for 30 minutes.

2 cups	uncooked long-grain rice	500 mL
2½ cups	cold water	625 mL
2 tbsp	butter	25 mL
½ tsp	salt	2 mL

1. Preheat the oven to 350 F (180 C).

2. Combine the rice, water, butter and salt in an 8-cup (2 L) ovenproof dish. Cover with foil.

3. Bake until the rice is tender, about 1 hour.

Makes 6 cups (1.5 L)

CORIANDER LIME RICE

Use a large quantity of water to cook the rice. This method removes the surface starch while the rice is cooking, so the rice is not sticky.

2 cups	uncooked long-grain rice	500 mL
1 tsp	salt	5 mL
¼ cup	butter	50 mL
2 tsp	ground coriander	10 mL
	Grated rind of 1 lime	

1. Bring a large pot of water to a boil on high heat. Add the salt and toss in the rice. Return to a boil and cook, uncovered, for 12 minutes. Drain, then rinse with hot water.

2. Melt the butter on low heat in the same pot. Add the coriander and lime rind. Stir together. Return the drained rice to the pot and toss with the butter mixture. Cover and steam for 5 minutes.

Serves 6

RISOTTO

The stock must be hot when added, or the rice will not absorb it properly. Add the stock slowly and stir the rice frequently to achieve the proper texture. Although this dish may seem fiddly, the end result is so good that it's worth the trouble.

2 tbsp	butter	25 mL
1	onion, finely chopped	1
1	clove garlic, finely chopped	1
1½ cups	short-grain Italian rice	375 mL
¾ cup	dry white wine	175 mL
5 cups	hot chicken stock	1.25 L
½ cup	grated Parmesan cheese	125 mL
	Salt and freshly ground pepper to taste	

Risotto is an Italian rice dish much favored by gourmets who love its creamy and slightly chewy texture. The best rice for risotto is the short-grain Italian rice, Arborio.

1. Heat 1 tbsp (15 mL) butter in a pot over medium-low heat. Sauté the onion and garlic until soft and golden, about 10 minutes. Add the rice and stir until translucent, then add the wine and cook, stirring, until the wine has almost evaporated.

2. Pour in the stock about 1 cup (250 mL) at a time, adding more as the rice absorbs each batch. Cook over low heat, uncovered, stirring from time to time.

3. Stir frequently during the last 10 minutes of cooking to keep the rice from sticking. (The total cooking time will be approximately 30 minutes.) The rice is done when it is creamy but firm, with the liquid absorbed. Stir in the remaining butter, cheese, salt and pepper. Serve immediately.

Serves 4 to 6

BARLEY CASSEROLE

This casserole makes a palate-pleasing and filling main course. Serve it with a salad. During the summer, use six fresh peeled and seeded tomatoes instead of canned.

3 cups	water	750 mL
1 cup	pearl barley, rinsed	250 mL
1	28-oz (796 mL) can tomatoes, drained and chopped	1
5	green onions, chopped	5
½ cup	black olives, pitted and chopped	125 mL
2	large zucchini, coarsely chopped	2
2 tbsp	finely chopped fresh dill, or 2 tsp (10 mL) dried	25 mL
1	fresh red chili pepper, seeded and chopped	1
½ cup	sour cream	125 mL
	Salt and freshly ground pepper to taste	
1 cup	grated Cheddar cheese	250 mL

1. In a heavy pot, bring the water to a boil on high heat. Sprinkle in the barley. Cover and turn the heat to low. Cook for 35 to 45 minutes, or until the barley is tender. Drain off any excess water.

2. Preheat the oven to 375 F (190 C).

3. In a bowl, combine half the tomatoes with the green onions, olives, zucchini, dill, chili and sour cream. Stir into the barley. Season well with salt and pepper.

4. Spoon the mixture into a greased 6-cup (1.5 L) casserole. Spread the reserved tomatoes on top. Sprinkle with the cheese.

5. Bake for 30 minutes, or until the casserole is bubbling and the cheese is browned.

Serves 4

KASHA AND MUSHROOMS

My Russian grandmother used to make toasted buckwheat or kasha as a side dish for chicken or meat. Sometimes she would serve it as a vegetarian main course and top it with lots of sour cream or cottage cheese.

¼ cup	vegetable oil	50 mL
1	onion, finely chopped	1
8 oz	mushrooms, sliced	250 g
1 ½ cups	kasha	375 mL
1	egg, beaten	1
3 cups	chicken stock	750 mL
½ tsp	dried thyme	2 mL
½ tsp	dried marjoram	2 mL
2 tbsp	finely chopped parsley	25 mL
	Salt and freshly ground pepper to taste	

1. Heat the oil in a pot on high heat. Sauté the onion until softened, about 2 minutes. Add the mushrooms and sauté until coated with the oil.

2. Add the kasha and egg; stir together until the kasha is dry, about 1 minute.

3. Pour in the stock. Stir in the thyme and marjoram. Bring to a boil.

4. Reduce the heat to low. Cover and cook for 15 to 20 minutes, or until the kasha is tender.

5. Stir in the parsley. Season with salt and pepper.

Serves 6

FETTUCCINE WITH PESTO

Pesto, which is made with fresh basil, captures the essence of summer. It should be served with fresh pasta, which will better absorb the flavors. Adding butter softens the sauce slightly. If you omit the butter, use an additional 2 tbsp (25 mL) olive oil.

2	cloves garlic, peeled	2
2 cups	fresh basil leaves, packed	500 mL
2 tbsp	pine nuts	25 mL
½ cup	olive oil	125 mL
½ cup	grated Parmesan cheese	125 mL
2 tbsp	butter	25 mL
	Salt and freshly ground pepper to taste	
1 lb	fresh fettuccine	500 g

1. Place the garlic, basil, pine nuts and olive oil in a food processor or blender. Process until smooth.

2. Remove from the food processor and beat in the cheese by hand. When incorporated, beat in the butter. Add salt and pepper.

3. Bring a large pot of salted water to a boil on high heat. Add the fettuccine, return to a boil and boil until *al dente*, about 2 minutes.

4. Add a large spoonful of the pasta cooking water to the pesto. Drain the pasta and serve topped with the pesto.

Serves 6

Pesto is a strong basil- and garlic-flavored paste. If you are making pesto to freeze, omit the cheese and butter. Beat them in after the sauce is defrosted; it will give a fresh flavor to the pesto.

VEGETABLE LASAGNA

A colorful and appetizing lasagna, great for hungry teenagers or ski chalet dinners. Serve it with a salad and garlic bread.

1	1-lb (500 g) package lasagna noodles	1
¼ cup	butter	50 mL
¼ cup	all-purpose flour	50 mL
2 cups	milk	500 mL
½ cup	grated Parmesan cheese	125 mL
½ tsp	nutmeg	2 mL
	Salt and freshly ground pepper to taste	

Filling:

2	10-oz (300 g) packages spinach	2
¼ cup	olive oil	50 mL
2	cloves garlic, finely chopped	2
1	onion, finely chopped	1
1 lb	mushrooms, sliced	500 g
¼ tsp	salt	1 mL
¼ tsp	freshly ground pepper	1 mL

To finish:

1	recipe Italian Tomato Sauce (see page 49)	1
1 cup	grated mozzarella cheese	250 mL
½ cup	grated Parmesan cheese	125 mL

If fresh lasagna or the new instant dried noodles are used, they do not need precooking.

1. Cook the lasagna noodles in a large pot of boiling salted water until *al dente*, about 10 to 12 minutes. Drain and place separately on waxed paper to prevent sticking.

2. Melt the butter in a pot on medium-high heat. Stir in the flour and cook for 1 minute. Turn the heat to low and gradually add the milk, whisking constantly.

3. When the milk is incorporated, stir in ½ cup (125 mL) Parmesan cheese, nutmeg, salt and pepper. Bring the sauce to a boil, stirring. Remove from the heat and reserve.

4. Remove the stems from the spinach. Wash well with warm water. Place the spinach in a large pot with the water that clings to the leaves. Cover and cook on medium heat until wilted, about 5 minutes. Drain and refresh with cold water, squeeze dry and cool. Chop coarsely and reserve.

5. Heat the oil in a large frying pan on high heat. Sauté the garlic and onion until softened, about 2 minutes.

6. Add the mushrooms and sauté until the mushrooms begin to exude water, about 2 minutes. Add the spinach and combine well. Season with salt and pepper. Blend into the white sauce. Reserve.

7. Preheat the oven to 350 F (180 C). In a 13 × 9-inch (3.5 L) pan, spread one-third of the tomato sauce. Cover with a layer of noodles and half the vegetable sauce. Repeat the layers, finishing with the tomato sauce. Sprinkle the mozzarella and Parmesan on top.

8. Bake for 45 minutes, or until the sauce is bubbling.

Serves 8 to 10

PENNE WITH PANCETTA

Plum tomatoes are preferable in this dish because they have a true Italian tomato taste. If penne is unavailable, use any short pasta.

4 oz	pancetta or bacon	125 g
2 tbsp	olive oil	25 mL
1	clove garlic, finely chopped	1
¼ cup	chopped onion	50 mL
2 cups	drained canned tomatoes	500 mL
2 tbsp	tomato paste	25 mL
2 tsp	hot pepper flakes	10 mL
½ tsp	dried sage	2 mL
	Salt and freshly ground pepper to taste	
1 lb	penne	500 g
¼ cup	grated Parmesan cheese	50 mL

1. Chop the pancetta coarsely.

2. Heat the olive oil in a frying pan on medium heat. Add the pancetta and sauté until golden, about 5 minutes. Remove from the pan and reserve.

3. Add the garlic and onion to the frying pan and sauté until the onion begins to color, about 5 minutes. Stir in the tomatoes, tomato paste, hot pepper flakes, sage, salt and pepper. Turn the heat down to low and cook gently, uncovered, for about 20 minutes, or until the sauce is thick. Stir in the pancetta.

4. Meanwhile, bring a large pot of salted water to a boil on high heat. Add the pasta, return to a boil and cook until *al dente*, about 10 minutes. Drain.

5. Return the pasta to the stove and turn the heat to low. Add the sauce, stir together and cook for 2 minutes. Serve the cheese separately.

Serves 6

SPAGHETTINI WITH TOMATO VINAIGRETTE

This unusual first course should be made in the summer with fresh tomatoes. For the best results, use a thin dried pasta such as spaghettini or angel hair, and serve the hot pasta with the cold sauce. (Angel hair takes less time to cook than spaghettini.)

8	tomatoes, peeled and seeded	8
⅔ cup	olive oil	150 mL
¼ cup	chopped fresh basil	50 mL
1 tsp	red wine vinegar	5 mL
	Salt and freshly ground pepper to taste	
1 lb	spaghettini	500 g
½ cup	grated Parmesan cheese	125 mL

1. Cut the tomatoes into chunks. In a large bowl, toss them with the oil, basil, vinegar, salt and pepper. Marinate at room temperature for 2 hours.

2. Bring a large pot of salted water to a boil on high heat. Add the spaghettini, return to a boil and boil for 10 minutes, or until the pasta is *al dente*. Drain.

3. Toss the sauce and the pasta together. Serve sprinkled with Parmesan.

Serves 6

To peel fresh tomatoes, drop them into boiling water for 30 seconds, then remove them and slip off the skins. I like to peel tomatoes before cooking them in a recipe; if they are not peeled, the skins float around in the dish looking nasty. After peeling, cut the tomato in half and squeeze out the seeds, which are occasionally bitter.

Pancetta is rolled, cured Italian bacon. If you can't find it, substitute bacon.

·15·
Vegetables

GRATED ZUCCHINI WITH BASIL

This is an easy stir-fried vegetable dish that is excellent with hamburgers or grilled chicken breasts.

3	zucchini	3
2 tbsp	olive oil	25 mL
1 tsp	dried basil	5 mL
	Salt and freshly ground pepper to taste	

1. Grate the zucchini in a food processor or by hand.

2. On high heat in a frying pan or wok, heat the olive oil. Add the zucchini and stir-fry until softened and beginning to brown, about 4 or 5 minutes.

3. Sprinkle on the basil, salt and pepper.

Serves 6

GREEN BEANS WITH GARLIC

Crisp-tender green beans complement any rich dish. If you wish, you can boil the beans ahead of time and run cold water over until they are cold. Reheat them in the butter/garlic mixture.

1 lb	green beans, topped and tailed	500 g
2 tbsp	butter	25 mL
1	clove garlic, finely chopped	1
	Salt and freshly ground pepper to taste	

1. Bring a large pot of salted water to a boil on high heat. Add the green beans and boil, uncovered, for 3 to 4 minutes, or until crisp-tender. Drain.

2. Heat the butter and garlic in a pot on medium heat. Toss in the beans. Turn to coat. Season with salt and pepper. Serve immediately.

Serves 6

POTATO AND MUSHROOM SOUFFLÉ

Try serving this soufflé with roast chicken or pork. It can be prepared ahead of time and left, covered, at room temperature until baking time. The original recipe comes from my mother's cooking school. Instead of mushrooms, you can also sauté three sliced leeks with the onions.

6	baking potatoes	6
	Salt and freshly ground pepper to taste	
⅓ cup	butter	75 mL
2	eggs, beaten	2
¼ cup	stock, milk or cream	50 mL
1	large onion, chopped	1
12 oz	mushrooms, sliced	375 g
¼ tsp	salt	1 mL
¼ tsp	freshly ground pepper	1 mL
1 tbsp	finely chopped parsley	15 mL

1. Peel the potatoes and cut them in half. In a large pot, cover the potatoes with cold salted water. Bring to a boil on high heat and boil until tender but firm, about 15 minutes. Drain and dry thoroughly by shaking over the heat until the moisture disappears.

2. Mash the potatoes with a potato masher or electric mixer. Add salt and pepper to taste, 2 tbsp (25 mL) butter, eggs and stock. Beat until fluffy.

3. Preheat the oven to 400 F (200 C).

4. In a frying pan, heat the remaining butter on medium heat. Sauté the onions for about 5 minutes, or until translucent.

5. Add the mushrooms, salt and pepper and sauté for another 3 minutes, or until the mushrooms are softened. Reserve.

6. Butter a 6-cup (1.5 L) soufflé dish. Line the bottom and sides with 1 inch (2.5 cm) of the potato mixture. Fill the center with the mushrooms, draining off any liquid, and cover with the remaining potato mixture. Bake for 15 to 20 minutes, or until golden brown. Garnish with parsley.

Serves 6

BROCCOLI WITH PINE NUTS

Look for broccoli that is a bright-green color with tightly closed florets.

1	bunch broccoli	1
2 tbsp	butter	25 mL
2 tbsp	pine nuts	25 mL
	Freshly ground black pepper to taste	

1. Separate broccoli into florets and peel the tough stalks.

2. Bring a large pot of salted water to a boil on high heat. Add the broccoli and boil until crisp-tender but still brightly colored, about 5 minutes. Drain and refresh under cold water.

3. On high heat, heat the butter in a frying pan until sizzling. Add the pine nuts and cook, stirring, until brown, about 2 minutes. Toss the broccoli with the pine nuts and season with pepper.

Serves 4

There are different kinds of potatoes. Baking potatoes are oval in shape and have a floury texture. Round potatoes have a waxy, firm texture. Use baking potatoes for mashing and baking; use round potatoes for boiling, potato salads and potato gratins.

STEAMED ZUCCHINI WITH YOGURT

A quick and easy zucchini dish. Because zucchini is watery, the juices mix with the yogurt to make a tangy sauce. Serve it with plain broiled dishes or simple sautés.

3	zucchini	3
2 tbsp	butter	25 mL
1 tbsp	finely chopped fresh dill	15 mL
1	clove garlic, finely chopped	1
1/2 cup	plain yogurt	125 mL
	Salt and freshly ground pepper to taste	

Fennel is a licorice-flavored vegetable; its taste mellows in cooking.

1. Thinly slice the zucchini in 1/8-inch (3 mm) rounds. Place in a steamer basket and steam over medium heat for 5 minutes, or until the slices are tender-crisp. Place in a serving dish.

2. On low heat, melt the butter in a small frying pan. Stir in the dill and garlic and cook for 1 minute. Stir in the yogurt and heat. Season with salt and pepper. Pour over the zucchini and serve at once.

Serves 4

BRAISED FENNEL

Serve this with chicken or veal roasts, veal scallopini or fish dishes. Use freshly grated Italian Parmesan instead of the sawdust-like pregrated domestic Parmesan.

2	large fennel bulbs, trimmed of all tough outer leaves and washed	2
1/3 cup	butter	75 mL
1/2 cup	chicken stock	125 mL
1/4 tsp	salt	1 mL
pinch	freshly ground pepper	pinch
1/4 tsp	ground ginger	1 mL
1/2 cup	grated Parmesan cheese	125 mL

1. Preheat the oven to 400 F (200 C). Cut each fennel bulb through the root into six wedges.

2. In a small pot, melt the butter on medium heat. Add the stock, salt, pepper and ginger.

3. Arrange the fennel wedges in an ovenproof dish. Pour over the stock mixture and sprinkle with Parmesan.

4. Bake, covered, for 1 hour, or until tender. Uncover and bake for a further 10 minutes to brown the top slightly.

Serves 6

CAULIFLOWER WITH CHEESE SAUCE

This cheese sauce goes well with cauliflower, broccoli and Brussels sprouts. It can be served with any broiled fish or meat, or can be eaten as a vegetarian main course with a grain dish to accompany it. The stronger the cheese, the stronger the taste. Mustard intensifies the cheesy flavor.

1	large cauliflower	1

Cheese Sauce:

2 tbsp	butter	25 mL
2 tbsp	all-purpose flour	25 mL
1 ¼ cups	milk	300 mL
pinch	nutmeg	pinch
1 tsp	Dijon mustard	5 mL
1 cup	grated Cheddar cheese	250 mL
	Salt and freshly ground pepper to taste	

1. Cut the cauliflower into even-sized florets.

2. In a pot, melt the butter on medium heat. Remove from the heat and stir in the flour. Return to the heat and cook, stirring, for 1 minute.

3. Add the milk and whisk until boiling. Turn the heat to low and add the nutmeg and mustard. Beat in the cheese. Season with salt and pepper to taste. Reserve.

4. Preheat the oven to 350 F (180 C). Bring a large pot of salted water to a boil. Drop the cauliflower into the boiling water. Boil for 3 to 5 minutes, or until the florets are crisp-tender. Drain well. Refresh with cold water until the cauliflower is cold. Drain well again.

5. In a buttered 11 × 7-inch (2 L) ovenproof gratin dish, place the cauliflower in a single layer. Coat with the cheese sauce. Bake at 350 F (180 C) for 10 minutes, or until the sauce bubbles and browns on top.

Serves 4 to 6

STIR-FRIED RED CABBAGE

The balsamic vinegar combined with the sweet red currant jelly creates a rich glaze that coats the cabbage. This side dish is especially good with roast pork, duck or sausages.

½	red cabbage	½
1	tart apple	1
2 tbsp	olive oil	25 mL
2 tbsp	balsamic vinegar	25 mL
1 tbsp	red currant jelly	15 mL
	Salt and freshly ground pepper to taste	

1. Thinly slice the red cabbage. Peel the apple and cut it into slivers.

2. Heat the oil in large frying pan on high heat. Add the cabbage and apples and stir-fry until the cabbage is limp, about 5 minutes.

3. Stir in the balsamic vinegar and red currant jelly. Combine well and bring to a boil. Season well with salt and pepper and serve.

Serves 4

Balsamic vinegar is a full-flavored vinegar that is aged in wood before being bottled. The longer it is aged, the more mellow the vinegar.

CREAMY STEAMED SPINACH

Wash the spinach in warm water to remove any grit. It is then steamed in its own juice and the water that clings to the leaves.

2	bunches spinach, or 2 10-oz (300 g) packages	2
2 tbsp	butter	25 mL
½ cup	whipping cream	125 mL
pinch	nutmeg	pinch
	Salt and freshly ground pepper to taste	

1. Strip the stalks from the spinach. Wash the leaves in warm water.

2. Place the spinach in a heavy pot. Cover. On medium heat, let the spinach steam in its own juices for about 5 minutes, or until limp.

3. Drain well, run cold water over the spinach to stop the cooking, then squeeze the moisture out of the leaves.

4. In a frying pan, heat the butter on medium heat. Add the spinach and sauté until heated through, about 1 minute. Add the cream and nutmeg. Boil on high heat until the cream has thickened, about 3 minutes. Season with salt and pepper to taste.

Serves 4

TURNIP AND ONIONS

If you think turnips are not to your taste, try the small white and purple ones before you venture into the stronger yellow rutabagas. Serve with roast lamb or beef.

This dish can be made ahead of time and reheated, covered, in a 350 F (180 C) oven for about 10 minutes, or until hot.

6	small turnips	6
1	large onion	1
3 tbsp	butter	45 mL
	Salt and freshly ground pepper to taste	

1. Peel the turnips and cut into ½-inch (1.25 cm) cubes. Place in a pot of salted cold water. Bring to a boil on high heat and boil until tender, about 5 to 10 minutes. Drain well.

2. Slice the onion into rings. In a large frying pan, melt the butter on medium-high heat until sizzling. Sauté the onions until golden, about 5 to 7 minutes.

3. Add the turnips and toss with the onions. Sauté for 2 minutes, or until the turnips brown slightly. Season well with salt and pepper.

Serves 8

Spinach retains a lot of water after cooking. It needs to be squeezed dry before being used in a dish.

There are two kinds of turnips—large waxed globes with orange flesh, which are often called rutabagas, or small white and purple rounds about the size of a baseball, with pure-white flesh.

SAUTÉED ASPARAGUS

This dish can be used as a first course, as an accompaniment to broiled lamb chops or any other sauceless meat. The same sauté and steam method works for broccoli and snow peas.

1 lb	asparagus spears	500 g
1/4 cup	butter	50 mL
1/2 cup	water	125 mL
1/4 tsp	salt	1 mL
1/4 cup	finely chopped parsley	50 mL

1. Remove the woody ends of the asparagus stalks and discard. Cut the asparagus into 1 1/2-inch (3.75 cm) lengths on the diagonal.

2. Heat 2 tbsp (25 mL) butter in a frying pan on medium-high heat. Sauté the asparagus for 1 minute. Add the water and salt. Cook, covered, for 1 minute. Then uncover and boil for 1 minute, or until the asparagus is crisp-tender.

3. Add the remaining butter and parsley, shaking the pan for 20 to 30 seconds. Serve at once.

Serves 4

BRAISED BRUSSELS SPROUTS WITH VINEGAR AND DILL

Cider vinegar and fresh dill heighten the fall flavor of Brussels sprouts. Discard any leaves that are brown-tinged or soft.

1 1/2 lb	Brussels sprouts	750 g
1 tbsp	cider vinegar	15 mL
2 tbsp	chopped fresh dill	25 mL
1/2 tsp	salt	2 mL
1/2 tsp	freshly ground pepper	2 mL
2 tbsp	butter	25 mL

1. Preheat the oven to 350 F (180 C).

2. Bring a large pot of salted water to a boil on high heat. Add the sprouts, return to a boil and cook for 6 to 8 minutes, or until barely tender. Drain, refresh under cold running water and drain again.

3. Butter an 11 × 7-inch (2 L) casserole dish. Add the sprouts, cider vinegar, dill, salt and pepper. Dot with the butter. Mix well.

4. Bake, covered, for 10 minutes. Uncover and bake for 5 minutes longer.

Serves 6

Before cooking Brussels sprouts, cut an X in the base of each sprout for even cooking and discard any leaves that are brown-tinged or soft.

·16·
Breads

ITALIAN PLUM BREAD

When fresh prune plums are in season, you won't find a better quickbread. You can freeze the second loaf.

1 cup	butter, at room temperature	250 mL
2 cups	granulated sugar	500 mL
4	eggs	4
1 tsp	grated orange rind	5 mL
1 tsp	vanilla extract	5 mL
3 cups	all-purpose flour	750 mL
1 tsp	salt	5 mL
1 tsp	cinnamon	5 mL
1 tsp	cream of tartar	5 mL
½ tsp	baking soda	2 mL
¾ cup	sour cream	175 mL
1 cup	chopped hazelnuts or walnuts	250 mL
3 cups	diced blue Italian plums	750 mL

1. Preheat the oven to 350 F (180 C).

2. Lightly grease two 9 × 5-inch (2 L) loaf pans.

3. In a large bowl, cream together the butter and sugar until light and fluffy. Add the eggs one at a time, and beat well after each addition. Add the orange rind and vanilla.

4. In a separate bowl, combine the flour, salt, cinnamon, cream of tartar and baking soda. Add the dry ingredients and sour cream alternately to the creamed mixture, beginning and ending with the dry ingredients.

5. Stir in the nuts and plums. Divide the batter between the two loaf pans.

6. Bake for 50 to 60 minutes, or until a toothpick inserted in the center comes out clean.

7. Let the pans cool on a rack for 10 minutes, then turn the loaves out of the pans and cool completely on the rack.

Makes 2 loaves

DOUBLE WHOLE WHEAT BREAD

This is the perfect whole wheat bread. It's nutritious and no-fail, and not too heavy.

2 cups	milk	500 mL
1/4 cup	butter	50 mL
1 cup	warm water	250 mL
1/3 cup	honey	75 mL
2	packages active dry yeast, or 2 tbsp (25 mL)	2
1 1/2 tsp	salt	7 mL
5 cups	whole wheat flour	1.25 L
1/4 cup	wheat germ	50 mL
3 cups	all-purpose flour, approx.	750 mL

1. In a small pot, heat the milk and butter on low heat, until the butter dissolves. Remove from the heat.

2. In a small bowl, combine the warm water and 1 tsp (5 mL) honey. Sprinkle the yeast over the top and let stand for 10 minutes, or until foamy.

3. In a large bowl, combine the remaining honey, milk/butter mixture and salt. Stir together. Cool for 5 minutes. Stir in the yeast mixture.

4. With a wooden spoon, beat in the whole wheat flour and wheat germ until smooth. Add enough of the all-purpose flour to make a soft dough.

5. Knead the dough for 10 minutes on a lightly floured surface.

6. Place the dough in an oiled bowl. Brush the top of the dough with vegetable oil. Cover and let rise until double in bulk, about 1 1/2 hours.

7. Punch down to remove the air and knead a few times. Cover and let rest for 10 minutes.

8. Divide the dough in half. Shape and place in two buttered 9 × 5-inch (2 L) loaf pans.

9. Cover and let rise in a warm place until doubled in bulk, about 45 minutes.

10. Preheat the oven to 400 F (200 C).

11. Bake for 40 minutes, or until the loaves are brown and sound hollow when tapped. Remove from the pans and cool completely on a wire rack.

Makes 2 loaves

Canada's Favorite Sandwich

Thickly slice a ripe tomato. Fry lots of bacon until crisp. Lavishly spread mayonnaise on a slice of whole wheat bread. Top with tomato, bacon, Romaine lettuce and a second slice of whole wheat — a BLT.

DARK PUMPERNICKEL BREAD

This is a healthy loaf in which cocoa and molasses give the bread a dark color and dense texture. The basil is optional, but gives a fragrant flavor. Serve the bread with cream cheese and smoked salmon for lunch.

1 tsp	granulated sugar	5 mL
1¼ cups	warm water	300 mL
2	packages active dry yeast, or 2 tbsp (25 mL)	2
2 tbsp	molasses	25 mL
1½ tsp	salt	7 mL
¼ cup	butter, melted and cooled	50 mL
1½ cups	rye flour	375 mL
2 tbsp	cocoa	25 mL
1½ cups	whole wheat flour	375 mL
3 tbsp	chopped fresh basil, or 1 tbsp (15 mL) dried	45 mL
1 cup	all-purpose flour, approx.	250 mL

For an elegant sandwich, spread dark pumpernickel with cream cheese and top with smoked salmon. For a kid-pleaser, combine one can tuna with lots of mayonnaise, diced carrots, celery and green onion. Spread thickly on the dark pumpernickel and serve with corn chips or potato chips.

1. In a large bowl, dissolve the sugar in the warm water. Sprinkle the yeast over the top. Let sit for 10 minutes.

2. Stir in the molasses, salt, butter, rye flour and cocoa. Beat until smooth. Stir in the whole wheat flour and basil and add enough all-purpose flour to make a soft dough.

3. Turn the dough onto a lightly floured surface. Knead until smooth, about 5 to 10 minutes.

4. Place the dough in an oiled bowl. Brush the top with vegetable oil. Cover and let rise in a warm place until doubled, about 1 hour.

5. Grease a large baking sheet.

6. Punch down the dough. Divide in half. Shape each half into a round, slightly flat loaf. Place the loaves on opposite corners of the baking sheet. Cover and let rise in a warm place for 1 hour.

7. Preheat the oven to 400 F (200 C).

8. Bake for 35 to 45 minutes, or until the loaves sound hollow when tapped. Remove from baking sheet and let cool completely on wire racks.

Makes 2 small loaves

CHALLAH

Esther Schwartz of the Canadian Jewish Congress demonstrated this bread at the 1986 Ontario Science Centre Food Show. Her secret is a vitamin C tablet, which helps the yeast work efficiently. Although this bread is made in the food processor, it adapts easily to the hand method; just follow the basic procedure for white bread (see page 112).

1	package active dry yeast, or 1 tbsp (15 mL)	1
¼ cup	granulated sugar	50 mL
1 cup	warm water	250 mL
1	vitamin C tablet (500 mg), crushed	1
3 cups	all-purpose flour	750 mL
1 tsp	salt	5 mL
1	egg	1
¼ cup	vegetable oil	50 mL

Glaze:

1	egg	1
2 tbsp	poppy or sesame seeds	25 mL

1. In a small bowl, combine the yeast, 1 tsp (5 mL) sugar, warm water and vitamin C tablet. Cover and let sit for 10 minutes, or until foamy.

2. Place the flour, remaining sugar and salt in the work bowl of a food processor fitted with the steel knife. Process with the on/off switch a few times, until blended.

3. With the machine running, gradually add the yeast mixture, egg and oil through the feed tube. Allow the machine to run until the dough forms a ball. If the dough is too sticky or the machine cuts off, add about 2 tbsp (25 mL) or more flour.

4. Turn the dough out onto a lightly floured board and knead for about 1 minute, until smooth and satiny. Place in an oiled bowl. Brush the top with oil and cover with a towel.

5. Let rise in a warm place for about 1½ to 2 hours, or until doubled in bulk. Punch down and shape into 1 large or 2 small loaves. Place on a greased baking sheet and cover with a damp towel; let the dough rise again in warm place for 30 minutes.

6. Preheat the oven to 375 F (190 C).

7. Bake for 35 to 40 minutes for a large loaf; 20 to 25 minutes for small loaves, or until nicely crusted and light brown.

8. About 10 minutes before the end of the baking time, beat the remaining egg and brush over the surface of the loaves. Sprinkle with the poppy or sesame seeds.

9. Remove the loaves from the baking sheet and let cool completely on a wire rack.

Makes 1 large loaf or 2 small loaves

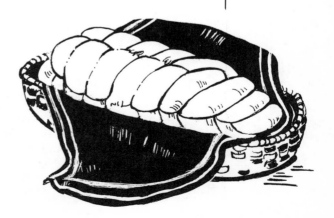

OATMEAL BREAD

This recipe is foolproof! You can eat one loaf and freeze the other.

2 cups	boiling water	500 mL
1 cup	rolled oats	250 mL
1	package active dry yeast, or 1 tbsp (15 mL)	1
pinch	granulated sugar	pinch
½ cup	lukewarm water	125 mL
½ cup	molasses	125 mL
1 tbsp	salt	15 mL
2 tsp	butter, melted	10 mL
5 cups	all-purpose flour	1.25 L

1. In a medium bowl, pour the boiling water over the oats and allow to rest for 2 hours or overnight.

2. In a small bowl, sprinkle the yeast and sugar over the lukewarm water and leave until foamy, about 10 minutes.

3. Place the oatmeal and yeast mixture in a large bowl and add the molasses, salt and butter.

4. Stir in the flour and beat with a wooden spoon until well mixed.

5. Shape into a ball, place in a buttered bowl, cover with a tea towel and allow to rise in a warm place for 1 hour and 15 minutes.

6. Punch down to remove the air, then beat again until smooth.

7. Divide the batter between two buttered 9 × 5-inch pan (2 L) loaf pans and allow to rise in a warm place until doubled, about 40 minutes.

8. Preheat the oven to 375 F (190 C).

9. Bake for 40 to 45 minutes, or until the loaves are golden and begin to pull away from the sides of the pans. Remove from the pans and let cool completely on a wire rack.

Makes 2 loaves

As a substitute for a cup of buttermilk, combine 1 cup (250 mL) milk with 1 tsp (5 mL) lemon juice.

SODA BREAD

This Irish bread is made with buttermilk and baking soda. The dough can also be divided into pieces and used to make scones. Serve with bacon and sausages for breakfast, or to dip into the gravy of a beef stew. If I have leftover bacon, I will crumble it and add it to the dry ingredients.

2 cups	all-purpose flour	500 mL
1 tsp	baking soda	5 mL
1 tsp	cream of tartar	5 mL
½ tsp	salt	2 mL
1 cup	buttermilk	250 mL

1. Preheat the oven to 425 F (220 C).

2. In a large bowl, sift together the flour, baking soda, cream of tartar and salt. Make a well in the center and add the buttermilk. Beat together until the dough has a soft, elastic consistency. Shape into a round 1½ inches (3.75 cm) thick. Flatten the top.

3. Sprinkle the dough with flour and place on a floured baking sheet. With a knife, score the top into six wedges.

4. Bake for 25 minutes, or until risen and lightly browned. Wrap in a damp tea towel to cool down. Serve warm or cold.

Makes 1 loaf

BLUEBERRY LEMON MUFFINS

These muffins can be made in a food processor, but fold the blueberries in later. Be careful not to overprocess when you add the wet ingredients.

3 cups	all-purpose flour	750 mL
1 cup	granulated sugar	250 mL
1 tbsp	baking powder	15 mL
¼ cup	butter, at room temperature	50 mL
2	eggs	2
1 cup	evaporated milk Grated rind and juice of 1 lemon	250 mL
1¾ cups	blueberries, washed and picked over	425 mL

1. Preheat the oven to 350 F (180 C).

2. In a large bowl, mix the flour, sugar and baking powder.

3. Cut in the butter until crumbly.

4. In a separate bowl, combine the eggs, milk, lemon rind and juice. Stir into dry mixture.

5. Gently fold in the blueberries.

6. Spoon the batter into greased 2¾-inch (7 cm) muffin pans.

7. Bake for about 30 minutes, or until lightly golden and a toothpick inserted comes out clean.

Makes 16 muffins

SOUTHERN CHEESE BISCUITS

Try serving these biscuits with stews, or for a breakfast or brunch treat. The dough freezes well unbaked. Cut the biscuits out, freeze, then bake when needed. Do not defrost; simply bake the frozen biscuits for an extra 5 minutes.

1 cup	grated Cheddar cheese	250 mL
1½ cups	all-purpose flour	375 mL
2 tsp	baking powder	10 mL
½ tsp	salt	2 mL
1	green onion, finely chopped	1
½ cup	butter	125 mL
¼ cup	milk	50 mL

1. Preheat the oven to 425 F (220 C).

2. In a bowl, combine the cheese, flour, baking powder, salt and green onion.

3. Cut in the butter until the mixture resembles coarse breadcrumbs. Beat in the milk and form into a ball.

4. On a floured surface, knead the dough for 1 minute. Roll or pat out to ¾-inch (2 cm) thickness. Cut into 3-inch (7.5 cm) rounds and bake for 10 to 12 minutes, or until golden. Any leftover dough should be gathered together, rerolled and used for more biscuits.

Makes 8 to 10 biscuits

·17·
Cakes and Cookies

LEMON CAKE

This is a lemony, moist cake from friend Sharon Evans. I think it's the best lemon cake I have ever eaten.

1 cup	butter, at room temperature	250 mL
1¼ cups	granulated sugar	300 mL
5	eggs	5
	Grated rind and juice of 2 lemons	
1¾ cups	all-purpose flour	425 mL
2 tsp	baking powder	10 mL
pinch	salt	pinch
1 cup	sifted icing sugar	250 mL

1. Preheat the oven to 350 F (180 C).

2. In a mixing bowl, with an electric beater or by hand, beat together the butter and sugar until light and fluffy. Beat in the eggs one at a time. Beat in the lemon rind. Reserve.

3. In a separate bowl, mix together the flour, baking powder and salt. Fold the dry ingredients into the wet ingredients.

4. Spoon the batter into a 9 × 5-inch (2 L) buttered and floured loaf pan. Bake for 1 hour. Loosen the cake and turn it out of the pan, then return it to the pan. (You do this to prevent sticking before pouring the glaze in.)

5. In a small bowl, mix together the icing sugar and lemon juice.

6. While the cake is still hot, make deep holes over the surface of the cake and pour in the glaze. When cool, turn out to serve.

Makes 1 loaf

POUND CAKE

This is a basic, mouth-watering pound cake that can be filled with chocolate mousse or fruit, or left plain. Flavor the batter with the grated rind of one lemon or orange, or top with a vanilla icing (see page 104), if preferred.

1 cup	butter, at room temperature	250 mL
2 cups	granulated sugar	500 mL
6	eggs	6
3 cups	all-purpose flour	750 mL
1 cup	light cream	250 mL
1½ tsp	vanilla extract	7 mL

1. Preheat the oven to 300 F (150 C). Butter and flour a 10-inch (3 L) bundt pan or tube pan, or a 10-inch (25 cm) springform pan.

2. In a large bowl, with an electric mixer or by hand, cream the butter until light. Gradually beat in the sugar. Beat at medium speed until light and fluffy.

3. Add the eggs one at a time, beating well after each addition.

4. Add the flour alternately with the cream, beating after each addition, ending with the flour. Add the vanilla. Beat a few seconds longer or until smooth. Do not overbeat.

5. Spoon the batter into the prepared cake pan and smooth out the surface. Bake for 1 hour and 15 minutes, or until a skewer inserted in the center comes out clean, and the cake is evenly brown.

6. Cool on a wire rack for 10 minutes. Remove from the pan. Allow to cool completely on the wire rack.

Makes one 10-inch (25 cm) cake

RICH CHOCOLATE CAKE

A rich, wet chocolate loaf similar to a chocolate mousse cake.

4 oz	bittersweet chocolate	125 g
½ cup	butter, at room temperature	125 mL
1 cup	granulated sugar	250 mL
4	eggs, separated	4
½ cup	all-purpose flour	125 mL
½ cup	cornstarch	125 mL
1 tsp	baking soda	5 mL

1. Preheat the oven to 350 F (180 C).

2. Melt the chocolate in a heavy pan on low heat. Remove and let cool.

3. In a large bowl, cream the butter. Add the sugar and cream together until light and fluffy. Blend in the egg yolks and melted chocolate. Reserve.

4. In a separate bowl, sift together the flour, cornstarch and baking soda.

5. Stir the dry ingredients into the chocolate mixture.

6. In a separate bowl, beat the egg whites until soft peaks form. Stir one-third of the egg whites into the chocolate mixture. Gently fold in the remaining egg whites.

7. Pour the batter into a buttered 9 × 5-inch (2 L) loaf pan.

8. Bake for 1 hour, or until a toothpick inserted comes out clean. Cool in the pan for 10 minutes. Remove and cool on a wire rack.

Serves 8

Pound cakes got their name because they were originally made with a pound of flour, a pound of sugar and a pound of butter.

APPLE CAKE

This is a wonderful recipe from friend Sandy Druckman, a great cook. Don't be alarmed if there does not seem to be enough batter to cover the filling. Just spread the remaining batter over the apples; once the cake is cooked, you will be surprised.

6	large cooking apples	6
½ cup	granulated sugar	125 mL
2 tsp	cinnamon	10 mL
2	eggs	2
¾ cup	granulated sugar	175 mL
1½ tsp	vanilla extract	7 mL
½ cup	vegetable oil	125 mL
3 tbsp	orange juice	45 mL
1½ cups	all-purpose flour	375 mL
2 tsp	baking powder	10 mL
¼ tsp	salt	1 mL
1 cup	sliced almonds	250 mL

1. Preheat the oven to 350 F (180 C).

2. Peel and slice apples into eighths. In a bowl, toss together the apples, ½ cup (125 mL) sugar and cinnamon. Reserve.

3. In a large bowl, beat the eggs, ¾ cup (175 mL) sugar and vanilla until light and fluffy. Blend in the oil and orange juice.

4. In a separate bowl, sift together the flour, baking powder and salt.

5. Gradually add the flour mixture to the egg mixture, folding together until the batter is blended and smooth.

6. Spread half the batter into a greased 11 × 7-inch (2 L) baking dish. Cover with the apple mixture. Spread the remaining batter over the top.

7. Bake for 40 minutes in the lower third of the oven. Scatter the almonds over the top and continue to bake

for 10 minutes, making sure the almonds do not burn. Cool in the pan. Cut in squares and serve warm or cold.

Serves 8 to 10

ORANGE ALMOND CAKE

A rich, moist cake that needs no embellishments. The cake keeps well for up to five days in the refrigerator.

1 cup	butter, at room temperature	250 mL
1 cup	granulated sugar	250 mL
4	eggs, separated	4
¾ cup	ground almonds	175 mL
¼ cup	fresh orange juice	50 mL
	Grated rind of 1 orange	
½ tsp	salt	2 mL
1½ cups	all-purpose flour	375 mL

1. Preheat the oven to 325 F (160 C).

2. Grease and flour a 9 × 5-inch (2 L) loaf pan.

3. In a large bowl, beat the butter and sugar until light and fluffy. Beat in the egg yolks, ground almonds, orange juice and rind. Set aside.

4. In a separate bowl, whisk the egg whites and salt until soft peaks form.

5. Mix one-quarter of the egg-white mixture into the butter/egg-yolk mixture. Fold in half the flour, the remaining egg whites, then the remaining flour. The mixture should be just mixed together.

6. Spoon the batter into the prepared pan and bake for 1 hour, or until a toothpick inserted comes out clean. Cool in the pan for 10 minutes, then turn out onto a rack.

Serves 6

Spy apples are my favorite cooking apples because they are tart and hold their shape. If they are unavailable, Granny Smith apples are my next choice.

MENU

COFFEE AND DESSERT AFTER THE THEATER

SOUR CREAM COFFEE CAKE

Coffee cakes are easy to make, and do not have to be iced or decorated. Serve warm and freeze any extra. Wrap in foil and reheat in a 350 F (180 C) oven until warm, about 15 minutes.

½ cup	butter, at room temperature	125 mL
1 cup	granulated sugar	250 mL
2	eggs, well beaten	2
1 tsp	vanilla extract	5 mL
1 cup	sour cream	250 mL
1 tsp	baking soda	5 mL
1¾ cups	all-purpose flour	425 mL
1 tsp	baking powder	5 mL
½ tsp	salt	2 mL
¼ cup	brown sugar	50 mL
1 tbsp	cinnamon	15 mL
2 tbsp	finely chopped nuts, optional	25 mL

1. Preheat the oven to 350 F (180 C).

2. Butter and flour an 8-inch (2 L) square cake pan.

3. In a large bowl, cream the butter. Add sugar and cream until light and fluffy. Add the eggs and vanilla. Beat well.

4. In a separate bowl, combine the sour cream and baking soda.

5. In another bowl, sift together flour, baking powder and salt.

6. Beat the dry ingredients into butter mixture alternately with the sour cream mixture, starting and ending with dry ingredients. Spread half the batter in the prepared pan.

7. In a small bowl or cup, combine the brown sugar, cinnamon and nuts. Sprinkle half the mixture on the batter. Cover with the remaining batter. Sprinkle with the remaining brown sugar mixture.

8. Bake for 45 to 50 minutes, or until a skewer inserted in the center comes out clean.

9. Cool in the pan. Run a spatula around the sides and lift onto a serving platter.

Makes one 8-inch (20 cm) cake

CLASSIC CHEESECAKE

Try this creamy, traditional cheese-cake, which can be baked without a crust, if preferred. It has a smooth, lux-urious taste.

Crust:

5 tbsp	butter, melted	65 mL
½ cup	Graham cracker crumbs	125 mL
1 tbsp	granulated sugar	15 mL
1 tsp	cinnamon	5 mL
2 tbsp	ground pecans or other nuts	25 mL

Filling:

1 lb	cream cheese, at room temperature	500 g
2 tbsp	butter, at room temperature	25 mL
¾ cup	granulated sugar	175 mL
3	eggs	3
1 cup	sour cream	250 mL
3 tbsp	all-purpose flour	45 mL
1 tsp	vanilla extract	5 mL
	Grated rind and juice of 1 lemon	

Topping:

1 cup	strawberries, hulled	250 mL
2	kiwi fruit, peeled and sliced	2
1 cup	raspberries	250 mL

Glaze:

½ cup	red currant jelly	125 mL
2 tsp	orange liqueur	10 mL

If your cheesecake cracks, it is because it has been cooled too quickly, or it has been left in a draft. Avoid this by cooling the cake in the oven, with the oven door open.

1. Spread 2 tbsp (25 mL) melted butter over the bottom and sides of an 8-inch (2 L) springform pan.

2. To make the crust, in a bowl, stir together the Graham cracker crumbs, sugar, cinnamon, pecans and remaining butter.

3. Knead the mixture together and pat into the bottom and sides of the prepared pan. Chill the crust in the refrigerator while you make the filling.

4. Preheat the oven to 350 F (180 C).

5. In a large bowl or food processor, cream the cheese and butter together. Add the sugar and beat until light and fluffy. Add the eggs one at a time, beating well after each addition. When the egg traces disappear, beat in the sour cream, flour, vanilla, lemon rind and juice.

6. Pour the filling into the chilled crust. Bake the cake in the center of the oven for 1 hour. Open the oven door, turn off the heat, and let the cake sit in the oven until cool. Leave at room temperature, and just before serving, unhinge sides of pan.

7. Top the cheesecake with the fruit.

8. Melt the red currant jelly and orange liqueur in a small pot. Brush over the fruit. Let the glaze set and serve.

Serves 8 to 10

BROWNIES

My friend Shirley Hawkins is an incomparable brownie maker; no family occasion is complete without her brownies. They are moist, chocolatey and not too sweet.

1 cup	butter	250 mL
4 oz	unsweetened chocolate	125 g
2 cups	granulated sugar	500 mL
4	eggs	4
2 tsp	vanilla extract	10 mL
1½ cups	all-purpose flour	375 mL
½ tsp	salt	2 mL
1½ cups	chopped pecans, optional	375 mL
	Sifted icing sugar	

1. Preheat the oven to 375 F (190 C).

2. Butter and flour a 13 × 9-inch (3.5 L) baking pan.

3. Place the butter and chocolate in a heavy pot on low heat. Heat, stirring, until the butter and chocolate melt. Cool.

4. In a large bowl, combine the chocolate mixture and the sugar. Add the eggs one at a time, beating after each addition. Stir in the vanilla.

5. Sift the flour and salt into the chocolate mixture and stir to blend. If using pecans, stir them in at this point.

6. Scrape into the baking pan and bake for 25 to 30 minutes, or until a skewer inserted in the side of the brownies comes out clean.

7. Cool on a rack in the pan. Sift icing sugar over top.

8. Cut in bars while still warm, but leave in the pan.

Makes about 2 dozen brownies

DENSITIES

The richest chocolate square ever eaten. My kids rate this an 11 out of 10.

4 oz	unsweetened chocolate	125 g
4 oz	bittersweet chocolate	125 g
1 cup	butter, at room temperature	250 mL
2 cups	granulated sugar	500 mL
4	eggs	4
1 cup	all-purpose flour	250 mL
½ tsp	salt	2 mL
2 tsp	vanilla extract	10 mL

1. In a small pot, on low heat, melt the chocolate. Reserve.

2. Preheat the oven to 350 F (180 C).

3. In a large bowl, cream the butter and sugar until fluffy. Add the eggs one at a time, beating well between additions.

4. In a separate bowl, sift together flour and salt. Beat the dry ingredients into the egg mixture.

5. Stir in the cooled melted chocolate and vanilla.

6. Pour the batter into a greased 13 × 9-inch (3.5 L) pan. Bake for 40 minutes, or until a skewer inserted in the side comes out clean. (The center should still be slightly moist.) Cool in the pan and cut into bars.

Makes about 4 dozen 2 × 1-inch (5 × 2.5 cm) bars

The secret to a good brownie is slight under-baking. Insert a skewer in the cake at the edge of the pan. It should come out clean, but the center should still be wobbly; the brownies will continue to cook while cooling.

TOFFEE CRUNCH COOKIES

These are the world's easiest cookies to make. They are good for Christmas gift-giving, because it takes such a short time to make dozens.

1	12-oz (400 g) package Graham crackers	1
1½ cups	butter, cut into small cubes	375 mL
1 cup	brown sugar	250 mL
2 cups	sliced almonds	250 mL

1. Preheat the oven to 400 F (200 C).

2. Line a cookie sheet with the Graham crackers.

3. In a pot, melt the butter and sugar together and bring to a boil.

4. Pour the butter/sugar mixture over the crackers. Sprinkle with the almonds.

5. Bake for 8 minutes, or until bubbling on top.

6. Cool slightly, cut into squares and remove from the cookie sheets. Cool on wire racks.

Makes about 30 cookies

A true Scottish shortbread uses rice flour combined with all-purpose flour to give the fine, crumbly texture associated with good shortbread.

SHORTBREAD COOKIES

If possible, use a food processor and process the granulated sugar for 30 seconds to give it a finer texture.

3 cups	all-purpose flour	750 mL
⅔ cup	rice flour	150 mL
1 tsp	salt	5 mL
¾ cup	granulated sugar	175 mL
1½ cups	butter, cut into ½ inch (1.25 cm) pieces	375 mL
	Sifted icing sugar	

1. Preheat the oven to 325 F (160 C). Lightly flour three cookie sheets.

2. In a large bowl, sift together the flours and salt. Stir in the sugar.

3. Using your fingertips, rub in the butter until the mixture resembles fine breadcrumbs. Knead the mixture until a ball can be formed, about 5 to 10 minutes. (You can also use a food processor or electric mixer to cut in the butter.)

4. Divide the dough into three portions and pat into three 9-inch (23 cm) circles or squares right onto the cookie sheet (or press the dough into an oiled and floured shortbread mold, then turn out onto the cookie sheet). Keep the top of the shortbread as smooth as possible, and make sure it is even in thickness.

5. Using a knife, mark into sections with lines like the spokes of a wheel if patted in circle shape. Prick all over with a fork. Decorate the edges with the tines of a fork.

6. Bake for 45 minutes, or until pale gold. The shortbread will not be firm to the touch. Re-mark the sections, sprinkle with sifted icing sugar and let cool on the baking sheets. Store in an airtight container for up to two weeks.

Makes three 9-inch (23 cm) rounds

COCONUT CRISPS

Leave out the coconut, and you will have oatmeal crisps.

1 cup	butter, at room temperature	250 mL
¾ cup	granulated sugar	175 mL
¾ cup	firmly packed brown sugar	175 mL
1	egg	1
1½ cups	all-purpose flour	375 mL
1¼ cups	rolled oats	300 mL
1 tsp	baking powder	5 mL
½ tsp	salt	2 mL
¾ cup	desiccated coconut	175 mL

1. Preheat the oven to 350 F (180 C).

2. In a large bowl, cream the butter and sugars. Add the egg and beat well.

3. In a separate bowl, combine the flour, oats, baking powder and salt. Beat into the creamed mixture. Stir in the coconut.

4. Drop by tablespoonfuls onto buttered baking sheets, about 2 inches (5 cm) apart. Press down the tops with a fork. Bake for 8 to 10 minutes, or until pale gold. Cool slightly before removing from the cookie sheets to wire racks.

Makes about 3 dozen cookies

MELTING MOMENTS

My mother-in-law, Margaret Mac-Dougall, makes perfect melting moments every Christmas. This is her grandmother's recipe.

1¾ cups	all-purpose flour	425 mL
¼ cup	cornstarch	50 mL
1 cup	butter	250 mL
¾ cup	icing sugar	175 mL
¼ cup	raspberry jam	50 mL
	Sifted icing sugar	

1. Preheat the oven to 350 F (180 C). Butter two cookie sheets.

2. In a bowl, combine the flour and cornstarch.

3. In a separate bowl, cream the butter and sugar until soft and smooth. Gradually beat in the dry ingredients.

4. Roll 1 tbsp (15 mL) dough at a time into small balls. Flatten slightly by lightly pressing cookies with a fork or your finger. Place on cookie sheets ½ inch (1.25 cm) apart.

5. Bake for 10 to 12 minutes, or until creamy-colored and firm to the touch. Cool on wire racks.

6. Spread ¼ tsp (1 mL) jam on half the cookies. Top with the remaining cookies. Sprinkle with the sifted icing sugar.

Makes 2½ dozen sandwich cookies

Thumbprint Cookies
Place 1 tbsp (15 mL) Melting Moment dough on a cookie sheet. Make an imprint in the dough with your thumb. Bake for 10 to 12 minutes, or until creamy colored. Cool, then fill the hollows with jam or lemon curd.

CRANBERRY CRUNCHIES

An especially good Thanksgiving or Christmas recipe, when cranberries are fresh.

Base:

2 cups	all-purpose flour	500 mL
½ cup	granulated sugar	125 mL
1 cup	butter, at room temperature	250 mL

Filling:

2	12-oz (340 g) packages cranberries	2
2½ cups	brown sugar	625 mL
4	eggs	4
2 tsp	vanilla extract	10 mL
1 tsp	baking powder	5 mL
⅔ cup	all-purpose flour	150 mL
¼ tsp	salt	1 mL
	Sifted icing sugar	

1. Preheat the oven to 350 F (180 C).

2. In a large bowl, sift together the flour and sugar. Cut in the butter until crumbly. Pat into a 13 × 9-inch (3.5 L) baking dish. Bake for 15 to 20 minutes, or until golden-brown. Cool.

3. Wash the cranberries well. In a pot, combine the cranberries with ¼ cup (50 mL) brown sugar. Cook over low heat until berries pop and soften. Let cool.

4. In a large bowl, beat the eggs lightly. Add the remaining sugar gradually, beating until thickened. Stir in the vanilla.

5. In a separate bowl, sift together the baking powder, flour and salt.

6. Add the dry ingredients to the egg mixture until blended. Fold in the cranberries.

7. Spread over the base and bake for 30 to 35 minutes, or until set.

8. When cool, dust with sifted icing sugar and cut into squares.

Makes about 32 squares

·18·
Desserts

POACHED PEARS WITH CHOCOLATE CURLS

This recipe is a sexy combination of pears, raspberries and chocolate—sure to please even the most jaded palate. Try to use Bartlett pears, since they have the best flavor for cooking.

3 cups	sugar syrup (see page 35)	750 mL
2	slices lemon	2
4	Bartlett pears, peeled, cored and halved	4
1	15-oz (425 g) package frozen raspberries in sugar syrup, defrosted	1
2 oz	bittersweet chocolate, at room temperature	60 g

1. In a heavy pot on high heat, bring the syrup to a boil. Turn the heat to low. Add the lemon and pears. Poach for 10 minutes, or until the pears are tender and a knife point slips in easily. Let the pears cool in the syrup.

2. Puree the raspberries in a food processor or blender. Sieve to remove the seeds. Chill.

3. With a vegetable peeler, scrape along the long edge of the chocolate to form curls. Chill.

4. Spoon the raspberry sauce on four plates. Place two pear halves core side down on each plate to form a heart shape. Sprinkle the pears and sauce with chocolate curls.

Serves 4

Professional bakers make chocolate curls by melting the chocolate, spreading it thinly on a sheet of marble and pulling a metal spatula across the chocolate to form curls. This works because the chocolate has been carefully heated and then cooled to exact temperatures, causing a change in the composition of the chocolate, which allows it to be worked. Home cooks don't usually bother with this, and make do with vegetable peelers and less than perfect curls.

PAVLOVA

This is my daughter Katie's favorite dessert. The dish is named after Anna Pavlova, the famous ballet dancer, because its white cloudy appearance reminds you of her dancing. Pavlova is soft inside and crisp outside. Top it with fruits in season or pureed dried apricots and grated chocolate.

4	egg whites	4
1 cup	granulated sugar	250 mL
1 tbsp	white vinegar	15 mL
pinch	salt	pinch
1 cup	whipping cream	250 mL
2 cups	strawberries, hulled	500 mL
2	kiwi fruit, peeled and sliced	2

1. Preheat the oven to 275 F (140 C).

2. Line a large cookie sheet with parchment paper or buttered foil.

3. In an electric mixer, beat the egg whites until stiff. Gradually add the sugar 1 tbsp (15 mL) at a time, beating well after each addition.

4. Add the vinegar and salt and beat the mixture until it is thick, glossy and stiff enough to support the beater.

5. Mound the meringue mixture onto the cookie sheet in a 10-inch (25 cm) circle.

6. Bake for 1¼ hours. The meringue should be creamy-colored and crisp. Bake for another 15 minutes if it is still sticky on the outside. Cool and remove from the paper onto a serving platter.

7. In a large bowl, whip the cream until stiff peaks form. Cover the meringue with whipped cream and decorate with strawberries and kiwi. The meringue can sit, uncovered, in a cool place for up to two days, but once it is garnished with the cream and fruit, it must be served within a few hours, otherwise it weeps.

Serves 8

CREOLE BANANAS

Serve these unusual bananas warm with a scoop of vanilla ice cream. Serve after Southern fried chicken or hamburgers.

¼ cup	butter	50 mL
	Grated rind and juice of 1 lemon	
½ cup	brown sugar	125 mL
¼ tsp	cinnamon	1 mL
3	bananas, sliced lengthwise and halved	3
¼ cup	Bourbon or Scotch	50 mL

1. Melt the butter in a frying pan on medium heat. Stir in the lemon rind and juice, sugar and cinnamon. Simmer together until the sugar dissolves.

2. Add the bananas and keep turning for a couple of minutes to coat them in the syrup.

3. Add the Bourbon just before serving and bring to boil. Serve immediately.

Serves 4

APPLE GINGER PUDDING

My husband, Bruce, considers this dessert the best in the book. For people who are apple and ginger lovers, this easy dessert is a must. Buy good-quality ginger cookies. Substitute pears for the apples and chocolate wafers for the ginger, and you have pear chocolate pudding—another taste sensation.

4	large apples	4
2 tbsp	butter	25 mL
	Grated rind and juice of ½ lemon	
½ cup	brown sugar	125 mL
1	7-oz (150 g) box ginger cookies	1
1 cup	whipping cream	250 mL

1. Preheat the oven to 350 F (180 C).

2. Peel, core and slice the apples.

3. In a large frying pan, heat the butter on medium-high heat. Add the apples and sauté until slightly softened, about 3 to 4 minutes.

4. Add the grated lemon rind, juice and ⅓ cup (75 mL) brown sugar. Cook until the sugar dissolves.

5. Break the cookies up into bite-sized pieces. Arrange a layer of cookies in a buttered 6-cup (1.5 L) soufflé or gratin dish. Cover with a layer of apple mixture and pour on a layer of cream. Continue until the dish is full, finishing with cream. Sprinkle with the remaining sugar.

6. Cover with foil and bake for 30 to 40 minutes, or until the apples are soft. Serve hot.

Serves 6

APPLES TATIN

A quick and easy, light dessert to serve after a heavy meal. Serve it hot over vanilla ice cream flavored with cinnamon to taste.

4	green apples	4
½ cup	butter	125 mL
½ cup	granulated sugar	125 mL

1. Peel, core and slice the apples.

2. Heat the butter and sugar in a frying pan on medium heat. Bring to boil, then simmer until the sugar turns pale gold, about 3 minutes. Add the apples and cook together until the apples are tender and the sugar is a rich brown color, about 5 to 8 minutes.

Serves 6

BERRY SALAD

Summer berries make an attractive dessert when the berries are layered in a glass bowl. Pour the dressing over as you spoon in each layer, because tossing the berries later will spoil the effect. If you have the patience and a cherry pitter, pit the cherries; discarding the pits while eating an elegant fruit salad is awkward.

½ cup	red currant jelly	125 mL
½ cup	port or sherry	125 mL
2 cups	strawberries, sliced	500 mL
1 cup	blueberries	250 mL
1 cup	raspberries	250 mL
2 cups	cherries	500 mL

1. In small pot on low heat, heat together the red currant jelly and port until the jelly dissolves.

2. Layer the fruits in a glass bowl, spooning some dressing on each layer.

3. Chill before serving.

Serves 6

BAKED FUDGE PUDDING

This dessert is halfway between a brownie and a steamed pudding. Serve it warm or cold with whipped cream.

2 cups	granulated sugar	500 mL
½ cup	all-purpose flour	125 mL
½ cup	cocoa	125 mL
4	eggs, beaten	4
1 cup	butter, melted	250 mL
1 tsp	vanilla extract	5 mL
1 cup	chopped almonds	250 mL

1. Preheat the oven to 325 F (160 C).

2. In a bowl, mix together the sugar, flour and cocoa. Stir in the eggs, melted butter, vanilla and nuts.

3. Place a large pan of hot water in the oven and bring to a simmer.

4. Pour the batter into a buttered 9-inch (23 cm) square baking dish. Place the baking dish in the larger pan; the water should come halfway up the sides.

5. Bake for 1 hour and 20 minutes. The pudding is done when the surface is lightly cracked and the center springs back when touched. Remove the baking dish from the larger pan to cool. The pudding has a custard consistency, which firms as it cools. Serve warm or cold in squares.

Serves 8

When a recipe calls for cooking in a *bain marie* or water bath, it means the dish is oven-poached. To oven-poach, half fill a roasting pan with hot water and place it in the oven. When the water simmers, place the dish to be cooked in the roasting pan. This creates steam in the oven and gently cooks delicate foods such as crème caramel, pâtés, or certain fish dishes.

CANADIAN APPLE PIE

This is the definitive apple pie.

1	recipe Basic Shortcrust Pastry (see page 94)	1
6	Spy apples	6
½ cup	granulated sugar	125 mL
½ cup	brown sugar	125 mL
1 tbsp	all-purpose flour	15 mL
¼ tsp	nutmeg	1 mL
1 tsp	cinnamon	5 mL
	Grated rind of ½ lemon	
	Grated rind of ½ orange	
1 tbsp	orange juice	15 mL
1 tbsp	butter	15 mL

1. Preheat the oven to 425 F (220 C).

2. On a floured board, roll out half the pastry and fit into a 9-inch (23 cm) pie plate (preferably a flan pan with a removable base).

3. Peel, core and slice the apples.

4. In a large bowl, combine the sugars, flour, nutmeg, cinnamon and grated lemon and orange rind. Toss the apples in the mixture. Sprinkle with orange juice. Pile into the pie shell, mounding the filling high in the center. Dot with butter.

5. Roll out the remaining pastry and fit over the apples. Trim and crimp the edges together. Make two vents in the center of the pie to allow steam to escape.

6. Bake for 10 minutes. Lower the heat to 375 F (190 C) and bake for a further 35 to 40 minutes, or until the crust turns golden and the filling is bubbling.

Serves 8

ALL-CANADIAN CHERRY PIE

I was addicted to cherry pie as a teenager, and consider myself an expert on good ones. Here is my favorite.

1	recipe Pearl's Meat Pie pastry (see page 96) or Basic Shortcrust Pastry (see page 94)	1
1 cup	granulated sugar	250 mL
2 tbsp	quick-cooking tapioca	25 mL
pinch	salt	pinch
4 cups	pitted sour cherries	1 L

1. Divide the pastry in two. Roll out one half. Line an 8- or 9-inch (20 or 23 cm) pie plate. Chill until needed.

2. Preheat the oven to 450 F (230 C).

3. In a large bowl, combine the sugar, tapioca and salt. Mix in the cherries until coated with the sugar mixture.

4. Fill the pie shell with the cherry mixture.

5. Roll out the other half of the pastry until it is 1 inch (2.5 cm) bigger than the pie plate. Drape the pastry over the cherries. Trim the pastry and seal the edges. Cut two or three slashes in the top.

6. Bake for 10 minutes, then reduce the heat to 350 F (180 C) and bake for 30 to 40 minutes more. Serve warm or cold.

Serves 6 to 8

BLUEBERRY PIE

Any berry works in this recipe. Blueberries can be sprinkled on top of the blueberry puree instead of folded in. Ribena is an English cordial made from black currants. It is available in health food stores.

4½ cups	blueberries, washed	1.125 L
½ cup	granulated sugar	125 mL
½ cup	water	125 mL
	Grated rind and juice of 1 lemon	
2 tbsp	cornstarch	25 mL
2 tbsp	water	25 mL
1 tbsp	butter	15 mL
2 tbsp	Cassis or Ribena	25 mL
1	9-inch (23 cm) baked Food Processor Pastry shell (see page 94)	1

1. In a pot, combine 1½ cups (375 mL) blueberries with the sugar, water, lemon rind and juice. Bring to a boil on medium heat and cook for 10 minutes. Puree in a food processor or blender. Return to the heat.

2. In a cup, combine the cornstarch and water. Add the cornstarch mixture and butter to the pot and stir until thickened. Remove from the heat. Cool.

3. Add the liqueur and fold in the remaining blueberries. Pile into the pie shell. Chill.

Serves 6 to 8

Fruit pies are baked at two temperatures to ensure a crisp bottom crust and properly cooked fruit.

PEACH SOUR CREAM PIE

A perfectly peachy pie with a custardy texture. There is no top crust to this pie, which is like a fruit-filled quiche.

1 cup	sour cream	250 mL
	Grated rind of ½ lemon	
½ cup	firmly packed brown sugar	125 mL
½ tsp	salt	2 mL
2	egg yolks, beaten	2
2 tbsp	all-purpose flour	25 mL
1	8- or 9-inch (20 or 23 cm) unbaked Basic Shortcrust Pastry shell (see page 94)	1
2½ cups	peeled sliced peaches	625 mL

1. Preheat the oven to 425 F (220 C).

2. In a bowl, mix together the sour cream, lemon rind, brown sugar, salt and egg yolks.

3. Sprinkle 1 tbsp (15 mL) flour on the pie shell. Sprinkle the remaining flour on the peaches and toss together. Pile the peaches into the pie shell.

4. Spread the sour cream mixture over the top. Bake for 15 minutes. Lower the heat to 350 F (180 C) and bake for 25 minutes more, or until the top is browned.

Serves 6

Quick-cooking tapioca is finely ground tapioca used to thicken pie fillings and puddings; it has a smooth texture and clear look. You can substitute flour, but the texture will not be as silky.

DEEP-DISH PLUM PIE

Use tart Italian blue plums for the best results. The crust is baked on top of the pie instead of underneath, so the plums need to be precooked. Peaches, cherries or apples can be substituted for the plums. This recipe looks attractive baked and served in a medium gratin dish.

12 to 16	plums, halved and pitted	12 to 16
½ cup	brown sugar	125 mL
½ cup	granulated sugar	125 mL
¼ tsp	ground cloves	1 mL
½ tsp	ground cardamom, optional	2 mL
pinch	salt	pinch
2 tbsp	quick-cooking tapioca	25 mL
2 tbsp	lemon juice	25 mL
1 tbsp	butter	15 mL
1	9-inch (23 cm) unbaked Sweet Pastry shell (see page 95)	1

1. Preheat the oven to 375 F (190 C).

2. Fill a 10-inch (25 cm) round cake pan with the plums, placed cut side down.

3. In a bowl, combine the sugars, cloves, cardamom, salt and tapioca. Sprinkle the mixture over the fruit and shake the dish so that the sugar sifts down through fruit. Sprinkle with the lemon juice and dot with the butter. Bake for 20 minutes.

4. Roll the pastry out and place over the pie. Trim the pastry and slash in three places. Bake for a further 20 to 30 minutes, or until the pastry is golden.

Serves 8

CHOCOLATE FRUIT FLAN

A chocolate lining stops fruit juices from leaking through the pastry, and it tastes great, too. To hull strawberries, remove the green stem with your fingers or a strawberry huller.

2 oz	semisweet chocolate	60 g
1	9-inch (23 cm) baked Sweet Pastry shell (see page 95)	1
4 cups	strawberries, hulled	1 L
1 cup	red currant jelly	250 mL
1 tbsp	brandy or orange liqueur	15 mL

1. In heavy pot on low heat, melt the chocolate slowly. Remove from the heat and brush the inside of the baked pastry shell with the melted chocolate. Cool.

2. Arrange whole strawberries attractively in rings inside the shell.

3. In a small pot, boil the red currant jelly and liqueur together for 1 minute. Cool until the glaze is at room temperature but still liquid. Brush the glaze on the fruit, making sure all the fruit is glazed and all the holes between the fruit are filled. Leave in a cool place until ready to serve.

Serves 6 to 8

RHUBARB STRAWBERRY CRUMBLE PIE

The first signs of spring are baked into this pie. Substitute sour cream for yogurt for a richer taste. The crumble topping takes the place of a top crust.

1½ cups	granulated sugar	375 mL
⅓ cup	all-purpose flour	75 mL
1 cup	plain yogurt	250 mL
4 to 4½ cups	diced rhubarb	1 to 1.125 L
2 cups	sliced strawberries	500 mL
1	9-inch (23 cm) unbaked Basic Shortcrust Pastry shell (see page 94)	1
½ cup	firmly packed brown sugar	125 mL
½ cup	all-purpose flour	125 mL
¼ cup	butter, at room temperature	50 mL

1. Preheat the oven to 450 F (230 C).

2. In a large bowl, combine the sugar, flour, yogurt, rhubarb and strawberries. Spoon into the unbaked pie shell.

3. In a small bowl, mix together the brown sugar and flour. Cut in the butter until the mixture has a crumbly texture. Sprinkle on top of the pie.

4. Bake for 15 minutes. Reduce the heat to 350 F (180 C) and continue baking for another 30 minutes. Serve hot or cold.

Serves 8

When using rhubarb in a recipe, add extra sugar if you are using garden-variety rhubarb instead of hot-house rhubarb, which tends to be sweeter.

KEY LIME PIE

Lime and ginger make a good finish to any spicy meal. This is a classic key lime pie with a strong, clean flavor.

Crust:

1¼ cups	Graham cracker crumbs	300 mL
1 tbsp	granulated sugar	15 mL
1 tsp	ground ginger	5 mL
¼ cup	butter, melted	50 mL

Filling:

5	egg yolks	5
1	10-oz (300 mL) can sweetened condensed milk	1
½ cup	lime juice	125 mL
1	egg white	1

Topping:

1 cup	whipping cream	250 mL
1 tbsp	icing sugar	15 mL
	Grated rind of 1 lime	

1. Preheat the oven to 350 F (180 C).

2. In a bowl, mix together the crumbs, granulated sugar, ginger and melted butter.

3. Pat the crust mixture onto the bottom and sides of a 9-inch (23 cm) tart pan.

4. Place the egg yolks in a large bowl and beat with a whisk until smooth. Slowly stir in the condensed milk and lime juice.

5. In a separate bowl, beat the egg white until stiff. Fold into the yolk mixture.

6. Pour the filling into the crust. Bake for 15 minutes, or until the filling is set. Test by shaking the pan. The filling should wobble slightly in the middle. Cool.

7. In a large bowl, whip the cream until it holds its shape. Beat in the icing sugar.

8. Spread the cream over the pie and sprinkle on the grated lime rind.

Serves 8

Menu Planning and Table Setting

MENU PLANNING

• Keep your menus simple and make sure you can handle them. Choose dishes that can be made ahead of time, and reheated or finished just before serving.

• Start with a light appetizer if you are having a substantial main course. If you start with a heavy appetizer, follow it with a light main course.

• If there is cream in one of the courses, do not have cream in any other. (I remember a dinner party I once went to where the hostess served a cream soup followed by chicken in a cream sauce. The dessert finished us—it was ice cream!)

• Consider contrasting textures if you are serving a stewy main dish. A crisp vegetable would be welcome with it.

• When the weather is hot, don't serve heavy foods. In cold weather, don't serve a cold soup with a salad main course.

• Menus today usually consist of an appetizer or soup, main course and dessert. The salad can be served either before or after the main course, though I prefer it after the main course to cleanse the palate.

• Cheese can be served before dessert, European style, or after dessert, American style.

TABLE SETTING

• Proper table setting follows specific rules. The cutlery used for each course is placed at the outside of the setting working to the inside. If the menu is an appetizer, soup, main course and dessert, the setting would be appetizer knife and fork on the outside, followed by the soup spoon, meat knife and fork and finishing with the dessert spoon and fork on the inside (or English style—at right angles to the other cutlery, over the plate).

• Wine glasses are placed over the knives, with the water glasses, if used, to the right of the wine glasses.

• If flowers are used, they should be low enough for people to see across them.

• Candles are great for the evening, but not acceptable at lunch or brunch.

• The bread and butter plate goes on the left side beside the fork. (Always eat your own roll; it's tacky to eat your neighbor's.) Bread and butter knives go on the bread and butter plates.

• Napkins go in the center of the setting between the knives and forks.

Glossary

Al dente: Cooked to the point where there is a touch of firmness left.

Au gratin: A dish that is sprinkled with breadcrumbs and/or cheese before being baked in the oven.

Bain-marie: To cook at a temperature just below the boiling point, in a pan standing in a larger pan of simmering water. This method is used in the oven or on the top of the stove to prepare sauces, custards and foods that should not be cooked over direct heat.

Bake: To cook with dry heat in an oven. Technically, baking and roasting are the same thing.

Baking blind: To prebake pastry by weighting down the base to prevent buckling and shrinking.

Baste: To pour liquid or fat over food to keep it moist.

Beat: To combine foods together thoroughly, incorporating air to make the mixture lighter. You can use either a wooden spoon, fork, electric mixer or food processor.

Blanch: To immerse food in boiling water for a minute to partially cook it.

Blend: To smoothly combine several ingredients.

Boil: To bring liquid to 212 F (100 C), at which point large bubbles form and steam rises.

Bouquet garni: A bay leaf, two stalks of parsley and a stalk of thyme (if available) are tied together with string or combined in a tea egg and used to flavor liquids.

Braise: To brown ingredients in fat and then cook them, covered, in a liquid.

Broil: A dry heat cooking technique where the intense heat of a grill or barbecue sears the outer surface of the food.

Chop: To cut up food into small pieces.

Coating a spoon: Refers to the thickness of sauces and custards. When you dip a metal spoon into sauce, you should be able to draw a distinct line through the liquid on the back of the spoon.

Cream: To beat an ingredient until it is soft enough to combine with others.

Crouton: A small square of fried bread.

Cut in: To combine fat and flour with two knives or your fingertips until the mixture resembles coarse breadcrumbs.

Deep-fry: To immerse food in hot fat to seal in juices and cook through.

Deglaze: To add liquid to a pan to scrape up all the cooking juices coagulated on the bottom.

Degrease: To skim fat off the top of soups or gravies.

Dice: To cut food up into small squares.

Dredge: To coat food with flour, breadcrumbs or sugar.

Dust: To sprinkle a fine coat of flour or sugar over food.

Flambé: To pour warmed spirits over food, ignite it and then continue to cook.

Fold: To combine a lighter mixture gently into a heavier one to retain volume and lightness. Use a large spoon or your hands.

Fry: To cook or brown in hot fat.

Garnish: To decorate a dish or a plate for eye appeal.

Glaze: To make foods shiny by brushing on egg white, milk or jelly.

Grate: To shred food into tiny pieces.

Grease: To brush fat on a pan to prevent food from sticking.

Grill: To broil.

Hold its shape: When a mixture is lifted with a spoon, it remains thick and full and doesn't fall off the spoon.

Julienne: To slice in thin matchstick-sized pieces.

Knead: To work a bread dough with the hands.

Marinate: To soak foods in an aromatic mixture to tenderize and flavor.

Mince: To chop foods very finely into tiny pieces.

Pinch: The amount of a dry ingredient that you can hold between thumb and first finger.

Poach: To cook food in liquid that is just shivering.

Proof: To test yeast for its ability to rise.

Puree: To break food down into a pulp with the help of a food processor, blender or food mill.

Reduce: To boil down a stock or sauce for maximum flavor and a satiny texture.

Refresh: To pour cold water over a hot food to stop the cooking and retain color.

Roast: To bake.

Roux: To combine and cook together equal amounts of fat and flour for sauces.

Sauté: To cook rapidly in an open pan with a small amount of fat.

Scald: To heat milk just until tiny bubbles appear at the edge of the pan.

Score: To slash meat or fish in its thickest part for even cooking.

Sear: To brown meat quickly.

Season: To flavor food with salt, pepper, herbs and spices to bring out taste.

Shred: To grate.

Sift: To eliminate lumps and aerate flour or other ingredients by passing through a sieve.

Simmer: To cook in a liquid just below the boiling point.

Skim: To remove surface scum or fat from the top of a stock.

Steam: To cook food indirectly in the steam rising from boiling water.

Stew: To cook less tender cuts of meat slowly in liquid.

Stir-fry: See Sauté.

Stock: A flavored liquid.

Whisk: To increase the volume of a mixture by beating with a whisk.

Zest: The rind, but not the white pith, of a citrus fruit.

Index

C

E

D

F

G

Q

R

S

T

U

V

W

Z